E. E. CUMMINGS

*The Magic-Maker*

*Books by* CHARLES NORMAN

The Muses' Darling: Christopher Marlowe

So Worthy a Friend: William Shakespeare

Mr. Oddity: Samuel Johnson, LL.D.

Rake Rochester

The Genteel Murderer

Ezra Pound

E. E. Cummings: The Magic-Maker

Selected Poems

# E. E. CUMMINGS
## *The Magic-Maker*

*by* CHARLES NORMAN

*Duell, Sloan and Pearce*
*New York*

*Affiliate of*
MEREDITH PRESS
*Des Moines & New York*

MANUFACTURED IN THE UNITED STATES OF AMERICA FOR MEREDITH PRESS

VAN REES PRESS • NEW YORK

*To My Daughter Nancy*

# Note to New Edition

This is a revised version of *The Magic-Maker: E. E. Cummings*, published in 1958. Much of the documentation, which I found on a rereading of that book to be excessive, has been eliminated. Some new material, and a final chapter dealing with Cummings' last years and his death in 1962, have been added.

C. N.

# Contents

|     |                                        |     |
| --- | -------------------------------------- | --- |
| I.   | *Portrait, With Views*                 | 3   |
| II.  | *"Conceive a Man . . ."*               | 12  |
| III. | *Harvard*                              | 30  |
| IV.  | *The Making of a Book*                 | 48  |
| V.   | *The Poet at War*                      | 62  |
| VI.  | *The Enormous Room*                    | 90  |
| VII. | *The Twenties: New York*               | 99  |
| VIII.| THE DIAL *and the Poet*                | 114 |
| IX.  | *The Twenties: Paris*                  | 137 |
| X.   | *The Poet as Playwright*               | 156 |
| XI.  | *The Poet as Painter*                  | 173 |
| XII. | *The Pilgrim and the Commissars*       | 182 |
| XIII.| *Portrait: More Views*                 | 207 |
| XIV. | *The Poet as Reader*                   | 217 |
| XV.  | *Harvard Revisited*                    | 225 |
| XVI. | *A Last Look*                          | 236 |
|      | *Index of Persons and Places*          | 241 |

E. E. CUMMINGS

*The Magic-Maker*

# I

## *Portrait, With Views*

### 1

Patchin Place is a cul-de-sac of three-story brick houses in Greenwich Village. It has an iron gate at one end, a wooden fence and lamp post at the other. The sidewalks are narrow; two may walk abreast if one is ready to step down. Between the sidewalks and brick walls thrust eight or nine ailanthus trees with curving trunks, giving the street a dappled shade in summer and afterwards strewing its pavement with seed pods and wrinkled leaves. The houses are all painted white. In them have lived a number of writers and artists, and the street is—or was before radio and TV—a quiet residential enclave with an old New York look. Across Tenth Street, on which Patchin Place abuts, stands Jefferson Market Court with its Victorian Gothic tower.

Daily from a house on the left-hand side of Patchin Place a man used to emerge, bound for Washington Square. A weathered hat rode high on a head seeking to soar from squared shoulders loosely draped in an old jacket, from the left pocket of which protruded the top of a black notebook. The face under the hat took daylight as though it and the light and air were friends. It was

a face without guile. Hazel eyes, which seemed abstracted—slight
acquaintances complained of not being recognized on the street
—could in the closer proximity of a room pierce disconcertingly or
brim with laughter or mischief like a child's. The nose was strong,
the mouth full and sensual, the chin arrogant. The ears were large
and seemingly tense with listening; they belonged to a born
eavesdropper of human speech or a dissolving sliver of birdsong.
On rainy days the slim figure of this man strode buoyantly under
an ancient black umbrella held aloft like a balloonman's bouquet
of balloons. He had beautiful hands.

Turning left on Tenth Street, and headed for Sixth Avenue—
now sans Elevated and officially "the Avenue of the Americas"
—he passed the florist shop on the corner where he and the proprietor, Mr. S. Psomas, had often bowed to each other among the
blossoms; for flowers were a necessity to him, and he thought his
friends—and sometimes strangers who had been charming or
kind—should have them, too. Diagonally across Sixth Avenue
from the florist shop stands the stationery emporium of Mr. A.
Schwartz, another friend. Now as he proceeded southward on the
avenue, a number of pedestrians became aware of his progress;
some turned to watch; others named him to ignorant companions,
having seen him plain. He was Edward Estlin Cummings, poet and
painter; or, as he has described himself, "an author of pictures, a
draughtsman of words."

The Village had long been aware of him. He had lived in this
quarter of New York four decades, with only occasional sojourns
abroad, and he had been celebrated virtually all that time, for he
leapt into fame with the first number of *The Dial* in January, 1920.
I have heard Villagers remark, over the years, that they had seen
him on his daily walk, and they remarked it with pleasure, as
though by this glimpse of him they had partaken of the aura which
surrounds famous men. His friends, too, have seen him, but left
him to his meditations—as a rule—by pretending blindness.

The entrance to Washington Square at Waverly Place and Macdougal Street is dominated by a towering English elm almost as
alive with sparrows as with leaves. Around it the ground lies bare

where pigeons with dusty feathers have taken over and multiplied. A pursuing child or an eager dog can make them rise with a windmill clatter, but after a brief centrifugal flight they always return—

SpRiN,k,LiNg an in-stant with sunLight

Buttonwoods, plane trees (which are little buttonwoods), and gingkos—which also line the streets surrounding the park—make small and pleasant groves. Most beautiful of all, catalpas, with heartshaped leaves and dangling "Indian beans," writhe into Oriental forms that an occidental painter can admire. In the center is a fountain; to the north of it, Washington Arch, statues of the first President in front and a memorable inscription across the top in back. And behind an iron fence north of the Arch, where Fifth Avenue begins, stood a crab-apple tree. Almost imperceptibly, on sleety days in late February or early March, it put forth sprinkles of tiniest red that grew and were blossoms.

Winter or summer, Cummings sketched the Square—quickly, skillfully—in a black-bound "Record" notebook of 180 lined and numbered pages measuring 7 by 4 1/4 inches—Mr. Schwartz has named it in his honor "the Cummings size." The sketches range from a disembodied head to full-length figures; one page contains a human cross-section of the park—a fat man lolling on a bench, spectacled intellectuals (male and female), several other pert, anonymous female faces, a girl with a doll carriage, a boy on a tricycle, a cop, two dogs, and two pigeons in flight. Snowfalls were sure to bring him there, he having been like Thoreau, an "inspector of snowstorms," and I have seen him standing in the snow, with a knitted wool cap on his head, feeding the pigeons and sparrows. For he was after all, a countryman in the city, and many of his poems are nests for birds—the chickadee

everywhere welcome
(but chiefly at home in
snowily nowheres
of winter his silence)

or the landscape remembered

> at dusk
>> just when
>> the Light is filled with birds

and for conclusion—

> may my heart always be open to little
> birds who are the secret of living
> whatever they sing is better than to know
> and if men should not hear them men are old

Shoulders squared, the handsome and arrogant head sculptured by Gaston Lachaise held proudly, Cummings in his sixties was not much different from the young blond poet who had appeared so spectacularly with his poems and drawings in *The Dial* a generation before. He had remained an individual in the age of conformity, and the *enfant terrible* (and magic-maker) of the twenties had stayed young doing so. For he was still the same solitary and dedicated man he had always been, not so much aloof, as supposed, as keeping himself to himself, painting by day, writing at night, dreading company, and then entertaining the company that came with tireless, exuberant talk. Then he might suddenly rise and, taking his notebook, ascend to his top-floor studio.

For he still had an inexhaustible box of tricks to astonish and delight those who are capable of being astonished and delighted—a necessary qualification in view of his history, in the course of which typesetters have quailed, book reviewers have spluttered, and letter writers have taken pen in hand (example: "Junior could do better on his new typewriter, and he's only four, and hasn't learned to type yet").

But the very things that baffled the barbarians had made Cummings a writers' writer and, for his typographical innovations, the particular idol of the young. When Cummings went to Bennington College in Vermont to give a reading, the entire audience of girls rose as he mounted the platform and chanted

"Buffalo Bill's/defunct" in unison. (He told me he was so surprised that all he could do was to take out his handkerchief and wave it. The girls cheered.) At Bennington, as in other schools, Cummings' typographical arrangements are being studied for what they are—devices to give readers a maximum of communication and excitement.

On the subject of his technique, Cummings himself wrote: "I can express it in fifteen words, by quoting The Eternal Question And Immortal Answer of burlesk, viz. 'Would you hit a woman with a child—No, I'd hit her with a brick.' Like the burlesk comedian, I am abnormally fond of that precision which creates movement" (from the foreword to *is 5*). His typography is sometimes a cover for his irreverences—towards other writers, patriots of the declaiming variety, politicos, and even Presidents:

> the only man woman or child who wrote
> a simple declarative sentence with seven grammatical
> errors "is dead"
> beautiful Warren Gamaliel Harding
> "is" dead

It is also, occasionally, a cover for coprology.

I have mentioned Thoreau; like him, Cummings was didactic, and a teacher. The most "modern" of the modern poets was anti-mechanistic:

> (While you and i have lips and voices which
> are for kissing and to sing with
> who cares if some oneeyed son of a bitch
> invents an instrument to measure Spring with?

He despised the radio and TV, did not have either. "Radio," he once said, "has taken the ears away from people completely."

He was against "progress," which he called "regression to barbarism." He was anti-scientific.[1]

---

[1] In an article entitled "Exit the Boob" (*Esquire*, June, 1935) he referred to science as "the omnipotent Genie of the uncorked Unknown."

> I'd rather learn from one bird how to sing
> than teach ten thousand stars how not to dance.

Unlike most of his contemporaries, however, he was not afraid of sentiment. He was the foremost celebrant of love among the poets of our time—

> be of love(a little)
> More careful
> Than of everything

—and "we're wonderful one times one" are reiterated themes. He had great admiration for the individual—

> any man is wonderful
> and a formula
> a bit of tobacco and gladness
> plus little derricks of gesture

—and his work is full of tender as well as savage portraits. In a time when it is seemingly fashionable to hate one's parents, he was refreshing. While his mother was still alive he wrote a poem in praise of her; and in recent years, at every reading he gave, he included a long elegy on his father, the late Rev. Edward Cummings, a Unitarian minister and sometime teacher at Harvard.

## 2

In their ground-floor apartment, thronged with books, hung with pictures, where herds of miniature elephants trek over bookcases and mantel, Cummings and his third wife entertained their friends at tea, occasionally dinner. Cummings liked to sit with crossed arms in a straight-backed chair, which he sometimes tilted against the wall. Crumpled bills, coins, and his notebook lay on a table where he dropped them when he returned from his walk, perhaps after an "assignation" with the crab-apple tree on the Square. He was an intense listener, and an eager talker. His tongue was sharp, and he talked occasionally at a rapid rate, out of the side of his mouth, with a mimic's art and the insistence of a barker. He was also earnest:

"The difference between a businessman and an artist is this: the businessman lives in a world which is completely outside him. That's his reality. When that world collapses, he collapses. But the artist never turns a hair. Why? Because the artist's country is inside him.

"The businessman is still secretly despised. Ask rich people how they made their money, and you will see by their reactions what I mean. I always ask them."

At the core of his position was his belief that only by doing or making things one's self can one be fulfilled, or at least grow:

"If a poet is anybody, he is somebody to whom things made matter very little—somebody who is obsessed by Making. Like all obsessions, the Making obsession has disadvantages; for instance, my only interest in making money would be to make it. Fortunately, however, I should prefer to make almost anything else, including locomotives and roses. It is with roses and locomotives (not to mention acrobats Spring electricity Coney Island the 4th of July the eyes of mice and Niagara Falls) that my 'poems' are competing.

"They are also competing with each other, with elephants, and with El Greco" (foreword to *is 5*).

To make things one's self means silence and solitude, a concept utterly at odds with the present epoch of sound. His own choice was made long ago:

> i will cultivate within
> me scrupulously the Inimitable which
> is loneliness . . .

Marion Cummings admires her husband's work, painting as well as poetry, and her "private" little collection of his oils and watercolors shows a discerning eye. She is an omnivorous reader, and has her own views about contemporary writers, particularly poets. Her camera portraits of Cummings are familiar to readers of his books. She is a tall, handsome woman and, as Marion Morehouse, was famous in her own right. Edward Steichen termed her "the best fashion model I ever worked with." She was probably also the most beautiful, as her pictures in *Vogue* and other magazines indicate. She appeared in two films, and I have heard that whenever she arrived on location, in a Long Island studio, spectators and technicians ceased watching the stars to watch her. When she married Cummings, she put her career behind her.

They had a pleasant ritual—really of convenience—about tea and meals; guests who arrived on time would see her take a little elephant bell from the mantelpiece, step into the hall, and ring it. He heard and descended, entering smilingly. How his eyes lit up at the sight of company! How delightful it was—always—to see him appear!

They spent their summers in New Hampshire, on a farm that Cummings inherited from his mother. Every May—the first week if the weather was warm, the second warm or cold—Cummings and his wife went there, going by plane to Boston, from Boston by train. Their sojourn at the farm was never under four months; often it was closer to five. Until 1957 there was no electricity in the house, and reading was done by kerosene lamps. Despite the wiring, no radio, no TV. For trips to the nearby village Cummings drove a 1929 Ford sedan, upholstered and roomy as an old-fashioned Pullman. It rode high over the narrow, winding dirt roads; cars of later design, he said, were too low-slung to be of use. Besides, he explained—smiling—should his car get stuck in a rut, only three pairs of hands could lift it out. On his farm, particularly in overalls, doing chores, he looked a bit more the Yankee he was.

Cummings had more than three hundred acres of woodland to roam in, which, despite the blandishments of regional lumbermen, had been left strictly alone. So had the grass and bushes around the house, with the result that thrushes were more numerous than chickadees or sparrows. Hummingbirds sipped from vials of sugared water outside the screen porch where Cummings and his wife took their meals. The stone floor of the porch was strewn with empty shells from peanuts in a cookie jar where chipmunks came three times a day, beginning with the first sound in the kitchen in the morning. There was also water for them in a glass dish.

Cummings had assured me that the hummingbirds "bowed good-by" to him when they were ready to take off for their long flight to the Caribbean at summer's end; and I hereby testify that it was so. On the last day of August, 1957, as we were sitting on the porch, which faces the mountains of the Sandwich Range, he called my attention to two hummingbirds outside the screen.

"They are bowing good-by," he said.

Like tiniest helicopters the hummingbirds rose straight up to the top of the screen, then descended, five or six times, turned, and were gone.

# II

## *"Conceive a Man..."*

**1**

> conceive a man,should he have anything
> would give a little more than it away....

Cummings did not believe in "the hyperscientific doctrine
that heredity is nothing because everything is environment." But it
is clear—from conversations with him; from his autobiographical
lectures at Harvard, from which the foregoing sentence is quoted;
and from a manuscript account by his sister of their childhood—
that his environment might have made a poet out of a foundling.

Consider his father and mother.

Replying to his friend Paul Rosenfeld, the music critic of *The
Dial*, who asked him for information about his father, Cummings
wrote:

> He was a New Hampshire man, 6 foot 2, a crack shot & a
> famous fly-fisherman & a firstrate sailor (his sloop was named
> The Actress) & a woodsman who could find his way through
> forests primeval without a compass & a canoeist who'd still-

paddle you up to a deer without ruffling the surface of a pond &
an ornithologist & taxidermist & (when he gave up hunting) an
expert photographer (the best I've ever seen) & an actor who
portrayed Julius Caesar in Sanders Theatre & a painter (both
in oils & watercolours) & a better carpenter than any professional
& an architect who designed his own houses before building
them & (when he liked) a plumber who just for the fun of it
installed all his own waterworks & (while at Harvard) a teacher
with small use for professors—by whom (Royce, Lanman,
Taussig, etc.) we were literally surrounded (but not defeated)
—& later (at Doctor Hale's socalled South Congregational really
Unitarian church) a preacher who announced, during the last
war, that the Gott Mit Uns boys were in error since the only
thing which mattered was for man to be on God's side (& one
beautiful Sunday in Spring remarked from the pulpit that he
couldn't understand why anyone had come to hear him on such
a day) & horribly shocked his pewholders by crying "the King-
dom of Heaven is no spiritual roofgarden: it's inside you."

Another Cambridge neighbor and professor was William James,
who introduced Cummings' father and mother to each other.

Edward Cummings, Harvard (*magna cum laude*, in philosophy),
1883, and after graduation a student of divinity, was the first
holder of the Robert Treat Paine fellowship in social science. He
studied abroad with the Reverend Samuel A. Barnett at Toynbee
Hall and Professor Estlin Carpenter at Oxford, in honor of whom
he named his son. On returning to this country, Mr. Cummings
was an instructor at Harvard in English, political economy, and
sociology for one year each, and, from 1893 to 1900, assistant professor of sociology in the Department of Economics. Of this period
of his life the *Dictionary of American Biography* says: "As a
teacher at Harvard he was human, alert, and stimulating."

In October, 1900, he was ordained minister of the South Congregational Society, Unitarian, of Boston, and became the colleague
of the Reverend Edward Everett Hale, a distinguished clergyman
and author of the nineteenth-century classic, *The Man Without a*

*Country.* Dr. Cummings succeeded Dr. Hale in 1909, and remained the pastor of the South Congregational church until 1925, when it merged with the First Church of Boston.

A number of Dr. Cummings' sermons, as well as treatises on trade unionism and industrial arbitration, were published in his lifetime. From a wide selection, I have chosen the following passage from "Lincoln, A Sermon," delivered by Dr. Cummings to his parishioners in 1909:

"If the great volume of Lincoln literature is significant, the great number of readers is still more significant, and the kind of readers is most significant of all. For the readers of Lincoln literature are not confined to any fastidious or specially educated class. Lincoln, fortunately, is the idol of what we sometimes call the common people. And by the common people I do not mean exclusively people of our older American stock, or even our native-born citizens. He is also, happily, the idol and the ideal of many of our newest, foreign-born recruits. It is one of the encouraging signs of the times that many of the most enthusiastic admirers of Lincoln are to be found among the so-called aliens who are flocking to our shores from every part of the old world. . . . And I know of no better evidence of their right to come here than this ability which they and their children show to recognize and choose the best. And I know of no greater or more important service than this which Lincoln is rendering his country today,—leavening all the diverse and incoherent elements of our population with the pervasive, democratic leaven of his own personality; binding all parts of the nation together in one organic, living whole, in spite of all the differences of race, language, religion and tradition."

But even with his father's precepts to guide him, Cummings could be very disconcerting. His friends are familiar with the way in which he triggered a shot; for whenever, in a pause in a discussion, he remarked, "Want to know what *I* think?" they learned to look around for shelter. One night—it was just after World War II—he remarked to a guest: "Know what *I* think? I think the only real Americans are those descended from the original stock that settled the Atlantic seaboard." His guest, who was not descended

from that original stock, but was still in uniform, did not pursue
the subject.

Of his mother, the former Rebecca Haswell Clarke, of Roxbury,
Massachusetts, Cummings said in his first Harvard lecture:
"Whereas my father had created his Unitarianism (his own father
being a Christian of the hellfire variety) she had inherited hers;
it was an integral part of herself, she expressed it as she breathed
and as she smiled. The two indispensable factors in life, my mother
always maintained, were 'health and a sense of humor.'" He also
said: "never have I encountered anyone more joyous, anyone
healthier in body and mind, anyone so quite incapable of remembering a wrong, or anyone so completely and humanly and unaffect-
edly generous." This is the poem he wrote:

if there are any heavens my mother will(all by herself)have
one.   It will not be a pansy heaven or
a fragile heaven of lilies-of-the-valley but
it will be a heaven of blackred roses

my father will be(deep like a rose
tall like a rose)

standing near my

(swaying over her
silent)
with eyes which are really petals and see

nothing with the face of a poet really which
is a flower and not a face with
hands
which whisper
This is my beloved my

                    (suddenly in sunlight
he will bow,

& the whole garden will bow)

2

Edward Estlin Cummings was born "at home," October 14, 1894, at 104 Irving Street, Cambridge, Massachusetts (astrologically: in Libra, the House of Marriage, his planet being Venus). The house is still standing, and looks today probably as it always did—a large, roomy, three-story house half-hidden by foliage in a quiet street of similar, amply spaced houses behind their iron or wooden fences. Its entrance is flanked by double pillars, and there is a veranda on one side facing a large oval garden ringed with a white-pine hedge and bounded on the outside by three curving streets: Farrar, Scott, and Irving.

"The third story," Cummings' sister Elizabeth, now the wife of Professor Carlton Qualey, has recalled, "had two very good places to play. One was a big room under the roof. It had a skylight at one end, and steps leading up onto the flat part of the roof. We could go up onto the flat roof if we were careful and walked softly. It was made of copper and had a railing all around it. If we ran or jumped, it was bad for the copper and might cause leaks. My brother made a box kite and a windlass for it, and used to take it up on the flat roof and fly it there. He let me help him turn the windlass. It was hard work, but very exciting. . . .

"The tool room was another good place to play. It was an unfinished room with a skylight, just off the landing, before you got to the third floor. Part of the room was fixed up with shades, a sink, and red and blue light bulbs. That was where my father developed and printed the pictures he took with his camera. Part of the room was used for storing things like extra bedding and trunks. There was a long tool bench with a vise and a rack full of tools and, of course, wood to make things of, and all sorts of nails and screws. I couldn't use the tools, but I loved to help my father and brother. I could blow sawdust away so that they could see the pencil line they were trying to saw along. I could pedal the big old grindstone, too, so they could sharpen tools."

A camera fan. The inhabitants of 104 Irving were progressive; the first telephone in Cambridge was installed there.

There was something progressive, as well, about the inhabitants' attitude toward children. The oval garden, which could have been a show place, was allowed to become, instead, a play place. There were about ten or twelve boys and girls in the neighborhood, and they all played in the Cummings "yard." Mrs. Qualey wrote: "Some people worried about children spoiling their lawns. My father liked to have us play in our yard, and used to say he was raising children and not grass. We could call and shout, but we were forbidden to scream unless we were hurt. My father did a lot of his work at home in his study. He said that happy noises, even loud ones, never disturbed him."

There was a swing, a bar, hanging rings, a sandpile, and "several good climbing trees." On one of these her father and brother built a tree house. "It was a sturdy little house, and cozy, too. You climbed up to the door by a strong ladder with wide rungs. There was a little stove with a real stove pipe, and a bunk big enough for my brother to sleep on, and a real window with a wooden shutter. There was room for at least six people [little people?] inside the house, and there was a small porch, with a railing around it, facing the street. We spent a lot of time in the tree house in all kinds of weather. The stove kept it warm in cold weather and, though it was a heating stove and not a cook stove, we could make toast, and cocoa, and pop corn on it. My brother used to go to the tree house to be alone, and sometimes spent the night there."

"Just in front of the house itself stood two huge apple-trees," Cummings told his audience at Harvard; "and faithfully, every spring, these giants lifted their worlds of fragrance toward the room where I breathed and dreamed. Under one window of this room flourished (in early summer) a garden of magnificent roses."

In her catalogue of the games played in the garden—football, tennis, "scrub" baseball, tag, hopscotch, jump rope, jacks, and marbles—Mrs. Qualey quotes this verse that her mother had learned as a little girl:

> "Inty, minty, kuty, corn,
>   Apple seed and apple thorn.
>   Wire, briar, limber lock.
>   Five geese in a flock.
>   Sit and sing
>   By the spring.
>   O-U-T spells out goes he (she)."

She also reveals the genesis of one of her brother's best-loved poems: "The first and most exciting sign that spring had really come was the balloon man. First you heard his whistle in the distance; then he would come walking down the street, carrying a basket full of balloons of all colors tugging at their strings." Cummings wrote:

> in Just-
> spring     when the world is mud-
> luscious the little
> lame balloonman
>
> whistles     far     and wee
>
> and eddieandbill come
> running from marbles and
> piracies and it's
> spring
>
> when the world is puddle-wonderful
>
> the queer
> old balloonman whistles
> far     and     wee
> and bettyandisbel come dancing
>
> from hop-scotch and jump-rope and
>
> it's
> spring
> and
>       the

                    goat-footed

balloonMan        whistles
far
and
wee

The Cummings children and their friends also played in
"Norton's Woods," where Charles Eliot Norton had his residence.
"Here, as a very little child," Cummings said in his second lecture,
"I first encountered the mystery who is Nature."

Mrs. Qualey also has an account of the circus, which came, like
the balloon man, every spring "and pitched a huge tent in an
open space outside the city of Boston. Before I was old enough to go
to the circus, I had heard my brother tell about going with my
father, and had seen the pictures he had made of the animals and
the acrobats."

In a *Vanity Fair* article about the circus in 1925 Cummings
wrote: "Although it was only once, and twenty-odd years ago, that
my eyes had the extraordinary honour to behold a slight young
man whose first name was DANGER DERIDING DEATH DEFYING DES-
PERATE DARE-DEVIL DIAVOLO LOOPS THE LOOP ON A BICYCLE (his last
name being, if I am not mistaken, PORTHOS: LEAPS THE GAP OVER
FIVE ELEPHANTS), I have not forgotten this person and shall never
forget him, simply because he was a great artist—who, like Paul
Cézanne, died the most fortunate and illustrious of deaths: died
at the *motif*, and in the execution of his art."

As for the elephants, he drew them over and over, and used to
astonish dinner companions by drawing them on the tablecloth
upside-down—that is, legs outward. In the article just mentioned
he suggested that everyone has an especially liked animal and confessed that "my own totem is the elephant." As a child, he had a
toy elephant that his father often mended, and at Harvard he wrote
a story entitled "The King," which was really a tribute to his un-
forgotten toy.

When Estlin and Elizabeth came down with measles, they

were put in the "big room" shared, usually, by their grandmother
and an aunt. Elizabeth wrote:

"My brother was great fun to be with. He could draw pictures,
and tell stories, and imitate people and animals, and invent
games, and could make you laugh, even when you thought you
felt very miserable. I think that we were in that room for several
weeks, but I had a wonderful time. It must have been then that
my brother arranged with his make-believe friend (Kingston) to
take me and my make-believe friend (Frimmon) up in Kingston's
new flying-machine. You are so used to airplanes that going up in
a make-believe one doesn't sound very exciting to you, probably.
But my brother and I had never seen an airplane. There was talk
about some men who were trying to invent a flying-machine, and
we had seen a picture of the one they were working on, but
nobody really expected that flying-machines would amount to
much."

Alas, they were mistaken. Her account continues:

"When we had the whooping cough we were sick for weeks and
weeks. After we got over the worst we didn't have to stay in bed,
and could even play in the yard on nice days. But we still coughed
like anything at times. About half the children in the neighborhood
had the whooping cough, or had been exposed to it. My brother
formed a club called the 'Whooper Club.' Anyone could belong
who had whooping cough or who expected to come down with it.
My brother was president, and editor of the 'Whooper Club'
paper, which he typed on mother's old Hammond typewriter.
Every member of the 'Whooper Club' had to write or dictate a
story for the paper. We had badges and a motto, too, and we all
played together and had so much fun that children tried to get
exposed to the whooping cough so they could join.

"My brother used to make different kinds of drawings, too,
sometimes ones (a little like the ones in the funny papers) that
he mounted on strips of cardboard. They told stories about us, our
animals, and all sorts of other things."

## 3

At the time Elizabeth Cummings was born, 104 Irving was occupied by her father, mother, brother, a grandmother and an aunt, and Uncle George, her mother's brother. Later there was another "aunt," a dear friend of her mother's. There were also Julia, the cook, and Sandy, "who did a little of everything." And there were two dogs, a cat, goldfish, and rabbits in a pen in the back yard.

"After myself and my father and mother," Cummings told a Harvard audience, "I loved most dearly my mother's brother George. He was by profession a lawyer, by inclination a bon vivant, and by nature a joyous human being. When this joyous human being wasn't toiling in his office, or hobnobbing with socalled swells at the Brookline country club, he always became my playfellow."

Of the two aunts, it may not be necessary to say more than that they kept an eye on their nephew. This collective eye was directed not so much to deportment as to neatness. In this, we may suppose Elizabeth Cummings to have been a little angel, as all little girls once were, and possibly are still. It was—and is—different with boys; and so it chanced with Estlin. Boys of half a century ago wore knickerbockers, and not long trousers, an item of apparel that even graces the tender legs of toddlers today. Knickerbocker trouser legs are fastened below-knee, and do not always stay fastened; sometimes one, sometimes both, will slip down and dangle, carrying a stocking along. Aunt Jane, and afterwards Aunt Emma, were insistent that they stay up. In time, by a domestic application of "divide and conquer," each assumed for herself the responsibility for one of the trouser legs; so that it was not unusual in that household, when Estlin hove in view, to hear one aunt say to the other: "There goes your leg."

Of the grandmother. I have heard from more than one visitor to 104 Irving Street her oft-repeated remark about the entire household: "I never feel easy until they are all safely in bed."

And now I should like to say something collective about the inhabitants; or rather, since he has said it better than I can, I shall quote Cummings, who told his Harvard audience: "I here devoutly thank a beneficent Providence for allowing me to live my childhood and my boyhood and even my youth without ever once glimpsing that typical item of an era of at least penultimate confusion—the uncomic nonbook. No paltry supermen, no shadowy space-cadets, no trifling hyperjunglequeens and pantless pantherwomen insulted my virginal imagination. I read or was read, at an early age, the most immemorial myths, the wildest wild animal stories, lots of Scott and quantities of Dickens (including the immortal *Pickwick Papers*), *Robinson Crusoe* and *The Swiss Family Robinson*, *Gulliver's Travels*, *Twenty Thousand Leagues Under the Sea*, poetry galore, *The Holy Bible*, and *The Arabian Nights*. One city winter I floated through chivalry with Mallory and Froissart: the following country summer—we had by then acquired a farm—I dressed as a Red Indian, slept in a teepee, and almost punctured our best Jersey cow with a random arrow; in emulation of the rightful inhabitants of my wrongful native land."

Elsewhere he adds *Lorna Doone* ("with whom I fell sublimely in love") and *Treasure Island* to his juvenile reading.

He was read to; he read *books*; the grandmother and the aunts sang and played the piano; his father painted, his mother "loved poetry; and copied most of the poems she loved best into a little book which was never far from her."

When does a poet emerge, if poet there is to be? All children utter and write lines of primeval brightness and beauty, provided, of course, that they are not beaten into silence and clenched hands. The organ of speech and the organ that scrawls at the hand's bidding are discoveries fraught with tremendous excitement, sometimes too fondly shared by doting parents. This, too, is inhibiting.

Of Cummings' earliest verse, there exists a couplet whose survival we owe to his mother; it might not have won a contest in *St. Nicholas*, but it is a good start, nothing clever in it, only observation and delight, as good ingredients for a poem as the most finicky critic could ask:

> O,the pretty birdie,O;
> with his little toe,toe,toe!

(It is always the hopping that does it.)

Cummings has told, in his second Harvard lecture, about the poetic periods through which he passed. The first he illustrated by the poem just quoted. The second had the somber cast of social-consciousness: "A good poem was a poem which did good, and a bad poem was a poem which didn't: Julia Ward Howe's Battle Hymn Of the Republic being a good poem because it helped free the slaves. Armed with this ethical immutability, I composed canticles of comfort on behalf of the griefstricken relatives of persons recently deceased; I implored healthy Christians to assist poor-whites afflicted with The Curse of The Worm (short for hookworm); and I exhorted rightminded patriots to abstain from dangerous fireworks on the 4th of July. Thus it will be seen that, by the year 1900, one growing American boy had reached exactly that stage of 'intellectual development' beyond which every ungrowing Marxist adult of today is strictly forbidden, on pain of physical disappearance, ever to pass."

The third poetic period began with a present from his Uncle George. It was *The Rhymester*, which, Cummings recalled, " diverted my eager energies from what to how: from substance to structure. I learned that there are all kinds of intriguing verse-forms, chiefly French; and that each of these forms can and does exist in and of itself, apart from the use to which you or I may not or may put it."

I take, from the lecture referred to, a chance meeting on Irving Street "one ever memorable day" when Cummings and Professor Josiah Royce came face to face. Royce was the man on whom "the mantle of philosophical authority had fallen at Harvard" and of whom Santayana was to write: "even without knowing that he had already produced a new proof of the existence of God, merely to look at him you would have felt he was a philosopher; his great head seemed too heavy for his small body, and his portentous brow, crowned with thick red hair, seemed to crush the lower part of his face."

" 'Estlin' his courteous and gentle voice hazarded 'I understand that you write poetry.' I blushed. 'Are you perhaps' he inquired, regarding a particular leaf of a particular tree 'acquainted with the sonnets of Dante Gabriel Rossetti?' I blushed a different blush and shook an ignorant head. 'Have you a moment?' he shyly suggested, less than half looking at me; and just perceptibly appended 'I rather imagine you might enjoy them.' Shortly thereafter, sage and ignoramus were sitting opposite each other in a diminutive study (marvellously smelling of tobacco and cluttered with student notebooks of a menacing bluish shade)—the ignoramus listening, enthralled; the sage intoning, lovingly and beautifully, his favorite poems. And very possibly (although I don't as usual, know) that is the reason—or more likely the unreason—I've been writing sonnets ever since."

Cummings has written a great many sonnets; and it is apparent from their variety that he could do anything with the sonnet form. Although he told me, "I did not decide to become a poet—I was always writing poetry," it was not until Harvard, the Harvard of his undergraduate days, that he became—in Johnson's sublime phrase—"irrecoverably a poet."

## 4

Perhaps, as the Bible says, there is a time to be born. For a future rebel, Cummings could not have been born at a better time or place. The world of his infancy and youth had still a moral atmosphere, and that atmosphere was laden with certain values and virtues seemingly made to be rejected:

the Cambridge ladies who live in furnished souls
are unbeautiful and have comfortable minds
(also, with the church's protestant blessings
daughters, unscented shapeless spirited)
they believe in Christ and Longfellow, both dead. . . .

It was also a world which was completely male-dominated, and in which the paterfamilias was the master of his house. Cummings never forgot the effect on everyone at 104 Irving Street the first time his father appeared as an ordained minister, however quickly the old cheerfulness broke through to reign as before.

Before Elizabeth was born, Dr. and Mrs. Cummings bought the farm in New Hampshire mentioned in the first chapter. It was called "the Joy Farm," after its owner, Ephraim Joy, "but it earned the name on its own account," as Mrs. Qualey afterwards wrote. There was a little frame house and an immense barn. "Some farmers think that it spoils the hay to let children play in it," she wrote. "Our horses and cows seemed to like our hay, though we did play a lot in the haymow." As was the case on Irving Street, neighbors' children came to Joy Farm to play.

The original house was plastered inside to keep out the cold and had floor boards ranging in width from eight inches to a couple of feet. A brick fireplace with two openings, like a primitive Moloch with two mouths, stood awkwardly, but efficiently, in the main room. Mount Chocorua was visible in the distance, but it was necessary to step outside to see it; Dr. Cummings put in windows from which the mountain could be seen, and added extensions and another story to the house, as well as a flat roof on the extension from which the sunset and stars could be observed. Here Cummings painted many of his oil landscapes and water-color sunsets.

"My father was always building something, or repairing something, or doing something special, and of course all of us wanted to help," Mrs. Qualey wrote. "He built a study at the edge of the woods. It was a very unusual one because it had so many sides that it was almost round. It had a big fireplace with a sunken hearth, and on each side of the fireplace were cement steps leading to a little room upstairs. Outside the upstairs windows was a wide walk that went all the way around the study and was like a sort of balcony. There were beds there, and downstairs my father built himself a desk where he could work during the day when he needed to be undisturbed.

"He built a little place for my brother to study, too. It was under a tree about half way from the house to my father's study. It was not a real building. There was a long plank the right height for a desk and about long enough for three people to sit at it at once. There was another long plank the right height for a bench. There was a wall at the back with a window in it, and walls at each end with cupboards and cubbyholes for books and things. Instead of an ordinary roof and door, there was a hinged roof that could be raised so as to stand out straight and give shade to the desk and the bench. It could be lowered to make the study into a sort of rain-tight box. My brother used the study a lot, and I used to use it sometimes when I did my lessons. I can remember learning my multiplication tables at that study."

This description of the "tree study" is of more than passing interest, for it is the prototype of the study which father and son afterwards built on the shore of a neighboring lake, and where *The Enormous Room* was written.

The Cummings children were taught self-reliance. Both were given compasses to carry when they went exploring in the woods, and Estlin had the additional honor and responsibility of carrying matches. If they were really lost, he was to build a small fire—"on a rock where it could not spread"—and someone at the house would see the smoke. But peril came to the children, not in the woods, but on the water.

On the shore of the lake Dr. Cummings built, chiefly with his own hands, an immense, roomy, rambling summerhouse with a flat-topped roof from which the surrounding countryside, its mountains mirrored in the lake, could be scanned. On a summer day in 1911, when Estlin was sixteen and Elizabeth ten, they went out in a canvas boat, guaranteed to be unsinkable, taking Rex, a bull terrier, with them. In the middle of the lake, where the water was forty feet deep, a sudden lunge of the dog tipped the boat over. It sank at once, leaving only paddles, floor boards, and two box seats floating. Rex started for the shore, and brother and sister held on to the boxes, managing to stay afloat despite their heavy clothes and shoes. Mrs. Qualey says they did not try to take them off, and could not have managed it if they had tried.

"It did not occur to me to be afraid," she wrote, "because my brother was cheerful and I had perfect confidence in him.

"Suddenly we realized that Rex had given up swimming for the shore and was swimming back toward us. He was thrashing around in a frightened way. He must have felt himself at the end of his strength and, hearing our familiar voices, turned back to us for help. My brother raised himself out of the water enough to shout loudly to Rex to go back. But Rex did not understand, and swam all the more frantically toward the voice he knew he could trust. By the time he got to me, he was in a panic and splashing so he could hardly see where he was going. He must have seen something that looked solid and have thought that he could climb out of the water onto it. I felt his weight on my shoulders; then lost hold of my box and went under water. I came up, spluttering, and got hold of the box again. Again Rex tried to climb on, and again I lost hold and went under water. My brother was swimming toward us and calling to Rex. The next thing I knew, Rex and my brother were struggling in the water; then I didn't see Rex any more. I could only guess how my brother must feel. I knew he would have done almost anything to save Rex, but he could not let Rex keep forcing me under water."

Back in the summerhouse, the rest of the family had been watching the sunset, when Dr. Cummings suggested a ride in the motor boat. Everyone went, including the grandmother, "who wasn't crazy about boats." Aunt Jane steered. Suddenly Dr. Cummings shouted to Aunt Jane: "Steer for those two heads in the water!"

"He explained to my mother, who was sitting next to him, that he could see two people swimming a long way from shore and was going to tell them it was dangerous, even if they were annoyed and thought it was none of his business. When the boat came close to the two heads in the water, the family could hardly believe their eyes. My brother's voice, telling them to pick me up first, sounded natural, but actually he was chilled and almost exhausted.

"For years my father insisted on keeping the two boxes we had hung onto. 'I keep them to remind me whenever things seem to me to be bad,' he said."

With advancing years one tends to remember who one is, and whence one sprang. To this father, the son has paid tribute in a long poem that was a fixed piece in his public readings. The poem ends:

> though dull were all we taste as bright,
> bitter all utterly things sweet,
> maggoty minus and dumb death
> all we inherit, all bequeath
>
> and nothing quite so least as truth
> —i say though hate were why men breathe—
> because my father lived his soul
> love is the whole and more than all

On November 2, 1926, Dr. and Mrs. Cummings left Cambridge for Joy Farm in a newly purchased automobile. Mrs. Cummings was at the wheel. In the region of the Ossippee mountains snow fell, and they stopped to wipe the windshield. A few minutes later, in a blinding snowstorm, the car came to a railroad crossing; a locomotive sheared the car in two, killing Dr. Cummings instantly and seriously injuring Mrs. Cummings. They were found by two brakemen from the train.

"These men took my sixty-six year old mother by the arms and tried to lead her toward a nearby farmhouse," Cummings said at Harvard; "but she threw them off, strode straight to my father's body, and directed a group of scared spectators to cover him. When this had been done (and only then) she let them lead her away.

"A day later, my sister and I entered a small darkened room in a country hospital. She was still alive—why, the head-doctor couldn't imagine. She wanted only one thing: to join the person she loved most. He was very near her, but she could not quite reach him. We spoke, and she recognized our voices. Gradually her own voice began to understand what its death would mean to these living children of hers; and very gradually a miracle happened. She decided to live."

I had the pleasure of meeting her at Patchin Place, a cheerful, informed, motherly woman enjoying the company of her son, his wife, and their friends. She had worked for a while, after her recovery, as a volunteer with the Travelers Aid in Grand Central Station; now she had her own apartment on Washington Square, where she continued to paste into scrapbooks any and every item that mentioned E. E. Cummings, a labor of love that has saved me many labors. Cummings once told me that, after reading the reviews of *The Enormous Room*, he decided he would never read another. It is probable that he did not read most reviews of his writings. The perceptive reader will find, toward the end of this book, excerpts from two reviews he did read, which—coming when they did—could not fail to upset him.

# III

## *Harvard*

1

Cummings, of course, was destined for Harvard. "As a baby," he has recounted, "I sported a white sweater, on which my mother had embroidered a red H." He first attended a private school in Cambridge where, he says, he learned nothing and "burst into tears and nosebleeds." Then came three public schools, the most important of which was the Cambridge High and Latin School, on Trowbridge Street, where he prepared for Harvard. One of the public schools had for principal a Negress "blessed with a delicious voice, charming manners, and a deep understanding of children." In his letter to Paul Rosenfeld, previously quoted, Cummings says his father sent him to that particular school because of her. Her name was Maria Baldwin. Cummings also pays tribute to a Mr. Cecil Derry, "one of those blessing and blessed spirits who deserve the name of teacher: predicates who are utterly in love with their subject; and who, because they would gladly die for it, are living for it gladly. From him I learned (and am still learning) that gladness is next to godliness. He taught me Greek."

From Irving Street, it was a short walk cross-lots to Trowbridge, through the little park where the Cambridge Public Library stands today, and which must have been more like a little wood at the beginning of the century.

Cummings entered Harvard in the fall of 1911. A member of the graduating class of that year was a diminutive—five feet four—bespectacled student named Joseph Ferdinand Gould, later to become "Little Joe Gould, the last of the Bohemians," after his translation to Greenwich Village.

Speaking to me of his memorable first year, Cummings related how he spent a rapturous afternoon and evening in the Harvard Union library reading his own discovery—Marlowe (probably in the great edition, Oxford University Press, 1910, of Professor Tucker Brooke). Forty-five years later he was still able to recite passages from *Hero and Leander* and the *Amores*. He told me that, as the evening wore on, the librarian began to appear more and more frequently to observe the phenomenon of a lone student actually reading for pleasure and unaware of the time; and he added, smiling, how surprised that librarian would have been had he known that Marlowe's and (through Marlowe) Ovid's eroticism were as titillating to the seventeen-year-old as the grandeur of the verse.

"Officially," Cummings said in "Nonlecture Three," "Harvard presented me with a smattering of languages and sciences; with a glimpse of Homer, a more than glimpse of Aeschylus Sophocles Euripides and Aristophanes, and a deep glance at Dante and Shakespeare."

By the end of his first year, Cummings was a contributor to the Harvard *Monthly*. He continued to contribute to it through his post-graduate year, 1916. He also appeared, though much less frequently, in the Harvard *Advocate*. At least one of his poems was signed "E. Estlin Cummings," but chiefly the signature was the familiar one of later years. The first of his poems to appear in the *Monthly* was entitled "Vision," and its inspiration was, not surprisingly, Harvard. It is in the heroic vein, and I give it here because it is the first of his poems to reach an audience in the great world, and also because it is itself not without interest for its structure and phrasing:

> The dim deep of a yellow evening slides
> Across the green, and mingles with the elms.
> A faint beam totters feebly in the west,
> Trembles, and all the earth is wild with light,
> Stumbles, and all the world is in the dark.
>
> The huge black sleeps above;—lo, two white stars.
>
> Harvard, your shadow-walls, and ghost-toned tower,
> Dim, ancient-moulded, vague, and faint, and far,
> Is gone! And through the flesh I see the soul:
> Coloring iron in red leaping flame,
> The thunder-strokes of mighty, sweating men,
> Furious hammers of clashing fierce and high,—
> And in a corner of the smithy coiled,
> Black, brutal, massive-linked, the toil-wrought chain
> Which is to bind God's right hand to the world.

It appears to be a sonnet, but lacks rhyme and has an extra line. Afterwards, there were sonnets in profusion, perfect enough to please the most academic eye, and something besides: past the striving for fresh images, fresh images—

> Great carnal mountains crouching in the cloud.

The influence of Rossetti and of the whole pre-Raphaelite brotherhood—"the fleshly school," as it was called—is apparent in many of the poems, with their ballad subjects and archaic language. "Ballade," a poem of six stanzas, published in the *Advocate*, ends:

> White stretched the north-land, white the south . . . A
> She was gone like a spark from the ash that chars; B
> And "After her!" he sware . . . C
> They found the maid. And her eyes were stars, B
> A starry smile was upon her mouth, A
> And the snow-flowers in her hair. C

Undergraduate verse reveals, better than anything else can, what discipline is needed to make a poet. There are enough Cummings poems in the Harvard *Monthly* and *Advocate* to make a book; but it would not be a good book. Yet by 1915 the phrases that are peculiarly his begin to leap out—

> Bluer are they than ponds of dream—

from "Ballad of Love," and

> A great, red, fearsome flower

from "Longing." There is also, in the refrain of "Ballade of Soul," a beginning awareness of the world outside the sheltering walls of Harvard and the warm family life in Irving Street:

> But are there Souls in winter garmentless,
> Be with them, God! and pity also me.

Almost as significant as his poems in the *Monthly* were the men he met in its office on the dusty third floor of the Harvard Union. A glance through the issues of this magazine, with its Fatima ad on the inside cover, reveals the following editors, Cummings among them, during his undergraduate years: J. Donald Adams, R. S. Mitchell, J. S. Watson, Gilbert Vivian Seldes, Robert Gruntal Nathan, J. R. Dos Passos, and Robert S. Hillyer. Of these men, afterwards celebrated in their own right, after a pruning of middle names or initials along the way, four became lifelong friends of Cummings. He was soon to meet another Harvard man, already an alumnus, with important results for all concerned. Cummings declared in "Nonlecture Three":

"Through Harvard, I met Scofield Thayer; and at Harvard, Sibley Watson—two men who subsequently transformed a do-gooding periodical called The Dial into a firstrate magazine of the fine arts; and together fought the eternal fight of selfhood against mobism, the immortal battle of beauty against ugliness."

Of this magazine, of which I shall give an account commensurate with its importance in the career of E. E. Cummings and the cultural life of the country, Stewart Mitchell became the first managing editor. He was, at the time of which I write, editor-in-chief of the *Monthly*. I am indebted to Robert Hillyer for this account of the way in which the *Monthly* board operated:

"It was the custom for the editors to write comments on the material submitted, signing their initials, and the piece was accepted or rejected according to the consensus. Some aspirant handed in a poem that began with the line: 'Thou hast faun eyes.' Cummings's comment took graphic form—a small horned deer with large and soulful eyes. On another poem he wrote, 'Good but poor.' That has always seemed to me an excellent phrase, accurately descriptive of much that is published."

Hillyer told me that when he was elected an editor, "John Dos Passos gave a party for the whole board in his rooms in Thayer Hall. Cummings lived in the same building. Several of us adjourned to his rooms, and after dinner we met there again. It was a Saturday night. We sat up drinking and reading poetry nearly all night, and—I think it was four or five of us—went to sleep where we were on chairs and couches. Early the next morning (or it seemed early) there was a knock at the door. Cummings rightly guessed that it was his father, the Reverend Dr. Cummings, the most famous Unitarian minister in Boston. The room was a shambles. What a to-do there was to whisk bottles and glasses into hiding places and bring some sort of order to the room before admitting the paternal divine! It went off all right; Dr. Cummings was either very unobservant or very wise."

One other meeting deserves mention. In 1913 the Cambridge Dramatic Club on Brattle Street produced Jerome K. Jerome's *Fanny and the Servant Problem*—in which Cummings was cast as Ernest, the second footman. Of this production—he also played Micah in *The Little Minister*—he recalls two things: that he was kissed "by the very beautiful leading lady," and that the hero, "Lord Somebody or other," was brilliantly played by a "cold and aloof" person. This person was T. S. Eliot. They met, formally, for the first time several decades later, in Patchin Place.

2

It was in his senior year that Cummings, who had been living at home, moved to Thayer Hall (south entry, second floor). He adorned his mantelpiece with four or five China elephants and his walls with "Krazy Kat" comic strips. It is just possible that the typographical arrangements in this famous funny-paper sequence suggested certain things to Krazy Kat's admirer. In this room he painted as well as wrote.

It was his first taste of independence. "Now I could roam that surrounding world sans peur, if not sans reproche: and I lost no time in doing so. A town called Boston, thus observed, impressed my unsophisticated spirit as the mecca of all human endeavors—and be it added that, in this remote era, Boston had her points." Some think it still has them: good speech, good manners. But Boston was only preparation for higher things, although I do not believe that he scanted the preparation. Malcolm Cowley has related (first in Sanders Theatre, introducing Cummings, who was to read, and then in the pages of the *Advocate*) how this "son of a famous minister was in revolt against ministerial standards, so that his father's car, with its clergyman's license plates, was found parked outside a famous joint near Scollay Square, to the embarrassment of the Boston police."

There were the delights of eating and drinking in German, Chinese, and Greek restaurants. S. Foster Damon recalled for me Charley Wirth's near Chinatown, where he and Cummings drank seidels of dark Kulmbacher beer; a bona fide Chinese restaurant whose specialty was a chop suey of lobster and pineapple, with no casualties listed; and the Parthenon and Athens, which live on in Cummings' poems. There were also Italian restaurants. And there was, of course, the Howard Athenaeum, affectionately called the "Old Howard," the throne and home of burlesque—whenever the Watch and Ward Society was not snooping around.

Damon, who accompanied Cummings on these Athenian ram-bles, met him first in a morning class in German literature in Cummings' junior year. "I was the first of the D's, he was the last of the C's," Damon said, and thus they became acquainted. He told me that Cummings was terribly shy, that he held a newspaper up to his face when riding in a street car, and that he would not be photographed with the *Monthly* staff. Cummings, he recalled, liked to talk about Shelley, and gave him a copy of Shelley's poems; about the Rossetti sonnet; and about Swinburne. At the time they met "Cummings was writing double ballades and all the trick forms."

Damon and Cummings also took Dean Briggs's famous course in poetic composition. Students were graded "inexplicably," Damon, who was to become a professor himself, related with a slightly quizzical look. One day Dean Briggs—who read Donne aloud "with great persuasiveness and charm," according to T. S. Eliot—read a poem by Damon, in which occurs this line:

Thy mouth is a fragrant wound of the twilight.

"Everybody, including the Dean," Damon told me, "shuddered."

Briggs told the class that he had shown the line to Professor Barrett Wendell, who termed it "putrescent." Whereupon Cummings stood up and asked:

"Dean Briggs, but why don't you like it?"

Damon said there was no reply—"just a look." But he was quick to add that "we all owe something to Dean Briggs for his teaching."

John Dos Passos and Robert Hillyer were also members of this class. Hillyer wrote me: "Our group in his courses was divided into the Ancients and the Moderns. I was an Ancient, of course; Cummings, Foster Damon and Dos Passos were Moderns." (Hillyer afterwards held the same chair as Dean Briggs—the Boylston Chair of Rhetoric and Oratory—and gave the same courses.)

Among themselves, the undergraduate poets were in despair. Damon told me: "We kept saying to each other that no more poetry could be written, that the best poems had already been written, and all the subjects were used up. There could be no more romantic poetry because there would be no more wars, the nations were so economically interdependent."

In the lecture from which I have been quoting, Cummings pays his respects to Damon, "who opened my eyes and ears not merely to Domenico Theotocopuli [i.e., El Greco] and William Blake, but to all ultra (at that moment) modern music and poetry and painting." Damon told me that Cummings, who had also become a member of the Musical Club, offered to teach him Greek in exchange for lessons in harmony. "Cummings," he recalled, "wrote several pieces of music for the piano, picking them out on the keys." Presumably Damon wrote them down, for he told me he still had them.

Dos Passos also remembers Cummings at the piano. He wrote me: "Let's see what I can remember about my *Monthly* days. Cummings's extraordinary verbal effervescence, the oldfashioned Cambridge household on Irving Street where his father presided at the head of the long table . . . I've cherished my recollection of it as a link with the Jameses and all the generations of old New Englanders back to Emerson and Thoreau . . . Italian restaurants and cheap Italian wine in Boston . . . Cummings improvising on the piano for the edification of his admiring family. Dr. Cummings booming from the pulpit—was it the Arlington Street church? or did I hear him preach there on some special occasion?"

It was probably Damon who showed Cummings the work of an almost forgotten poet named Donald Evans, the author of five books of verse, the first of which, *Discords*, appeared in 1912. Evans was a type of aesthete who moved in uptown society circles as well as downtown literary ones. He wrote with elegance but was smothered by facility. He was the enthusiastic publisher of Gertrude Stein's *Tender Buttons*, which he issued under the imprint of "Claire Marie" at 3 East Fourteenth Street in 1914. This, too, found its way to Harvard, where Cummings read it.

"Practically everything I know about painting and poetry came to me through Damon," Cummings told me. It was Damon who showed him a little book that was to have a profound influence on his work—*Ripostes*, by Ezra Pound, published in 1912. Perhaps equally important was the Imagist credo, in which Pound and his group in England stated certain aims, among them: "To produce poetry that is hard and clear, never blurred nor indefinite."

Cummings was also grateful to another student, Theodore Miller, who introduced him not only to the poems of Catullus, Horace, and Sappho in the original Latin and Greek; "but the token of whose most memorable kindness was a volume combining poems and letters by that glorious human being who confessed:

I am certain of nothing but of the holiness of the Heart's affections, and the truth of Imagination.

Whereupon—deep in those heights of psychic sky which had greeted my boyish escape from moralism—an unknown and unknowable bird began singing" ("Nonlecture Three").

The quotation is from Keats's letter to Benjamin Bailey, dated 22 November, 1817. Less than a year later, on July 18, 1818, Keats wrote to Bailey, among other things: "when I see you, the first thing I shall do will be to read that about Milton and Ceres, and Proserpine."

I asked Cummings if he was aware of the resemblance between the passage in *Paradise Lost* to which Keats here refers and his own beautiful "Tumbling-hair," and quoted both. He expressed genuine surprise. This is from Book IV of *Paradise Lost*:

> Not that fair field
> Of Enna, where Proserpin gathering flowers,
> Herself a fairer flower, by gloomy Dis
> Was gathered—which cost Ceres all that pain
> To seek her through the world. . . .

And this is Cummings' poem written while at Harvard:

Tumbling-hair
        picker of buttercups
                violets
dandelions
And the big bullying daisies
                through the field wonderful
with eyes a little sorry
Another comes
        also picking flowers

One other slight but curious echo in Cummings' poetry is also from Milton; I refer to the last two lines of "The Hymn" in Milton's "On the Morning of Christ's Nativity":

And all about the courtly stable
Bright-harnessed angels sit in order serviceable.

Cummings wrote:

(and i imagine
never mind Joe agreeably cheerfully remarked when
surrounded by fat stupid animals
the jewess shrieked
the messiah tumbled successfully into the world
the animals continued eating. And I imagine she, and
heard them slobber and
in the darkness)

stood sharp angels with faces like Jim Europe[1]

There were also direct influences from the poems of Keats. This passage by Cummings is from "Longing":

                The Christlike sun
Moves to his resurrection in rejoicing heights,
And priestly hills partake of morning one by one.

[1] A famous colored band leader before World War I. Gilbert Seldes wrote in *The Seven Lively Arts*: "Jim Europe seemed to have a constructive intelligence and, had he lived, I am sure he would have been an even greater conductor than Whiteman." A drummer shot him dead.

"The one use of a man's knowing the classics is to prevent him from imitating the false classics," wrote Ezra Pound to Margaret Anderson.

### 3

Cummings was graduated from Harvard, June 24, 1915, *magna cum laude* like his father before him, but in English and the classics instead of philosophy. Although he did not "make" Phi Beta Kappa, he was invited to speak at the Commencement Celebration in Sanders Theatre. The exercises began earlier than was usually the case in order to include the ceremony that marked the presentation of the Widener Memorial Library to the University. The following is from the official account in the Harvard *Alumni Bulletin* of June 30, 1915, but I shall also give an "unofficial" version so far as the effect of Cummings' talk was concerned:

"The weather was unseasonably cool, and the Yard seemed less filled with graduates than in other years. The presence of women as invited guests at the Library exercises made good the deficiency in numbers.

"At the morning exercises in Sanders Theatre, Paul Perham Cram, '15, delivered the Latin Oration; Henry Parkman, '15, had for the subject of his part, 'Neutralization: its Past and its Future'; Edward Estlin Cummings, '15, spoke on 'The New Art'; and Clarence Belden Randall, A.B., of the Law School, on 'The Undertow in Education.'

"President Lowell conferred 1124 degrees."

The original manuscript of Cummings' talk in the Harvard archives is a rewarding document. It afterwards appeared in the *Advocate* with some slight changes. If the reader will bear in mind the age of the speaker and the date of the speech, he will be struck by the extraordinary perception Cummings displayed (and which could hardly be entirely appreciated). His composition begins:

"The New Art has many branches [in the published version he added "painting, sculpture, architecture, the stage, literature, and music"]. In each of these there is a clearly discernible evolution from models. In none is there any trace of that abnormality or incoherence which the casual critic is fond of making the subject of tirades against the new order. It is my aim to sketch briefly the parallel developments of the New Art in the fields of painting and sculpture, music, and literature.

"Anyone who takes Art seriously, who understands the development of technique in the last half century, accepts Cézanne and Matisse as he accepts Manet and Monet. But this brings us to the point where contemporary criticism becomes, for the most part, rampant abuse, and where prejudice utters its storm of condemnation. I refer to that peculiar phase of the New Art called indiscriminately 'Cubism' and 'Futurism.'

"The term Cubism, properly applied, relates to the work of a small group of ultra-modern painters and sculptors who use design to express their personal reaction to the subject, and who further take this design from geometry. By using an edge in place of a curve a unique tactual value is obtained. . . .

"The painter Matisse has been called the greatest exponent of Cubist sculpture. At the 1913 Exhibition, the crowd around Brancusi's 'Mlle. Pogany' was only rivalled by that which swarmed around the painting called 'Nude Descending a Staircase,'[2] which Walter Pach has analyzed as 'phrasing of the elements of motion, mass, and accentuation.' "

Of music, he said: "While Germany has the honor of producing one of the greatest originators and masters of realism, Richard Strauss, it is a French school, inspired by César Franck, which brought new life to music. One of the most interesting of the modern composers is Erik Satie. Twenty-five years ago[3] he was writing what is now considered modern music. The most striking aspect of Satie's art is the truly extraordinary sense of humor which prompts one of his subjects, the sea-cucumber, to console himself philosophically for his lack of tobacco."

[2] By Marcel Duchamp.
[3] 1890.

He also praised Schönberg and Stravinsky.

In introducing the portion of his talk dealing with literature, Cummings declared: "I shall discuss only the most extreme cases, quoting three contemporary authors to illustrate different phases and different degrees of the literary parallel to sound-painting [in the published version he added, "in a rather faint hope that the first two may prepare the way for an appreciation of the third"]. First Amy Lowell's 'Grotesque' offers a clear illustration of development from the normal to the abnormal:

> Why do the lilies goggle their tongues at me
> When I pluck them;
> And writhe and twist,
> And strangle themselves against my fingers,
> So that I can hardly weave the garland
> For your hair?
> Why do they shriek your name
> And spit at me
> When I would cluster them?
> Must I kill them
> To make them lie still,
> And send you a wreath of lolling corpses
> To turn putrid and soft
> On your forehead
> When you dance?

"In this interesting poem we seem to discern something beyond the conventional. The lilies are made to express hatred by means of grotesque images. But there is nothing new in the pathetic fallacy."

It is doubtful if anyone was listening; the audience had not yet recovered from the shock of the first quoted line coming, as it did, on the heels of Cummings' remark that the poem offered "a clear illustration of development from the normal to the abnormal." Professor Damon, the biographer of Miss Lowell, wrote: "Sanders

Theatre shuddered in sibilant horror as he recited: 'Why do the lilies goggle their tongues at me,' " and adds:

"One aged lady (peace be to her bones!) was heard to remark aloud: 'Is that our president's sister's poetry he is quoting? Well, I think it is an *insult* to our president!' Meanwhile the president's face, on which all eyes were fixed, was absolutely unperturbed. But one of the Boston newspapers, which did not truckle to the Brahmins, came out with the headlines recalled as 'Harvard Orator Calls President Lowell's Sister Abnormal.' "

Leaving Amy Lowell, probably to the relief of her august brother and Damon's "aged lady," Cummings quoted eight lines from a sonnet by Donald Evans, and I give them chiefly for the comment with which he followed them:

> Her voice was fleet-limbed and immaculate,
> And like peach blossoms blown across the wind;
> Her white words made the hour seem cool and kind,
> Hung with soft dawns that danced a shadow fête.
> A silken silence crept up from the South,
> The flutes were hushed that mimed the orange moon,
> And down the willow stream my sighs were strewn,
> As I knelt to the corners of her mouth.

Cummings said: "With the figure 'her voice was fleet-limbed,' and the phrase 'white words,' it is interesting to compare Dante's expressions, occurring in the first and fifth cantos of the *Inferno:* 'dove il Sol tace,' and 'in loco d'ogni luce muto.' But even Dante would not have dared 'the corners of her mouth' [the last sentence is omitted from the printed text].

"From Donald Evans to Gertrude Stein is a natural step, up or down, and one which I had hoped we might take in security. Gertrude Stein is a Futurist who subordinates the meaning of words to the beauty of the words themselves. Her art is the logic of literary sound-painting carried to its extreme. While we must admit that it is logic, must we admit that it is Art?

"Having prepared the way as best I can for a just appreciation,

I now do my best to quote from her book, 'Tender Buttons,' as follows:

(1) A Sound.
> Elephant beaten with candy and little pops and chews all bolts and reckless, reckless rats, this is this.

(2) Salad Dressing and Artichoke.
> Please pale hot, please cover rose, please acre in the red stranger, please butter all the beefsteak with regular feel faces.

(3) Suppose an Eyes.

. . . . . . . . . . . . . . . . . . . . . . . . .
> Go red, go red, laugh white.
> Suppose a collapse is rubbed purr, is rubbed purget. Little sales ladies little sales ladies little saddles of mutton.
> Little sales of leather and such beautiful beautiful, beautiful, beautiful.

Here we see traces of realism similar to those which made the 'Nude Descending the Staircase' so baffling. The book from which these selections are taken is undoubtedly a proof of great imagination on the part of the author, as any one who tries to imitate her style will discover for himself. But as far as these 'Tender Buttons' are concerned, the sum and substance of criticism is zero, for the reason that criticism is impossible. The unparalleled familiarity of the medium precludes its use for the purposes of aesthetic effect. And here, in their logical conclusion, impressionist principles are reduced to absurdity.

"The question now arises: How much of all this is really Art?

"The answer is: We do not know. The great men of the future will undoubtedly profit by the experimentation of the present period [in the published version he added here: "An insight into the unbroken chain of artistic development during the last half century disproves the theory that modern is without foundation"], for this very experimentation is the logical unfolding of sound tendencies. That the conclusion is in a particular case absurdity does not in any way vitiate the value of the experiment provided we are dealing with sincere effort. The New Art, discredited though it be by fakirs and fanatics, will appear in its essential spirit to the unprejudiced critic as a courageous and genuine exploration of untrodden ways."

## 4

Cummings stayed on at the Harvard Graduate School of Arts and Sciences for another year, and emerged an M.A. During his final year he helped to organize the Harvard Poetry Society, which met on the top floor of the Union. I am indebted to Malcolm Cowley for this freshman's-eye glimpse of Cummings and his circle at this time:

"I didn't know him when he was in college. By the fall of 1915, Cummings was already a graduate student, outside the horizon of a freshman, but I must have seen him at two or three meetings of the Poetry Society, held in the sanctum of the Harvard *Monthly*. I can't remember whether he read his poems, though I clearly remember readings by others—for example, Foster Damon, whose voice became flat and matter-of-fact when he recited an especially outrageous line; and Robert Hillyer, looking like a wicked cherub; and John Dos Passos, speaking in very low tones as he peered at a manuscript from behind very thick lenses."

The formation of the Poetry Society apparently engendered a certain amount of spiteful or malicious gossip on the campus. Among those who gossiped most were undergraduate poets who were not members. Although its founders were chiefly contributors to the *Monthly*, it was the rival *Advocate* that struck back with an indignant editorial (which incidentally reveals some of the things that were being said):

"There has been gossip abroad concerning just what sort of an organization the Harvard Poetry Society is. There have been hints of effeminacy, of desires on the part of its members to grasp the flickering halo of aestheticism that hovers about the long locks of pseudo-geniuses. The falsehood of such gossip is something that is not to be discussed. But the seeming malice of what has been the current libel is something to be deplored and to be stopped at once. The Harvard Poetry Society is doing its small best to gain more intellectual and artistic benefit, by their meetings and the privilege of listening to well-known poets, than is required to enter 'the brotherhood of educated men' by reason of English A and sixteen other courses. If those who disapprove of such endeavor do not care to join the society, or who, by lack of ability, are unable to secure admission, let them by all means remain absent. And let the howling, that is seemingly so much in vogue, cease. It ill-befits students with any claim to seriousness. Let those who scoff ape gentlemen, or let them at least swallow their sour grape scorn in silence."

A feeling admonition.

On the evening of February 28, 1916, Amy Lowell came to address the new society. In her honor a festive board, consisting of beer and pretzels, adorned the big table at which she was to sit in massive superiority. Also, in order to provide a respectable audience, as regards numbers, the meeting was officially denominated "a candidates' meeting," so that undergraduates who were not members of the *Monthly* staff or of the Poetry Society might hear her. The room was consequently full. Miss Lowell talked about her favorite subject and practice—*vers libre*.

"I suppose you think that Whitman wrote it; well, he didn't." That was that.

At the end of her talk she read "Patterns" and "The Cross-Roads" from the manuscript of her forthcoming book, *Men, Women and Ghosts*. This was followed by a discussion.

John Brooks Wheelwright, one of the Society poets who was later to refer to Miss Lowell as "Biggest Traveling One-Man Show since Buffalo Bill caught the Midnight Flyer to contact Mark Twain," and who had a flair for showmanship himself, rose to ask a question. It had probably been much considered for its "shock" value.

"Miss Lowell, what do you do when you want to write a poem and haven't anything to write about?"

All eyes were on the questioner, who looked—as Horace Gregory has described him—like "a pre-Revolutionary Bostonian," slender, with "a fine head with a nearly 'hawklike' nose, thin lips, and slightly slanted, narrowed eyes," while the two New England blue-bloods peered at each other over an immense silence. But Miss Lowell never answered.

It was now Cummings' turn. He, too, had framed a question. But whether from shyness, or Miss Lowell's abrupt departure, he almost missed his chance. Damon says in his book: "As she was leaving, with a regretful glance at the centerpiece of beer and pretzels, which nobody offered to disturb, E. E. Cummings asked her what she thought of Gertrude Stein.

" 'Do *you* like her work?' Miss Lowell replied, Yankee-wise.

" 'Why—yes—.'

" 'I don't!' "

And she swept massively out into the night, where her carriage waited.

(Twenty-two years after his Harvard talk and this exchange with Amy Lowell, I innocently asked Cummings what *he* thought of Gertrude Stein. This was his reply: "I tried to read her. I can feel some things, but she doesn't give me as many things as some people get. [Here, I noted at the time, his eyes brightened.] She's a symbol —she's an excellent symbol, like a pillar of Portland cement. You can't budge her. Philistines bump into her and get bruised.")

In the Harvard *Monthly* for March, 1916, appeared "All in green went my love riding," and it must have been apparent at once, to all his associates, that Cummings was not only the chief poet of the Society he had helped to found, but one to challenge all his contemporaries.

# IV

## *The Making of a Book*

1

It was Stewart Mitchell who conceived the idea of putting into permanent form the work of some of the men with whom he had been associated during this memorable period. Thus was born *Eight Harvard Poets*, a collection that appeared in 1917 and whose contributors were blazoned on the title page in the following order:

> E. Estlin Cummings
> S. Foster Damon
> J. R. Dos Passos
> Robert Hillyer
> R. S. Mitchell
> William A. Norris
> Dudley Poore
> Cuthbert Wright

But while the moving spirit behind this project was Mitchell, it was John Dos Passos, ably seconded by his father, who kept the project from foundering.

For a little book—118 pages, in gray boards with a cloth back stamped with crimson lettering—*Eight Harvard Poets* appears to have been as involved a production as any in the history of publishing. In part it was due to the number of contributors, but mostly it was due to the peculiar nature of the undertaking.

Laurence J. Gomme, under whose imprint the book appeared, had been an associate of Mitchell Kennerley, whom he succeeded as proprietor of "The Little Book Shop Around the Corner," at 2 East Twenty-ninth Street, across the street from the church with the similar name. Some time in 1916, he told me, Stewart Mitchell brought him the manuscript of *Eight Harvard Poets*. Gomme said his poetry readers were Joyce Kilmer and Clement Wood, and it was to the latter that the manuscript was sent. Mr. Wood, whose first volume of verse had just been published by Gomme, was a critic as well as a poet; he once showed me his copy of *The Waste Land*, in which he had written—beside the opening lines—"No rhythm." On October 19, 1916, from his residence at 510 Audubon Avenue, New York City, Wood reported to Gomme. Of Cummings he wrote: "Take him all in all, he is only fair."

With the words "To the better ones," he found Mitchell "a delight," and liked Norris "almost as much." Poore "belies his name in the 2nd poem," "one or two" of Wright's pieces passed muster; "Hillyer's 'Sea Gull,' his Scarlatti thing, his excellent 'My Peace I Leave With You' sonnet—these are indeed good. Damon I find more like Cummings, inclined to be too much only a fair distiller of overused poetic material; and Dos Passos is good, particularly in his second and third poems, and in certain lines of 'Memory' and 'Nightpiece.'

"As a whole, the collection is good; and I hope you make it sell," was Wood's conclusion. Between his report and the publication of the book one of the most involved correspondences on record took place.

2

Mr. Gomme wrote for Mr. Mitchell on the occasion of the latter's presentation of the book to Harvard in 1941:

In May 1917, "The Little Book Shop Around the Corner" closed its doors and with it came the end to my publishing business.

As I was already under contract for the "Eight Harvard Poets" which was at this time in the process of printing, I took temporary quarters in the old Washington Irving House, corner of 17th Street and Irving Place, occupying the front room on the ground floor of this historic mansion. "Eight Harvard Poets" was produced from there. It was the last book I published before going into war work.

Early in June of 1917, Mr. Dos Passos sailed for Europe for the American Red Cross Ambulances, he therefore did not see the book until his return. Under the contract thirty copies were sent to each of the authors for their own use.

I have been informed that one of the authors who up to this moment I have been unable to identify, has not thought so well of his appearance in the volume and has destroyed all copies that came within his grasp. Perhaps this accounts for the rarity of this small but interesting contribution to American poetry.

The unidentified author referred to by Gomme was William A. Norris, who became a businessman, and is reputed to have bought up all copies of *Eight Harvard Poets* he could lay hands on in order to destroy them. It explains why, in the copy of the book deposited at Harvard by Stewart Mitchell, there are only seven autographs. It also explains Mitchell's letter, which accompanied the book:

This volume was planned at first as *Seven Harvard Poets*. Owing to the insistence of one of the seven, however, an eighth contributor was added—William Allis Norris, of Milwaukee, Wisconsin, of the Class of 1917.

Having secured the autograph of Cuthbert Wright late in September, 1940, I wrote to Norris, asking him if he would be willing to put his name in the volume, which I was going to present to the Harvard College Library. I did not receive the courtesy of a reply.

Obviously the feeling that the appearance of Norris in this book was a mistake is now mutual.

To return to 1916: on November 3 Gomme wrote to John R. Dos Passos, the novelist's father, a well-known lawyer with offices at 120 Broadway:

For the purpose of my records, I would outline the details discussed in our conversation regarding the book we are publishing under the title "Eight Harvard Poets."

We are to print five hundred copies with plates. It is understood that permission has been granted by the various holders of the rights. Upon publication, I am to supply thirty copies to the eight authors at a price of $1.00 less 1/3%. The first five hundred copies will be published free of royalty. All copies sold after five hundred have been disposed of, will be on a 10% royalty basis.

The price of the book will be $1.00, unless at the time of manufacturing the price of paper is so advanced as to make this impossible. In that case we will have to make the price $1.25, and the price of the book to the eight authors will have to be advanced in proportion. As this was a point I did not take up with you, I submit it to you for your approval now.

The acknowledgment of this letter will be sufficient contract on both sides.

To this, Mr. Dos Passos replied, November 9, as follows:

Your letter dated November the 3rd was directed to me, whereas it was intended for my son, John R. Dos Passos Jr. He is now in Madrid, having gone there to enter the University to perfect himself in Spanish and other courses. He told me all about the terms of the publication of the book, the "Eight Harvard Poets." Your version of the understanding is correct and you can assume this to be a confirmation of the same on behalf of my son. If you will kindly write me about any matter relating to the book I shall be glad to act for my son as to its publication. I am forwarding your letter to him with a copy of this letter also.

The letters were duly forwarded; on December 22, 1916, John Dos Passos wrote to Gomme from Madrid:

Your letter—to which my father replied—has just reached me. If anything should come up in regard to the Anthology—Dudley S. Poore or R. S. Hillyer—Cambridge would be the best people to get in touch with. Still, I hardly think anything will—except the small "i's," which you may be as high handed about as you like as far as I am concerned.

By the way, the terms are completely satisfactory, that is:— each of the eight are to take thirty copies—at the retail price minus a third, and if another edition is thought advisable we are to get 10% royalty.

Lastly, please don't let them forget the "Junior" at the end of my name on the title page. It would be too bad to saddle my father with my poems!

Thus ended the old year. The new began with trepidations on the part of Gomme, which he seems to have communicated to several of the contributors.

Mr. Gomme's correspondence, which he kindly placed at my disposal, includes a letter from Cuthbert Wright that was in reply to one of his, unfortunately missing. But its subject can be guessed —Cummings' typography, to which Dos Passos had briefly referred. Wright, who seems to have been the only member of the Eight not on the move or march, wrote on Harvard Union stationery, January 13:

In regard to *Eight Harvard Poets,* I find that Cummings has gone to N.Y. and can be addressed in care of Collier's Weekly. If he makes any difficulty about the poem I should suggest that it be dropped out. If you will address me as above I shall be glad to read the proof and be personally responsible for getting it back expeditiously. I am sorry not to report on the man to write the preface but will do so as soon as possible. Mr. Wendell has re- tired and may not do it, but either Bliss Perry or W. A. Neilson would consent I am sure.

I hope I may serve you in the matter if you need any help at this end.

## 3

It is not easy at this late date to determine which poem Dos
Passos and Wright had reference to. Cummings led off the book,
as he did the roster of contributors, with eight poems, which
occupy pages 3 to 10. There were four sonnets, which are among
Cummings' best: "Thou in whose swordgreat story shine the
deeds," "when thou hast taken thy last applause," "this is the
garden: colours come and go," and "it may not always be so."
The first and third appeared afterwards in *XLI Poems*; the
second and fourth, in *Tulips and Chimneys*. The four remaining
poems were : "i will wade out," "Over silent waters," "your little
voice," and "Tumbling-hair." The first appeared in *XLI Poems*;
the third and fourth, in *Tulips and Chimneys*. The second, entitled
"Finis" in *Eight Harvard Poets*, has never been collected:

>Over silent waters
>
>                    day descending
>
>                                        night ascending
>floods the gentle glory of the sunset
>In a golden greeting
>                    splendidly to westward
>as pale twilight
>                    trem-
>                        bles
>                            into
>                                Darkness
>comes the last light's gracious exhortation
>                                Lifting up to peace
>so when life shall falter
>                    standing on the shores of the
>eternal
>god
>        May I behold my sunset
>Flooding
>            over silent waters

There was one final flurry. Cummings told me that Dos Passos came to see him just before going abroad on war service. "As I remember it Dos was greatly agitated," he said. "He asked me what I proposed to do about the lowercase 'i's' in the poems, and I replied—I heard myself with surprise—that the poems must stand as they were.

"It was," he added, "the beginning of my style."

But while the typographical arrangements were allowed to stand, someone—Gomme thinks the printer—capitalized all the "i's" when the book went to press.

The flurry among the poets was followed by a bombshell from Gomme, who wrote to the senior Dos Passos on February 8:

On November 3rd I wrote to you in regard to the publication of "Eight Harvard Poets." Since that time I find that it has become more and more difficult to publish books, owing to the very high cost of material; and conditions make possibilities of sales extremely uncertain.

It is with this feeling I am writing to ask you to release me from the obligation to bring this book out. Conditions have changed to such an extent recently that I doubt very much whether there will be sufficient demand for books of this character to justify the expense of production. It is with great regret that I am writing to you in this vein as I looked forward with a good deal of pleasure to producing what I feel would be a very worthy collection of poems.

On March 29 Gomme addressed a second letter to 120 Broadway. The tone of both suggests that he, like the poets concerned, was not altogether desirous of having the project dropped. The communications might be termed "feelers," without offense to anyone. They proved successful. John Dos Passos wrote me (September 29, 1957):

"My recollection is that I induced my father John R. Dos Passos, the lawyer, to put up $750 to guarantee the printing costs."

Dos Passos had returned to this country from Spain and, following the death of his father, had enlisted in the Norton Harjes

Ambulance Corps. "A Bord de 'Chicago' " of the French Line on June 20, 1917, he scribbled a hasty note to Gomme:

My dear Mr. Gomme—

I didn't get a chance to get to see you this morning—my wild rush for the boat.

Enclosed is the letter about the upwards $200.

Will you please send your letter to my aunt, Mrs. J. R. Gordon at the address I gave you.

Also, when that millenial day arrives and the Eight finally see the light, will you please write Mr. Mitchell to find out how many copies he wants. If you send me five copies—or perhaps six—it will be sufficient. Then I shall send Mr. Poore two & Mr. Hillyer two, as I shall know where in France they will be.

Best wishes,<br>J. R. Dos Passos

Address
    —c/o American Red Cross Ambulance
        7 Rue François Premier
            Paris

It would appear that Gomme wrote to Mrs. Gordon without delay. On June 21, from 214 Riverside Drive, she replied:

Your note of June 20 was rec'd this morning. Mr. Dos Passos asked me to pay you the balance on the printing bill of the volume on its completion—which I shall be glad to attend to for him. He said that he thought the volume would be ready next week.

But it was not until July 12 that the first copy was ready. Gomme wrote Mrs. Gordon:

Dear Madam,

I have pleasure in sending by this mail the first copy of Eight Harvard Poets off the press. The book is now ready for distribution.

I would esteem it a favour if you would send me a check for

the balance on the printing bill as indicated on the enclosed invoice.

I hope you will like the appearance of the book. It has been a very great pleasure to me to see the book through the press and I feel sure it will receive the attention good verse deserves.

Yours very sincerely,
Laurence J. Gomme

He also notified some of the contributors that the book was "about to be published in a few days." It may be that Norris was already feeling some uneasiness about his role as a published poet. I do not know how many letters Gomme sent him in all; I know that he wrote him on June 26 and July 9 and 12, after appealing to Wright, who replied:

Norris is still in the Harvard Regiment and can be addressed either at his old rooms or care of *Harvard Reserved Officers Training Comp., Harvard University.*

Dr. Cummings' address is *Irving Street, Cambridge, Mass.*

On July 12, which seems to have been a busy day in the life of Gomme, another letter went to Norris at his new address, as well as one to Dr. Edward Cummings, who replied on stationery of the World Peace Foundation, 40 Mt. Vernon Street, Boston, of which he was General Secretary:

Dear Sir:

It gives me pleasure to enclose check for twenty dollars, in accordance with the arrangement made by Mr. Dos Passos, with the understanding that you will forward me thirty copies of the volume entitled "Eight Harvard Poets."

Sincerely yours,
Edward Cummings

On the same day, Damon wrote Gomme on the letterhead of the Reserve Officers' Training Corps, Harvard Barracks, requesting that one copy of the book be sent to "Company K, Barre, Mass., and the rest to the address I sent you before."

A long delay now ensued, vexing to all concerned. Dr. Cum-mings went to New Hampshire, and returned from New Hampshire, and there was still no sign of the book. On September 19, from his home in Irving Street, he addressed Gomme once more, this time in stern vein. After quoting the whole of Gomme's letter to him of July 12, he said:

On July 23, I sent you a check for $20, with directions for forwarding the books by parcel post or by express.

More recently, I wrote stating that the check had come back to me with your endorsement, showing that it had been cashed; but that I had received no word with regard to the books which you assured me ready for distribution on July 12. I heard nothing from this letter.

Do you wish me to begin legal proceedings, or may I have the favor of a prompt reply?

Sincerely yours,
Edward Cummings

However these matters were finally straightened out, the mystery surrounding the publication of *Eight Harvard Poets* persisted as late as 1949, when Jack Potter, a Chicago bookseller specializing in British and American nineteenth- and twentieth-century first editions, wrote to Gomme for information:

I can find no record, in fact, that the book was ever formally published. There is no listing of it in the copyright annals, nor was a copy sent to *Publisher's Weekly*. Further, it was apparently never reviewed, as it is not mentioned in *Book Review Digest*.

I do know that the Library of Congress acquired a copy in 1923, but this was evidently a copy they bought rather than the copyright deposit copy.

The size of the printing is not so vital a matter as knowing the approximate date of publication. I have always assumed that this latter was Spring, 1917, but the fact that I am unable thus far to trace it at all has made me wonder if it was delayed indefinitely.

To this, Gomme replied:

> Regarding the *Eight Harvard Poets*, it was published in August
> 1917.... Two thousand copies were printed, one hundred copies
> of which were sent to each of the contributors.... There is one
> thing in your letter I cannot quite understand, that the Library
> of Congress' copy sent to them for Copyright is not in their
> files—I entered the Copyright in accordance with the Law.

### 4

Neither Professor Neilson, an eminent Shakespeare scholar
and teacher, nor Professor Perry wrote a preface for *Eight Harvard
Poets*; the book appeared without one. But one day in Cambridge
Neilson asked Cummings whether he would like a job in New
York. Cummings jumped at the chance. It was not, however, with
*Collier's Weekly*, as Wright supposed, but with the parent firm of
P. F. Collier & Son, Inc., which ran a mail-order business in books,
usually in sets. Its offices were at 416 West Thirteenth Street, and
there Cummings went to work for fifty dollars a week, an enormous
sum in those days, particularly for a young man. His job was to
answer letters elicited by advertisements in *Collier's Weekly*.
Cummings recalled for me the substance and spelling of some of
these untutored epistles; in one of them, a woman complained that
her "husban" could not stand the "noyz" of her sewing machine.
This stumped him, and he turned to his boss, who told him to look
at the ads—there was sure to be one of a silent machine. His
boss, Cummings told me, used to strike out most of his sentences,
with the result, he said, "I learned how to write a business letter."
Whenever someone came into the office, he said, his boss stood up,
and he did likewise because "I was brought up that way," but this
was deprecated by his boss, who, he added, was a Yale man. Most
of the time, Cummings said, he had nothing to do.

"I read both Eddas in the three months I worked there," he told
me.

During this period he lived at 21 East Fifteenth Street, just off

Fifth Avenue, with Arthur ("Texas") Wilson, a friend of his
college days who had shocked Harvard by a short story called "The
Girl Who Advertised." Wilson was also a poet, and later appeared
in *The Dial*; then he became a painter specializing in seascapes.
Of his first home in New York, Cummings recalled that there was
a photographer's studio upstairs where young women posed in the
nude. The women soon discovered that there were no plates in the
camera, and that they were being paid merely to display themselves
while the photographer, covered with a large hood, made a pretense
of pressing the bulb. As they were models, it made no difference
to them so long as they were paid. Cummings explained that this
was in the days before sex magazines, and the "photographer"
simply liked to look at nudes.

Thus it happened that, in his twenty-second year, Cummings
plunged exuberantly—if briefly this first time—into the city that
was henceforth to be his home.

"After Harvard," he declared in "Nonlecture Three," "I thank
(for self discovery) a phenomenon and a miracle. The phenomenon was a telemicroscopic chimera, born of the satanic rape of
matter by mind: a phallic female phantasm, clothed in thunderous
anonymity and adorned with colossally floating spiderwebs of traf-
fic; a stark irresistibly stupendous newness, mercifully harboring
among its pitilessly premeditated spontaneities immemorial races
and nations."

The miracle was to come: Paris.

Cummings had arrived in New York not only with Professor
Neilson's introduction, which resulted in a job, but bearing three
other letters to magazine editors from Amy Lowell, who also wrote
to the editors themselves. In his biography of her, Professor Damon
gives the form she used in addressing the editors of the *Century*,
*Scribner's Magazine*, and *Craftsman*:

> I am taking the liberty of giving a letter of introduction to
> you to a young Harvard graduate, named Erstline [sic] Cum-
> mings. He has been specializing in English I believe, and had
> one of the Commencement parts last year, in which I hear he

was very brilliant. He is extremely interested in all forms of the
New Poetry, but I do not think confines himself to that branch
of literature. He is very anxious to get something to do on a
magazine, and although I have very little hope that you will
have anything to give him, perhaps you would be so kind as to
see him for a few minutes and give him some excellent advice.
At any rate, I hope that I am not trespassing upon a very slight
acquaintance; if I am, pray ignore both this note and the letter
he will bring you.

It is not likely that her notes were ignored, or that the letters
Cummings bore would have been. He simply did not present
them.

After three months at Collier's, Cummings "fired" himself—
"the most intelligent thing I could possibly have done." He had
learned, he told me, once and for all, what "having a job" means,
how it feels to "earn your living" in a country "where nothing
outranks the almighty dollar," and what price a human being pays
for "security." Meanwhile, he said, "America was becoming less
and less secure."

Arthur Wilson, one day, joined the American Army as an
aviator. It was now, of course, a question of time before Cummings
would be called up for service. He journeyed to 2 Rector Street
and signed up as a volunteer ambulance driver with the Norton
Harjes Ambulance Corps. Among the other volunteers at this
time was a good-looking devil-may-care product of Webster,
Massachusetts, and Columbia University. His name was William
Slater Brown. (When I asked Brown how a New Englander got
to Columbia University, he replied: "I couldn't get out of New
England fast enough, and the first chance came with college.")
He was then twenty years old. Cummings was twenty-three.

Young Americans slipped into Canada to enlist in the Royal
Flying Corps, among them William Faulkner; they enlisted in the
French Army, like Alan Seeger, or in the French military transport,
like Malcolm Cowley. Many of them, being in Cummings' phrase
"neither warrior nor conscientious objector," enlisted in the

American Field Service or the Norton Harjes Ambulance Corps. Cowley wrote in *Exile's Return*: "We were eager to get into action, as a character in one of Dos Passos' novels expressed it, 'before the whole thing goes belly up.' " Dos Passos wrote me:

Although I was an enthusiastic pacifist I wanted to get into the ambulance service to see what the war was like. There hadn't been any great wars for some time. The attraction was enormous. My eyes were so myopic that it was the only way I could get anywhere near action. Another motive was that I had a horror of serving in the army . . . a good many other young men of my generation felt the same way. Everybody's idea was to get into the war without getting into the army. Later, after I'd seen the front lines a little, I felt quite differently. In fact I went to a great deal of trouble to get into the army after the volunteer services were disbanded and I've always been glad that I did. It was the most valuable part of my education during these years.

Cummings felt the same way. He has great sympathy for conscientious objectors, but never could understand those who were not and yet avoided service, or were resentful over having to serve.

"World War One," he told me, "was the experience of my generation."

He went on to explain that those who had consciously shut themselves off from it were ever afterwards "outsiders." He admitted that he volunteered with Norton Harjes to avoid the U. S. Army. "It was an opportunity to do something useful and to see France at the same time. Of course," he added, smiling, "the Army got me afterwards; but I didn't mind."

# V

## *The Poet at War*

**1**

Cummings and William Slater Brown sailed, the last week in April, 1917, on *La Touraine* of the French Line. They had not yet met. Brown told me that he was talking to another volunteer ambulance driver, who asked Cummings, about to pass them on a stroll around the deck, for a light. Perhaps Cummings was wearing the fur coat that was to figure so comically in *The Enormous Room*. Introductions followed. (Malcolm Cowley was also on board, but did not meet them during the voyage.) After this chance encounter Brown and Cummings became inseparable, with the ship's bar a frequent background for their talks. They were still talking when they landed at Boulogne. But eagerly as they looked forward to Paris, little did they suspect that by a missed signal, to which all organized effort is susceptible, they would have a fairly lengthy stay there. It happened as follows.

On the boat-train, the leader of their group became more and more excited as they neared Paris. Just before the capital he rushed through the cars, shouting for all to be ready to detrain, and all—

incredible as it may sound—detrained at the next stop, which was not Paris at all, but a suburb. Brown and Cummings, busy with their own affairs, paid no attention, and consequently arrived where they were supposed to. But when they reported at 7, rue François Premier, they were told to await orders, as they could not be sent to the front as individuals. This was—in Brown's recollection—May 7 or 8. The rest of their group reported as a body after they left, and were quickly assigned and shipped out. Still awaiting assignment, Brown and Cummings spent a blissful month in Paris.

"I participated in an actual marriage of material and immaterial things," Cummings afterwards wrote; "I celebrated an immediate reconciling of spirit and flesh, forever and now, heaven and earth. Paris was for me precisely and complexly this homogeneous duality: this accepting transcendence; this living and dying more than death or life. Whereas—by the very act of becoming its improbably gigantic self—New York had reduced mankind to a tribe of pygmies, Paris (in each shape and gesture and avenue and cranny of her being) was continuously expressing the humanness of humanity. Everywhere I sensed a miraculous presence, not of mere children and women and men, but of living human beings" ("Nonlecture Three").

He was to return to Paris again and again; but it was to New York that he returned to live.

In that incredible month he and Brown took in all that Paris had to offer. Among their more memorable experiences was Stravinsky's *Petrouchka*. Brown purchased a number of Cézanne prints and placed them in a suitcase, which he left at the Red Cross. He never saw them again. In uniform at last, they were assigned together to Section Sanitaire Vingt-et-Un, Ambulance Norton Harjes, Croix Rouge Américaine. They left Paris for the Noyon sector of the front in an ambulance convoy. After an overnight stop in Compiègne they proceeded to a village outside Noyon called Ham, which was to be the scene of their debacle. To this, two things contributed: their *chef de section*, and Brown's indiscretion as a letter-writer in wartime.

First, the *chef de section*. He was soon looking with a furious eye on two happy nonconformists who thought nothing of letting grease spots stay where they had splattered; and of these there must have been a great many, for they were constantly attending to vehicles. Also, to his furious eye, it appeared from time to time as though Brown and Cummings had set out to grow beards. They were "a disgrace to the section."

"In this, I am bound to say," Cummings wrote in *The Enormous Room*, "Mr. A. was but sustaining the tradition conceived originally by his predecessor, a Mr. P., a Harvard man, who until his departure from *Vingt-et-Un* succeeded in making life absolutely miserable for both B. and myself. Before leaving this painful subject I beg to state that, at least as far as I was concerned, the tradition had a firm foundation in my own predisposition for uncouthness plus what *Le Matin* (if we remember correctly) cleverly nicknamed *La Boue Héroïque*."

Mr. A.'s advice was, "you boys want to keep away from those dirty Frenchmen" and "we're here to show those bastards how they do things in America." His name was Anderson.

These pungent remarks bring us to the second cause of the debacle. Brown and Cummings, perhaps not so much disliking their compatriots as preferring the French, easily and quickly made friends with the eight Frenchmen attached to their section, particularly the cook and provisioner (when arrested, Cummings was actually domiciled with the Frenchmen, who had made room for him "on their own initiative"). And since the section itself was attached to the French Army, they had quickly and easily made friends among the *poilus*. From the latter they heard some disquieting rumors. Brown, who had attended the Columbia School of Journalism, flashed them in letters home. (*Flashed,* however, is hardly the word, for the letters were never delivered.) There was also a letter written jointly by the two friends and a third American to the Under-Secretary of State in French Aviation offering to enlist in l'Escadrille Lafayette, in order to continue their fraternization with the French now that the United States was in the war (and had taken over the Red Cross). All letters from section members, of course, were dropped unsealed so they could be inspected for security reasons.

Three months after their arrival in Ham the blow fell. Brown and Cummings had just finished cleaning and greasing the *chef de section*'s car, a form of punishment, when a Renault drove up. In it were a police officer and two helmeted soldiers. The two friends were taken to Noyon in separate cars, which also carried their belongings. And they were interrogated separately. Cummings met Brown coming out looking, he afterwards wrote, "peculiarly cheerful." Brown, he added, cheerfully announced, "I think we're going to prison all right."

Cummings found himself looking into three pairs of eyes, not all of them unfriendly. One pair belonged to "Monsieur le Ministre de Sûreté de Noyon." He was asked his name.

" 'You are Irish?'—'No,' I said, 'American.'—'You are Irish by family?'—'No, Scotch.'—'You are sure that there was never an Irishman in your parents?'—'So far as I know,' I said, 'there never was an Irishman there.'—'Perhaps a hundred years back?' he insisted.—'Not a chance,' I said decisively. But Monsieur was not to be denied: 'Your name it is Irish?'—'Cummings is a very old Scotch name,' I told him fluently; 'it used to be Comyn. A Scotchman named The Red Comyn was killed by Robert Bruce in a church. He was my ancestor and a very well-known man.'—'But your second name, where have you got that?'—'From an Englishman, a friend of my father.' This statement seemed to produce a very favourable impression in the case of the rosette, who murmured: 'Un ami de son père, un anglais, bon!' several times."

The case against him, if case there was, did not go very well; if he had dissociated himself from Brown, he could have walked out of the interrogation almost at any point. But this he refused to do —he even insisted, after hearing the interrogator's view of Brown, that his own be put into the record: "Write this down in the testimony—that I, here present, refuse utterly to believe that my friend is not as sincere a lover of France and the French people as any man living! Tell him to write it."

He was told instead that "We have the very best reason for supposing your friend to be no friend of France."

To this Cummings replied: "That is not my affair. I want my opinion of my friend written in; do you see?"

It was written in.

Finally he was asked: *"Est-ce que vous détestez les boches?"*

In *The Enormous Room* he wrote: "I had won my case. The question was purely perfunctory. To walk out of the room a free man I had merely to say yes. My examiners were sure of my answer. The rosette was leaning forward and smiling encouragingly. The moustache was making little *oui's* in the air with his pen. And Noyon had given up all hope of making me out a criminal. I might be rash, but I was innocent; the dupe of a superior and malign intelligence. I would probably be admonished to choose my friends more carefully next time, and that would be all. . . .

"Deliberately, I framed the answer:

" '*Non. J'aime beaucoup les français.*' "

An effort was made to extricate him. If only he would admit that the Germans were hateful. "But you are doubtless aware of the atrocities committed by the *boches?*" "I have read about them." "You do not believe?" "*Ça se peut.*" "And if they are so, which of course they are, you do not detest the Germans?" "Oh, in that case, of course anyone must detest them."

It was all over. "I breathed freely once more. All my nervousness was gone. The attempt of the three gentlemen sitting before me to endow my friend and myself with different fates had irrevocably failed.

"At the conclusion of a short conference I was told by Monsieur:

" 'I am sorry for you, but due to your friend you will be detained a little while.'

"I asked: 'Several weeks?'

" 'Possibly,' said Monsieur."

With this, Cummings as well as Brown disappeared. The Red Cross was, seemingly, indifferent to their fate. It took the combined efforts of their families, friends in the government, the American

Embassy in Paris, the State Department in Washington, and a letter to the President, to find them. By a species of poetic justice, a man named Anderson was to be instrumental in bringing them aid. Meanwhile, from the Enormous Room, Cummings sent an account of what had befallen him and Brown to his mother.

Dearest of Mothers!

At 11 A.M. Monsieur le ministre de Sureté plus 2 or 3 gendarmes convoyed my friend and me in separate voitures to his abode in N. Here we dined,each with his gendarme,still apart, and later were examined. Then removed to separate cells where we spent the night. My friend must have left the following day: I spent another night in my cell(sans sortir)having enjoyed a piece of bread,a piece of chocolate(thanks to friend)a small pail(or marmite)of grease-meat soup,more bread,ditto of beans, ditto soup & bread. This sound[s] like a lot. At 10 A.M. I left in the company of 2 gendarmes for the station of N. A distance of about ½ mile. Had some trouble with a gendarme,who told me if I didn't want to carry my baggage I could leave it(I had a duffle-bag,chockfull,a long ambulance coat,a fur coat,a bed-roll,&blankets,total + 150 lbs.)by the wayside—which I naturally refused to do. We finally compromised by my hiring a sweet kid to lug bed-roll(which he did with greatest difficulty). Chemin-de-fer till 5 o'clock when landed at G. where supped on grease-meat-soup in a better cell,and slept on planks in blankets (other baggage forbidden)till 4 A.M.,when another pair of gendarmes took me to the station of G.(I with baggage)where we boarded c.def. for Paris,arriving at 6 A.M. Wait till 12 noon. In interval coffee & newspapers. At 1 train left for B.,where we arrived at 9:30 PM,I having dined on bread. All this time my friend was 1 day ahead of me. Arrived at B.,we checked big duffle-bag & roll in gare,and set off on foot for la Ferté Macé, I carrying this time merely a small bag of letters,n.books,& souvenirs,which a gendarme had always carried hitherto. Douze kilometres. Arrived midnight. Given a straw pallet & slept on floor sans blankets. In morning found self in hugely long room with my long-lost friend and about 30 others as I guess—very cosmopolite group.

The following program is ours now till 15th October,when a commission comes to examine us for pacifism or something of the sort:6—up. Coffee. 7—down to yard. 9:30 up. 10 down to salle a manger. 10:30-3:45 yard. 3:45 up. 4 down to salle a manger. 4:30-7 yard. 7 up. 9—lights out. I am having the time of my life. Never so healthy. Our meals are both soup,but we are allowed a spoon,which is better than eating with fingers,as we did in prison. By the way,a gendarme assured me this is not prison.

By the time this reaches you I shall have been out for some time. It's a great experience. Monsieur le Surveillant is a fine man. We(my friend & I) have instituted "3 old cat",which we all play in the yard when it's fair. I couldn't possibly want anything better in the way of keep,tho' you have to get used to the snores,and they don't allow you a knife,so you can't cut the air at night which is pretty thick,all windows being shut.

Elos's[1] letter I got before leaving the "front" and please thank her & give her my much love,as to all.

You can't imagine,Mother mine,how interesting a time I'm having. Not for anything in the world would I change it! It's like working—you must experience it to comprendre—but how infinitely superior to Colliers! If I thought you would excite yourself I wouldn't write from this place,but I know you will believe me when I reiterate that I am having *the time of my life!*

Always—<br>Estlin

P.S. my bagg[ag]e has been given back. I have
    my bed and am finely off! No more floor-sleeping.
P.P.S. arrested a week ago today.

[1] Elizabeth Cummings.

2

I have before me the personal and official correspondence dealing with the arrest and detention of Cummings and Brown, including Brown's intercepted letters. With the exception of Dr. Cummings' letter to President Wilson, and another by him to an officer on the staff of the Judge Advocate General, A. E. F., in Paris (parts of which appear in the Foreword to *The Enormous Room*) none of this material has ever been published before. Although at the time, which was of course a period of great anxiety for the families of the two young men, nothing appeared to be happening in their behalf, the documents reveal an extraordinary amount of activity, and this in very high quarters.

The first word of the plight of his son reached Dr. Cummings in the form of a cablegram from Paris, dated October 17, 1917:

> EDWARD E. CUMMINGS HAS BEEN PUT IN A CONCENTRATION CAMP AS RESULT OF LETTERS HE HAD WRITTEN STOP AM TAKING UP THE MATTER THROUGH EMBASSY TO SEE WHAT CAN BE DONE.

It was signed "Norton." This was Richard Norton, head of the Norton Harjes Ambulance Corps, the son of Charles Eliot Norton and a friend of Dr. Cummings. Two pencil drafts of replies survive. The first one, from Dr. Cummings, reads:

> Thanks—Do everything—Draw on me Advise me what to do— Will come if needed Cable progress.

The second one is addressed to "E. E. Cummings care Richard Norton" and reads:

> Please act on Norton's advice Take greatest care for my sake Cable immediately.

It is signed "R. H. Cummings," the poet's mother.

On October 20 Norton dispatched another cablegram to Dr. Cummings:

NOTHING TO BE DONE FOR PRESENT UNDERSTAND COMMISSION WILL
PASS ON YOUR SONS CASE NO NEED TO COME WILL MYSELF DO ANY-
THING THAT IS POSSIBLE TO BE DONE

Again there is a draft of the reply, the date—"Oct. 21"—in pencil,
the text in ink:

Norton Ameredcross Paris
Unless Ambassador is assured of prompt release provide best legal
counsel for defence. Am prepared to take up Case at Washington
[here "and appeal to country" is crossed out] if necessary France
cannot afford to alienate American sympathy by disregarding
rights of Citizens or dealing harshly with youths who volunteered
to help her [here "Notify French Govt" has also been crossed
out].

The word "youths" indicates that Dr. Cummings had learned,
possibly from Brown's family, that Brown was also involved. The
note is signed "C," which greatly resembles the famous single-
letter signature of his son.
Norton replied by cable October 25:

SO FAR AS I AM INFORMED EVERYTHING GOING SLOWLY BUT WELL
STOP YOU MUST NOT FORGET ALL PERSONS IN THE SEASON [? SERV-
ICE] OF THE ARMIES WHETHER VOLUNTEERS OR CIVILIANS ARE
SUBJECT TO MILITARY LAW STOP CAN SEE NO HARM IN EMBASSY
BEING ASKED TO AND [? AID] YOU.

This cablegram indicates that Norton had not yet turned for
assistance to the United States Embassy in Paris, which seems
strange for an official used to "chains of command" and "chan-
nels." (As it turned out, the Embassy had requested information
on the matter from the American Expeditionary Force, Liaison
Group, on October 24.) A note, in ink, in Dr. Cummings' handwriting, dated "27 Oct.," and presumably the draft of a cable in
reply, reads:

Taking no action—Relying entirely on you—Grateful for good
report—.

Two days later, on the 29th, Norton wrote to Arthur Hugh Frazier, First Secretary, American Embassy, 5, rue Chaillot, as follows:

Dear Mr. Fraser [sic],

I enclose a letter for young Cummings who as you know is locked up by the French.

I have a cable from his father to-day, and he is awaiting my report as to what can be done. I have told him that for the present, he has to be patient and that there is nothing to do but await the action of the French. If you have any later information you can give me, I shall be very grateful for it.

Very truly yours,
Richard Norton
Director Red Cross Ambulance Service

Mr. Frazier replied the next day:

My dear Norton,

Your letter of October 29th 1917 with enclosure, relating to the father of Cummings has been received.

The Embassy has made repeated representations both through the 2$^e$ Bureau and the American General Headquarters, to ascertain the status of the case against Cummings and another young ambulance driver under detention. At the present time the Embassy has received nothing definite beyond the fact that letters which these two young men wrote to their parents were intercepted by the French authorities and that their detention was the direct result of statements made in such letters. I will, however, not fail to communicate with you on receipt of definite news.

Very sincerely yours,
Arthur Hugh Frazier

On the same day that Norton wrote to Mr. Frazier, he also wrote a long letter to Dr. Cummings. (The envelope bears this note in Dr. Cummings' handwriting: "NB complains of 'amazing lack of action on part of Red Cross.' ") Norton's letter follows:

7, rue François 1$^{er}$
Paris, le October 29th, 1917.

My dear Dr. Cummings,

I entirely sympathize with the shock you must have had when you received my cable about your son. I am sorry not to have been able to write to you before. The fact was I could not get sufficient information to be able to write intelligently. This was partly due to the fact that I was tied here and could not myself go to the Front and talk with the Leader of the Section in which your boy and a fellow named Brown who was also taken in charge by the authorities were, but it was still more due to what seemed to me an amazing lack of perception on the part of the Red Cross authorities. I could not induce them to do anything in any efficient and vigorous manner for a long time. I have at last got the matter cleared up.

It turned out that your boy and Brown attracted attention to themselves by always being together, by never going with the Americans, but always with the French, and by a great deal of what seems to have been extremely foolish talk. The letters that the men in our sections write are always censored. It is in the power of the American Leader of the Section to do this, himself, or turn the duty over, as is generally done, to one of the French officers attached to the section. It was a Frenchman who was censoring the letters of Section 21 to which your boy and Brown belonged. His attention was attracted one day by a letter addressed to the Minister of War. It is contrary to all military law for an individual in the position of a soldier, as these two boys were, to write directly to the Minister of War. He opened this letter and found that it was a request to the Minister from your boy and Brown to be accepted in the Aviation Corps. Why they should have thought this was the way to go about things I do not know [note in margin, by Dr. Cummings: "They did so on the advice of the French lieutenant attached to the Section. E. C."]. It seems to me to show that they are both of them lacking in common sense, to a marked degree. This led to talk. It appeared that they were both desirous of getting into Aviation, but said that they would not want to drop bombs or do any damage to the Germans [marginal note: "Nonsense!"]. This might be for a professional pacifist, a possible point of view, but naturally the Frenchmen in the Section now became suspicious and this apparently led to the letters of these two boys being regularly censored.

It turned out that Brown certainly, (and I am not sure about your son) was writing frequently to a German Professor in Columbia College and according to accounts that have come to me, expressing generally most traitorous sentiments. At any rate, the letters were considered so bad that one day two gendarmes appeared at the camp and took the boys away for an examination. As a result of this examination, they have both been put in a concentration camp where they are, as I understand it, merely under surveillance until their papers can be properly gone into, and the whole matter settled. The Embassy are looking after their interests and my impression is that the authorities will merely recommend that the two boys be shipped out of the country, dishonourably discharged from the Service, and probably with a warning to the American authorities that owing either to lack of common sense or to crooked education, they are at present, dangerous people.

I will do the best I can to keep you informed of anything that turns up but I believe it is a matter where you will simply have to be patient.

> Believe me,
> Very truly yours,
> Richard Norton

Before this letter arrived, another cablegram from Norton reached Dr. Cummings. Dated November 6, it read:

HAVE BEEN RELIEVED OF ALL WORK WITH REDCROSS STOP IMPOSSIBLE FOR ME TO DO MORE FOR YOU STOP ADVISE USING ALL INFLUENCE TO STIR AUTHORITIES TO MORE VIGOROUS ACTION

A note in ink on a small sheet of pad paper gives Dr. Cummings' reply:

Asking help from Washington Please inform boys and visit them if you can. Am still sending mail your care.

To get help from Washington, Dr. Cummings turned to another friend, the Hon. George W. Anderson, head of the Interstate Commerce Commission, who proved a friend indeed. There is no written record of the first communication between the two men, which was probably by telephone. But on November 8 the following telegram was received at 104 Irving Street:

STATE DEPARTMENT CABLES PARIS TODAY FOR FULL REPORT WILL SEE YOU TOMORROW IN BOSTON

G W ANDERSON

Their meeting probably took place in the office of the World Peace Foundation, 40 Mt. Vernon Street, Boston, of which Mr. Anderson was a trustee.

## 3

No mere routine communication from the State Department followed. The cable to Paris was signed by Robert J. Lansing, Secretary of State, and the United States Ambassador took charge. The American Military Mission in France, by direction of General J. G. Harbord, Chief of Staff, sent the Embassy its dossier on Cummings and Brown. It read as follows:

From:     The Chief Liaison Group, G.Q.G.
To:       The American Embassy in Paris
          (Thro' the Chief of Staff, A.E.F.).
Subject:  Two American volunteers sent to distribution center.

October 26, 1917.

1. Reference telegram from U.S. Embassy in Paris, signed Lt. R. Simmons and dated 24 October.

The following is the report on the two Americans BROWN and CUMMINGS mentioned therein.

BROWN, William Slater, born November 15, 1896, at Webster, Massachusetts, U.S.A., resident at Webster. College man. Bachelor. Volunteer attached to Automobile Sanitary Section N° 21.

CUMMINGS, Edward Estlin, born October 14, 1894, at Cambridge, Massachusetts, U.S.A., resident at Cambridge. College man. Bachelor. Volunteer attached to Automobile Sanitary Section N° 21.

They arrived at S.S.U. N° 21 on June 15, 1917.

They generally lived quite by themselves, not mixing with their American comrades.

2. On September 7, 1917, the French Postal Control stopped the accompanying letters written by W. S. BROWN to:

    1.—Charles Francis Phillips, New-York.

    2.—Lewis G. Levenson, New-York, Journalist School, 2940 Broadway [Columbia School of Journalism].

    3.—Dr. Gerhardt Lower, New-York [ditto].

3. M. ANDERSON, Chief of the S.S.U. N° 21, to whom BROWN was signaled as Germanophile by another American volunteer, thinks that Brown is an undesirable in the Zone of the Armies, that he should not be permitted to go freely in France and that his immediate return to America would be dangerous. Declaration was made officially by Mr. Anderson to this effect.

4. BROWN's letters are forwarded herewith without comment.

5. CUMMINGS is the friend of BROWN. Although his correspondence was not censored, his intimacy with Brown, under whose influence he seems to be and whose ideas he seems to approve, has made him similarly suspected. His Chief, Mr. Anderson, thinks that he is as undesirable as Brown in the Zone of the Armies and that his immediate return to America would be dangerous.

On the other hand, it has been proved that on several occasions he expressed pro-German feelings and endeavoured to come into contact with French soldiers with suspicious intentions.

6. By order of the Commander in Chief, both BROWN and CUMMINGS were evacuated separately to the distributing center for such cases, La Ferté Macé (Orne), the first on the 22nd September 1917, the second on the 23rd September 1917.

Moreover, request was made by the French General Headquarters that both should be sent to a concentration camp under surveillance.

The Interministry Committee which examines suspects, at its meeting of 17 October 1917 has concluded as follows:

With regard to BROWN, that he be sent to a concentration camp;

With regard to CUMMINGS, that he be set free.

The French Home Ministry, in agreement with the French War Ministry, will take final decision.

Frank Parker
Colonel U. S. Army

The following are excerpts from Brown's letters:

At present the French Division to which we are attached is on repos and we are quartered in a small village in the North of France doing nothing. There is a Church here, a pump, seven or eight houses, a chateau and a café. At the café one can buy beer that tastes as if it had been brewed in the stomach of a horse. It is rather a nice place and we are within four kilometers of a city—a very ugly one where one drinks white wine au Grove.

For a month I have not heard the screaming and whistling of a shell and I am gradually dropping into a state of ennui. Everybody in France is terribly tired of the war and if it does not end very soon there will be all kinds of trouble. The war will [not] end with victory for either side. That is impossible—and every one despairs of a revolution in Germany.

. . . . . . . . . . . . . . .

How is Bishop and the rest of my friends getting along? Have any of them been conscripted? If they have already been and are among the first troops to get over here, they might as well do away with themselves now, for the first large contingent of American troops is going to have hell handed to them by the Germans.

.    .    .    .    .    .    .    .    .    .    .    .    .    .    .

As soon as the Americans arrived in France, people at once began telling stories about them which of course have not the slightest ground of truth to them. One of them is that syphilis in the American training camp is spreading like an epidemic, and of course this is laid to the work of spies. It is said that the syphilis is of the virulent variety and is contracted through cuts and open places in the skin. There is another story of less truth than this one however, and you know Americans too well to consider the story of the slightest truth. It is said that the Americans are already considering shooting of the officers whom they do not like. From what I hear, the French who are in their camp have taught them this. It is a well known fact that this has happened to a large extent in the English Army, due to the fact that the superior officers used to charge "over the hill" with their men, which gave their men a good chance to shoot them if they felt like it. It is rather easy to shoot the officers, or at least so I am told. It would be the simplest thing to follow out Bernard Shaw's advice on this matter it would cure all.

A propos of this story a French soldier told me the other day that in his company there were two officers whom the soldier did not like and one night they were both found dead. When the doctors examined them they found French bullets in their backs. I guess the man was a liar. The French soldiers adore their officers, as any one with a little observation would see.

.    .    .    .    .    .    .    .    .    .    .    .    .    .    .

Every one is sick of the war here and I look forward to a revolution in France soon. The French soldiers are all despondent and none of them believe that Germany will ever be defeated. They maintain the war just as they hold on to the Church, or marriage, or any senescent institution. I remember seeing senescent in a poem by Poe. Have I used it correctly?

I hope that none of my friends will ever have to come over to this damn place and fight. It makes me feel very ill when I think how many fellows are going to be killed for no reason whatsoever. How any one can hate the Germans is more than I can imagine. While I have been here I have not heard a French soldier say anything against the Germans, in fact they admire the Germans very much. I think the French dislike the English a great deal more than they do the Germans.

The dossier reached the Embassy on November 12. On the 15th, Brown's twenty-first birthday was "celebrated" with cups of cocoa that he and Cummings made on top of the stove mentioned in Chapter IX of *The Enormous Room*. On the 16th, Ambassador Sharp cabled Lansing as follows (State Department paraphrase):

2755 Nov. 16, 10 p.m. Your cable No. 2789 in reference to Edward Estlin Cummings and William Slater Brown, who were evacuated from Section 21 Norton Harjes Ambulance Corps, on September 22nd and 23rd, to Ferté Macé, because of letters Brown had written to persons in the United States, who authorities considered pro-German. Cummings was suspected because of his intimacy with Brown, but wrote no letters of this kind. On Oct. 17th Examining Board decided that Cummings be released and that Brown be interned. Final decision will be made by Ministry of Interior. Have endeavored, through this Ministry, to learn present whereabouts of Cummings and will cable you reply. Copies of letters written by Brown and preliminary report will be sent by next pouch.

Sharp

4

On the same day—November 16—Norton cabled Dr. Cummings, who sent the new information to Commissioner Anderson in the form of a telegram, of which the following is the draft:

Just received Cable as follows Letters for son arrived and put in hands of Embassy stop Believe everything going smoothly and boy will shortly return signed Norton So your efforts seem to be bearing fruit. Many thanks—

Mr. Anderson did not reply until November 19. It would appear that he checked with the State Department and was promised additional information. On that date he was given a paraphrase of Sharp's report, which he forwarded to Dr. Cummings.

From Paris, on the 21st, came more welcome news in the form of a cablegram from Norton, apparently filed on the 20th:

HAVE FINALLY SEEN ALL PAPERS IN CASE ABSOLUTELY NOTHING AGAINST YOUR BOY WHO I UNDERSTAND AFTER CERTAIN FORMALITIES WILL BE IN FEW DAYS HIS OWN MASTER.

Norton appears to have had an interview with the Ambassador, and afterwards with an Embassy secretary, who showed him the files in the case. For he now wrote Dr. Cummings as follows:

November 20th, 1917

My dear Dr. Cummings,

After endless trouble, I have just seen all the papers regarding your son and his friend Brown, at the American Embassy. There is nothing whatever of the slightest description against your boy except that he was an intimate friend of Brown whom I judge to be a bumptious ass. I am told by the Embassy that your boy has been recommended to be sent home, and as soon as certain formalities are gone through, that he will be, as I have cabled you today, his own master. I hope to see him and have a talk, possibly ram a few ideas into his head.

As for Brown, unless I can persuade the powers that be to take strong measures, he will, I am afraid, be kept in a Concentration Camp. Knowing my own compatriots as I do, this seems to me ridiculous. There is nothing of any criminal intent, of any possible sort in his letters; he obviously has, however, little breeding or education and "gasses" in his letters about stories he has heard in regard to officers being shot, everybody being sick of the war, and propounds very unbaked philosophical doctrines, and quotes idiotic poetry.[2] It looks to me as if most of the trouble had come from people reading his letters who did not know English, and certainly did not know the American nature, possibly also, because he had made himself unpopular with his section as I am told your son did too, from a general lack of neatness—in fact, I will put it stronger and say that they have been reported to me, both of them, as being dirty and unkempt. I do not know whether you have passed much life under canvas; if you have (as I have many years) you will realize that this is a real sin and may well get on people's nerves, so that they cannot bear the sight of a person who shows these faults, and are apt to think worse of such a person than he deserves. I do not vouch for the absolute truth of what I say, but merely give it to you as a suggestion to explain the conditions, believing that you would rather know anything I can possibly tell, or suggest, than that I should keep anything hidden from you.

With best regards,
Yours sincerely,
Richard Norton

On the envelope are the following notations in Dr. Cummings' handwriting:

Quote "After endless trouble ... & there is nothing whatever of the slightest description against your boy except that he was an intimate friend of B."

NB One month before release!

Quote Cable Nov. 12
" " " 16
" " " 6

---

[2] "Thought of a fine poem last night which for its simplicity of diction, its freedom from classical rhyme, its feeling for social equality is unrivaled in literature, it is:

The moon is very democratic
It sits in pools so people can look at it"

(letter to Phillips). T. E. Hulme had made the moon a famous Imagist subject in the appendix to Pound's *Ripostes*. As for the other complaints, "oh said the other, my dear you forget we were young then" (*The Autobiography of Alice B. Toklas*).

These notations were made several weeks later, and they were made because of certain developments that impelled Dr. Cummings to seek help from the President himself. The first of these developments was a telegram to Mr. Anderson, who was again in Boston, from the Assistant Secretary of State in Washington:

FOLLOWING TELEGRAM JUST RECEIVED FROM PARIS QUOTE HAVE
LEARNED FROM AMERICAN NAVAL AUTHORITIES THAT EDWARD
ESTLIN CUMMINGS EMBARKED FOR UNITED STATES ON THE ANTILLES
AND THAT HE IS REPORTED AMONG THOSE LOST END QUOTE

WILLIAM PHILLIPS

It was received by Mr. Anderson practically simultaneously with the receipt of Norton's cablegram at 104 Irving Street on November 21. It was now Mr. Anderson's painful duty to communicate the dreadful news to his friend. They must have met at once to confer, as indicated by the following telegram from Mr. Anderson to Mr. Phillips:

TELEGRAM RECEIVED NEWS INCONSISTENT WITH CABLE FROM
NORTON SENT CUMMINGS FATHER TODAY SAYING CUMMINGS IN-
NOCENT AND SHORTLY RELEASED KINDLY CABLE FOR CORRECTION
OR VERIFICATION

Dr. Cummings also set out to get information, as his notations show:

Camb. Nov. 21, 1917 to Norton
        Ameredcross Paris—
Informed son sailed on Antilles and reported lost Cable truth immediately

Cummings

Following receipt of this cable, Norton wrote to Ambassador Sharp:

Paris, le 22. Nov. 1917.
To H. E.
        The American Ambassador:
Sir:
    Confirming our conversation of two days ago may I ask you to look into the matter of Messrs. Cummings (E. E.) & Brown

(W. S.) formerly in Section 21 of the American Red Cross Ambulance Service. These two men were arrested by the French authorities because of the character of letters they wrote to friends in America. Your secretary, Mr. Wiley, tells me that he has been informed that Cummings was to be liberated but that Brown was to be interned, the reason for the difference in treatment being that Cummings' only fault was his friendship for Brown. Mr. Wiley has shown me copies of the letters which form the basis of the charge against Brown & while they are unquestionably extremely foolish I cannot but feel that a serious error would be committed were Brown to be interned.

Yesterday Mr. Wiley informed me that the American Military authorities had told him that Cummings lost his life when the *Antilles* was torpedoed. I find it hard to believe that the boy could have been sent out of the country without either you or the Red Cross authorities being informed.

Respectfully yours,

Richard Norton

Norton, apparently, was of the opinion that Cummings was still in France, and does not appear unduly alarmed.

Three days were to pass before additional word came to Dr. Cummings from Washington, four before additional word came from Norton in Paris. (Cummings told me that during this period of anguished suspense his mother never faltered in her belief that he was still alive.) At four fifteen on the 24th, Mr. Phillips dispatched the following telegram to Dr. Cummings:

TELEGRAM JUST REC'D FROM PARIS STATES H H CUMMINGS AND NOT E E CUMMINGS LOST ON ANTILLES AMBASSADOR IS RENEWING ENDEAVORS TO LOCATE YOUR SON AND WILL REPORT LATER

5

On December 8 Dr. Cummings addressed a letter to President Woodrow Wilson, using the various notations he had made as a guide to his principal points. This letter appears in the Fore-

word he wrote to *The Enormous Room* in somewhat abbreviated
form; I give the full text from the original in the State Department
files.

104 Irving Street,
Cambridge, December 8, 1917.

President Woodrow Wilson,
White House,
Washington, D.C.

Mr. President;

It seems criminal to ask for a single moment of your time. But
I am strongly advised that it would be more criminal to delay
any longer calling to your attention a crime against American
citizenship in which the French government has persisted for
many weeks,—in spite of constant appeals made to the American
Minister at Paris; and in spite of subsequent action taken by the
State Department at Washington, on the initiative of my
friend Hon. George W. Anderson, of the Interstate Commerce
Commission.

The victims are two American ambulance drivers,—Edward
Estlin Cummings of Cambridge, Mass., and William Slater
Brown, of Webster, Mass., son of a Contract Surgeon in the
United States Army, and nephew of Spaulding Bartlett, prob-
ably known to you as a member of the Textile Commission.

More than two months ago these young men were arrested,
subjected to many indignities, dragged across France like criminals, and closely confined in a Concentration Camp at La
Ferté Macé; where according to latest advices they still remain,
—awaiting the final action of the Minister of the Interior upon
the findings of a Commission which passed upon their cases as
long ago as October 17.

Against Cummings both private and official advices from Paris
state there is no charge whatever. He has been subjected to
this outrageous treatment solely because of his intimate friendship with young Brown, whose sole crime is,—so far as can be

learned,—that certain letters to friends in America were mis-interpreted by an over-zealous French censor.

It only adds to the indignity and irony of the situation, to say that young Cummings is an enthusiastic lover of France, and so loyal to the friends he has made among the French soldiers, that even while suffering in health from his unjust confinement, he excuses the ingratitude of the country he has risked his life to serve, by calling attention to the atmosphere of intense suspicion and distrust that has naturally resulted from the painful experience which France has had with foreign emissaries.

Be assured, Mr. President, that I have waited long—it seems like ages—and have exhausted all other available help before venturing to trouble you:—

1. After many weeks of vain effort to secure effective action by the American Ambassador at Paris, Richard Norton of the Norton-Harjes Ambulance Corps to which the boys belonged, was completely discouraged, and advised me to seek help here.

2. The effort of the State Department at Washington resulted as follows:

i. A cable from Paris saying there was no charge against Cummings and intimating that he would speedily be released.

ii. A little later a second cable advising that Edward Estlin Cummings had sailed on the Antilles and was reported lost.

iii. A week later a third cable correcting this cruel error, and saying the Embassy was renewing efforts to locate Cummings,—apparently still ignorant even of the place of his confinement.

After such painful and baffling experiences, I turn to you,—burdened though I know you to be, in this world crisis with the weightiest task ever laid upon any man.

But I have another reason for asking this favor. I do not speak for my son alone; or for him and his friend alone. My son has a mother,—as brave and patriotic as any mother who ever dedicated an only son to a great cause. The mothers of our boys in France have rights as well as the boys themselves. My boy's mother had a right to be protected from the weeks of horrible anxiety and suspense caused by the inexplicable arrest and imprisonment of her son. My boy's mother had a right to be spared the supreme agony caused by a blundering cable from Paris saying that he had been drowned by a submarine. (An error which Mr. Norton subsequently cabled that he had discovered six weeks before). My boy's mother and all American mothers have a right to be protected against all needless anxiety and sorrow.

Pardon me, Mr. President, but if I were president and your son were suffering such prolonged injustice at the hands of France; and your son's mother had been needlessly kept in Hell as many weeks as my boy's mother has,—I would do something to make American citizenship as sacred in the eyes of Frenchmen as Roman citizenship was in the eyes of the ancient world. Then it was enough to ask the question, "Is it lawful to scourge a man that is a Roman, and uncondemned?" Now, in France, it seems lawful to treat like a condemned criminal a man that is an American, uncondemned and admittedly innocent!

Very Respectfully,

Edward Cummings

Dr. Cummings' letter to the President is stamped in the upper left hand corner "RESPECTFULLY REFERRED FOR ACKNOWLEDGMENT AND CONSIDERATION," and signed "J. P. Tumulty," the President's secretary. In a copy of this letter in the National Archives there is a typed notation at the end: "Hon George W. Anderson delivered this letter by *Messenger* from his office, Washington (Dec. 10?)."

There is no record of a reply by the President. But on December 15 Secretary of State Lansing dispatched the following cablegram (given here in Embassy paraphrase) to Paris:

2952 Dec. 15 5 p.m. Other telegraphic correspondence and your 2755 regarding Brown and Cummings. The Department has not received the promised preliminary report. Reasons for failure of Embassy to follow up matter cannot be understood Cable reply promptly

While the Embassy, presumably, was seeking clarification from the Foreign Office, Cummings left La Ferté Macé and was proceeding to Paris with a police pass. He was released on December 19, and arrived at the Embassy on the 20th, apparently at the very moment when Ambassador Sharp was dictating a reply to Secretary Lansing's cable:

2926 Dec. 20, 7 p.m. Referring to your 2952 information has been received from the Foreign Office that definite orders have now been given for the internment of Brown at Ferte Mace and that Cummings' release has been ordered stop This case has been followed with close attention by me in order to try and get in touch with Cummings but in spite of repeated and energetic representations to Foreign Office and Ministry of the Interior I have been unable to obtain any information from these two departments of the French Government until today when I learned that in accordance with my request he was being sent to Paris stop Cummings reported at Embassy just now and on Saturday will leave on the Espagne for the United States stop Departure will be facilitated by me stop By next pouch copies of letters which Brown has written will be forwarded.

The next day the Ambassador set out to explain by letter:

Sir:
Referring to my telegram No. 2926 of the 20th instant, relative to the release by the French authorities of Mr. Edward Estlin Cummings who has been interned at Ferté Macé and recently at the College de Presigny (Sarthe) and reporting his approaching departure for the United States on board the "Espagne," sailing tomorrow the 22nd, I have the honor to transmit herewith a copy of a report on the arrest drawn up by Colonel Parker as well as copies of letters addressed by Mr. William Slater Brown to persons in the United States. These letters had been intercepted by the French censors and were believed by them to express progerman sentiments and they

served as evidence in the proceedings against both Cummings and Brown.

As will be noted in the enclosed report, suspicion was only directed against Mr. Cummings because of his intimacy with Mr. Brown and these suspicions have been ascertained to be unfounded.

The internment of Mr. Brown has been definitely ordered and he is now confined at Presigny.

I am now investigating his case and shall report thereon in a separate communication.

I have the honor to be, Sir,
Your obedient servant,
Wm. G. Sharp

The separate communication in the case of Brown was filed from Paris January 23, 1918, and reads (in paraphrase):

3084 Jan. 23 4 P.M. With reference to my despatch 5889 dated December 21'st, I decided after a talk with Cummings to make informal representations to the French Government having in view the release of Brown. I have just received a communication from the Foreign Office in which it is stated that instructions which have in view the assurance of his departure to the United States have been given.

As in the case of Cummings, powerful influences had been brought to bear to bring about Brown's release, including that of Senator Henry Cabot Lodge of Massachusetts. Brown had been taken to the prison at Précigné about the middle of December. There were approximately four hundred prisoners there, including several who had been with him and Cummings at La Ferté Macé. The food there consisted only of bread, beans, and potatoes, Brown told me, and he came down with scurvy. He said:

"I was at Precigné until the middle of February [1918], when I was taken to Bordeaux, held in prison for a week and then placed aboard the 'Niagara' of the French Line, which brought me to

New York. I stayed with my family in Webster for a couple of months recovering from scurvy, and then joined Cummings who was living on Christopher Street."

Meanwhile, on Christmas Eve, Dr. Cummings had received a letter from the Assistant Secretary of State, the address on the envelope—"104 Irving Street, Boston"—having been corrected in pencil by the Boston post office:

> Washington
> December 21, 1917
>
> Dear Sir:
>
> At the request of Commissioner Anderson, to whom I have read the telegram, I beg to send you enclosed a paraphrase of the cable just received from the American Embassy at Paris with regard to your son. You will note that he has now been released and is about to sail for the United States.
>
> Very truly yours,
> William Phillips

The enclosure repeated the information contained in Ambassador Sharp's cable to Secretary Lansing.

The last item in the documents from which I have drawn the foregoing correspondence is the draft of a telegram from Dr. Cummings to Mr. Phillips:

> Cambridge, Dec. 24, 1917
>
> Your letter just received enclosing Cable brings the most welcome of Christmas gifts. Profoundly grateful for good offices. Please accept holiday greetings and best wishes from Mr. and Mrs. Edward Cummings. Correct address 104 Irving St. Cambridge—not Boston.

Cummings arrived in New York on New Year's Day, 1918. Here is his second glimpse of his future home (from the last paragraph of *The Enormous Room*):

"The tall, impossibly tall, incomparably tall, city shoulderingly upward into hard sunlight leaned a little through the octaves of its

parallel edges, leaningly strode upward into firm, hard, snowy sunlight; the noises of America nearingly throbbed with smokes and
hurrying dots which are men and which are women and which are
things new and curious and hard and strange and vibrant and
immense, lifting with a great ondulous stride firmly into immortal
sunlight. . . ."

# VI

## *The Enormous Room*

1

All classics have this in common—each one, being unique, contributes to a community of uniqueness. There is something else: they all have a life of their own, regardless of current tastes, and this life they share. *The Enormous Room* is indubitably a classic, and does not resemble any other. It has survived many vicissitudes, and shows the right kind of durability. It is very much alive today, and my readers as well as I may be hard put to it to name a book published in 1922 that has lasted at all or lasted as well. Like all true classics, *The Enormous Room* easily passes the supreme test: it can be reread, and it is reread with all the attendant excitement of its first appearance.

It has often been pointed out that the best preparation for a writer of prose is the writing of verse, and it is true that a great many prose writers, particularly in Europe, have begun their careers with the proverbial slim volume. Cummings, after leaving Harvard, not only continued to write poems—he wrote them steadily, voluminously even at the Front. But *The Enormous*

*Room* is not only the work of a poet—it is a poet's work; no mere writer of prose could have written it. For the beauty and surprises of many of its pages are of the same sort, the same quality, that afterwards made Cummings' books of verse so memorable. Indeed, were certain of his poems and certain paragraphs from this book placed side by side, it would be seen at once that their authorship is the same.[1] Here, it may be useful to point out that Cummings— whether in conversation or letters, in poetry or prose, including the drama—had only one style, and that style, an instrument of great range and flexibility, was his own. It did not exist before him, and falls flat when imitated. The reason is simple—Cummings' style springs from what he was. He expressed it in *The Enormous Room* as follows:

"There are certain things in which one is unable to believe for the simple reason that he never ceases to feel them. Things of this sort—things which are always inside of us and in fact are us and which consequently will not be pushed off or away where we can begin thinking about them—are no longer things; they, and the us which they are, equals A Verb: an IS."

## 2

The book was written at the insistence of Dr. Cummings, whose indignation did not abate with the passing months or years. He has related, in the Foreword, what shape his son was in when released—"very much under weight [and] suffering from a bad skin infection." However, he added, "a month of competent medical treatment here seems to have got rid of this painful reminder of official hospitality."

There was one other reminder. Philip Hillyer Smith, a Cambridge neighbor who was a senior at Harvard in 1918, told me he used to see Cummings take a live coal from the grate with his fingertips, light his cigarette with it, and set the coal down without burning his fingers—a trick picked up at La Ferté Macé, where matches were scarce.

[1] The same is true of the play *Him* and the Russian diary, *Eimi*.

In the fall of 1920, at his New Hampshire farm, Dr. Cummings finally persuaded his son to set down the record of his imprisonment. William Slater Brown was there to jog his memory when Cummings started to write. Cummings also drew from notes he had made at La Ferté Macé, for he never went anywhere without a notebook, not even to prison. In Chapter Five of *The Enormous Room* there is an example of a note made on the spot, together with its "interpretation"—i.e., expansion. Although Cummings refers to this note as a "specimen of telegraphic technique," and Robert Graves terms it "telegraphese" in his Introduction to the English edition of the book, it is really, in language and construction, a portrait like the portraits to be found among Cummings' early poems under the heading of "Realities." When Dr. and Mrs. Cummings went back to Cambridge, Cummings and Brown stayed on in New Hampshire; and in the tree-house previously mentioned, on a spur of land called Hurricane Point, the book was written in two months. A letter to Stewart Mitchell describes Cummings' procedure:

> Here I've been working (as worked the sons of Egypt to build the pyramids, you understand—in other words like H.) upon a little historical treatise of vast import to my Family and Nobody in General—comprising my experiences in France, or more accurately *en prison*. Honestly to say, I haven't done nawthing else. Strenuous is no name therefor—3 pages a day, since my family left, on an average 2 hours to a page. ID EST, a six hour day, splendid for the good of humanity, and if so, and so forth.

The letter is dated October 6, 1920. Mitchell, at this time, was managing editor of *The Dial*, in which Cummings had made his sensational debut as a poet with the first—January, 1920—number.

Some time in 1921 the manuscript of *The Enormous Room* was taken to Boni & Liveright by Dr. Cummings. When I asked Cummings why this particular firm had been chosen, he replied: "It was a good firm at the time." I have been told by several authors published by this firm that when Horace Liveright finally met

Cummings at a party, he rushed towards him, exclaiming: "Your father turned my hair white!"

It is an inclusive remark. Cummings, having finished his book, gave it to his grateful and enthusiastic father—instructing him to allow no publisher to make any change whatever in the manuscript—and left for Paris. A letter from him, from Autun, France, authorized Dr. Cummings to sign the contract for him; this, Dr. Cummings did. In sending the contract back to Liveright, he wrote, November 4, 1921: "There are a few sentences to be added to the end of one chapter. My son seems to attach considerable importance to having this addition made. I will see that it is forwarded at once." He also sent the letter from Cummings, saying: "The sketches to which my son refers in his letter are, as I recollect them, rough pencil portraits of some of the characters he describes, made on small slips of paper which happened to be available. Do you want to consider using them?"

To this, Liveright replied: "I think it would help the book very much if we use the sketches your son did. I hope that there are a number of them. Please send them all." He also suggested a title for the book—*Hospitality*. One sketch was reproduced on the jacket. There is no further mention of the suggested title in the surviving correspondence. On April 8, 1922, Liveright wrote that he expected copies of the book from the binders on the 18th and that he was "endeavoring to have the New York *Times* give Dos Passos the book for review."

Thus far, and until after the book appeared, the correspondence between Liveright and Dr. Cummings appears cordial. On June 5 Liveright had some disquieting news to impart:

> I have just learned through a friend of your son, Estlin Cummings, who had word from him from Paris, that he cannot understand why we have omitted two or three chapters from The Enormous Room. This is the first I have heard of any omissions other than a few phrases or words which we felt it was necessary to delete in order to make the publication of the book possible in this country.

I would appreciate it very much if you would let me hear from you at once regarding the mysterious missing chapters. It may be that you in your great good judgment edited the book before it came here and I have no reason to believe that there is any complaint to be found with your editing; but, naturally, I want to be in position to intelligently answer your son's inquiry.

Dr. Cummings' reply, dispatched the next day, is sufficient to account for Liveright's rueful remark a few years later. Dr. Cummings wrote:

My son, E. E. Cummings, wrote me in regard to the omissions of certain parts of THE ENORMOUS ROOM, about which you make inquiry in your letter of June 5. He wanted to know who was responsible for these omissions,—as well as for certain pretty obvious and rather stupid mistakes in spelling, punctuation, etc.

I wrote him that I accepted entire responsibility; because the proofs submitted to me did not contain these passages, and because the passages in question had been deleted from the manuscript returned to me with proofs, and because under the circumstances I did not think it worth while delaying the publication of the book and trying to persuade you to reinstate the omitted passages. If any passages had to be omitted, those which you had deleted seemed to me less of a sacrifice than any others which could have been chosen.

All you have to do to verify my statement with regard to the deletion of the passages in question, is to consult the manuscript, which you asked me to return with the corrected proof. Incidentally, I would suggest that if there is no serious objection to so doing, you return the original manuscript to me.

So you will perceive that "your great and good judgment edited the book" before it came to me,—not the reverse, as your letter suggests. So, also, you will pardon me for expressing some surprise at the statement that the information recently received from Paris was "the first you had heard of any omissions other than a few phrases or words which we felt it was necessary to delete in order to make the publication of the book possible in this country." I suppose you also may have been ignorant of the pressure that was brought to bear upon me to return the proofs immediately, on the ground that I was delaying your publication schedule, etc., etc. All of which had considerable to do with my decision as above stated.

Please observe that in writing to my son I have accepted entire responsibility. I further reminded him that if anyone was to blame beside me, it was himself; because I cabled him to come back at my expense and see the book through the press. He said he was too happy where he was. I daresay he would be happier now if he had come. I hope you have seen the review of THE ENORMOUS ROOM in the *Nation* of June 7. It is superb.

The author of it was Ben Ray Redman, a scholarly critic, translator, essayist, and poet, in later years the best of the contributors to the *Saturday Review* when it was the *Saturday Review of Literature*. I mourn his untimely death.

Isidor Schneider, a poet employed by Boni & Liveright, told me that, at the last moment, just before the book went out to reviewers, a report came that John S. Sumner, Secretary of the New York Society for the Suppression of Vice, planned a raid because of a four-letter word on page 219. The passage read:

" 'You don't say! Look, the king of England is sick. Some news! ...What? The queen, too? Good God! What's this? —My father is dead! Shit. Oh, well. The war is over. Good.' —It was Jean le Nègre, playing a little game with himself to beguile the time."

Schneider told me the offending word was inked out to avoid entanglement with Sumner.

"A little girl in the office had to go through the copies—the whole edition—inking out the word," he said.

The passage is now in French, as Jean le Nègre spoke it (Modern Library edition, page 271).

3

The question of Cummings' style in *The Enormous Room* and possible influences on it has interested writers and critics ever since the book appeared. At the beginning of this chapter I tried to show that Cummings' prose style grew naturally out of his poetic one, plus a factor to which I have also called attention—namely, his extraordinary reportorial skill. If other influences were at work, I have not been able to find them; nor has anyone else.

Cummings himself has confirmed that his book "just growed." The confirmation occurs in an exchange of letters with Malcolm Cowley in the spring of 1951. Cowley wrote him:

> I'm putting together a book of which the real subject is the contributions to prose fiction of the new writers who appeared in the 1920s. They were big and varied contributions, if you add them all together or even if you take them separately. You never wrote any prose fiction that I know of, but The Enormous Room comes into the story because it had a very great influence on other writers. It was something absolutely new when it appeared, as your poems in the first issue of the monthly Dial were absolutely new. There had been a big change since 1915, when you were a kid writing for the Advocate, and the question I wanted to ask was how the change came about. It isn't the old question of literary influence, as if I wanted to end by saying that Cummings "was influenced by" or "derives from" and so on. You found something that was new and your own—the real question is what started you to looking for it? Was it mostly your reading (and of whom?) or was it partly because you started painting and wanted to get some of the same immediate effects in words?

To this, Cummings replied, April 30, 1951, on the eve of sailing to Paris with his wife:

> TheER wrote itself as a(n however microscopic)
> gesture of thankfulness toward my father;who,

despite every effort of Norton Harjes & l'armée
francaise, boosted not only me but B out of hell.
B & I were together at the writing, which sans
his memory of events would have proved impossible.
And he can probably tell you when this happened

as for the "big change": (1)our unhero wrote for a
literary mag called The Harvard Monthly, not for
a special sheet called The ditto Advocate—whatever the Advocate "Anthology" 's editor may say or
not(2)perhaps,& here's hoping,I Just Growed

The experience at La Ferté Macé was decisive. Pound said to
Cummings in St. Elizabeths Hospital: "How fortunate for you
to have served your term of imprisonment when you were young!"
Cummings would have rebelled, in any case, against the coming
society of anonymous mass-men with rubber-stamp inanities and
cruelties; as it happened, he became, on the very threshold of his
career, a champion of the individual man and a spokesman for the
universal underdog. Bunyan did not glimpse the Delectable Mountains until his release from prison; Cummings found them inside,
the individual and the underdog in combination.

It may come as a surprise to new readers of *The Enormous Room*
that concentration camps were not the peculiar property of the
latter-day Germans, and that guilt by association was not invented
in the United States:

"For who was eligible to La Ferté? Anyone whom the police
could find in the lovely country of France (*a*) who was not guilty
of treason, (*b*) who could not prove that he was not guilty of treason. By treason I refer to any little annoying habits of independent
thought or action which *en temps de guerre* are put in a hole and
covered over, with the somewhat naive idea that from their cadav-
ers violets will grow whereof the perfume will delight all good
men and true and make such worthy citizens forget their sorrows.
Fort Leavenworth, for instance, emanates even now a perfume
which is utterly delightful to certain Americans."

This, presumably, is a reference to political prisoners and con-

scientious objectors immured in World War I, a procedure repeated in World War II, when there was somewhat better treatment. It appears, then, that Cummings was liberal without labeling
himself. Those who have criticized him as politically ignorant or
naive can only have meant that he did not share their views. In
the light of events he has been, at least, consistent, while those
intellectuals who became most vociferous politically were at last
struck dumb or sick, or turned into informers, their own choice
having been an unmitigated catastrophe.

# VII

## The Twenties: New York

1

In the spring of 1918 Brown joined Cummings in New York, in a tumbledown wooden building of three stories at 11 Christopher Street. There was an outhouse in the back. The building has long since disappeared, and the space it occupied is now a parking lot.[1] In the summer Cummings was drafted and reported to Camp Devens, Massachusetts, where he underwent training as an infantry soldier until the Armistice. It was at Camp Devens that he became acquainted with Olaf, the "conscientious object-or" of his poem. Brown was also drafted, but "scurvy had left my health, particularly my teeth, in such bad shape that I was discharged when I reached camp," he told me. In the fall he resumed his studies at Columbia, and when Cummings was mustered out they took a studio together at 15 West Fourteenth Street, opposite Hearn's department store—both now also gone. They were there about a year. Brown told me that Cummings painted "all the time."

[1] 1963.

Brown said he and Cummings "walked for hours" all over New York and "sat for hours" in New York restaurants. It was not the city's "stark irresistibly stupendous newness" (as Cummings phrased it at Harvard) that fascinated them, but the quarters that had more of the Old World in them than the New, the enclaves of "immemorial races and nations." Of these, the Jewish section on the lower East Side, whose Fifth Avenue was Second, drew them daily to its streets. And gradually a pattern evolved.

At the southwest corner of Second Avenue and Twelfth Street was the Café Royale, the rendezvous of Yiddish writers and actors; this might be said to have marked the northernmost bounds of the quarter, as Fourteenth marks that of the Village. At the Café Royale, now defunct, Cummings and Brown soon made friends, despite language barriers. Brown told me that, in 1919 at least, he and Cummings saw more of Yiddish writers than American ones. He was particularly impressed, he said, that when he and Cummings walked down Second Avenue with a Yiddish writer, everybody on the street—"even the pushcart peddlers"—said "hello."

"It was very pleasant to walk with them," Brown said.

At the southern, or lower, end of Second Avenue, at the corner of Houston, was the National Winter Garden Burlesque theater, and past the theater, also on Houston Street, was Moscowitz' Romanian restaurant. The restaurant, which had a cosmopolitan clientele, and a Middle European atmosphere, served the "little meats," or *mititei*, of Romania (a little like hot dogs, of finest meat spiced with garlic) and filet mignon broiled over charcoal. I have been told that the broiling of steaks in the Romanian fashion was so fine an art that even in that remote period the chef was handsomely paid. This restaurant drew European visitors as well as celebrities from the American literary, theater, and film world, among them Charles Chaplin. Moscowitz himself, tall, mustachioed and distinguished-looking—"with the very look of a great gallant and ladies' man," as a Romanian habitué described him to me—was not only host but entertainer; he played, for his own delight and his clients' pleasure, skillfully and triumphantly, upon an instrument known as a cymbalon. His most sensational number was the "Poet and Peasant" overture, which always brought down the house. Mr. Moscowitz was no amateur, for he gave solo concerts uptown.

In the warmth of their welcome among people so different from themselves, and who spontaneously took the two attractive gentiles to their hearts, Cummings and Brown basked in continual pleasure and surprise. In a prose poem that belongs to this period—"my eyes are fond of the east side"—Cummings has catalogued the sights, smells, colors—and tastes—of the quarter, which he observed with the eyes of a painter and the mind of a poet. He remembers a scarlet pepper that he ate. Result: "my eyes were buttoned with pain." In another poem: "I have not eaten peppers for a week."

The two friends also spent many afternoons and evenings drinking ale in McSorley's saloon, now "McSorley's Old Ale-House," fronting Hall Place east of the Bowery on Seventh Street. McSorley's was already in business when Abraham Lincoln spoke at Cooper Union, a bottle's toss away, in 1860. It has two rooms, each with its individual admonitory sign, "Be Good or Be Gone." The walls are crowded with photographs and lithographs in which a vanished city dwells, and dead, buxom ladies and derbied men. The room in front has the bar, but the room in back boasts a famous lady of a smooth and beautiful nudeness. She does not receive too much competition from the other decorations on the wall—Gilbert Stuart's Washington, the American flag, and a Dublin Horse Show poster. She is propped on visible and invisible bolsters, recliningly, and is looking at a parrot. The parrot is looking at her. She is a durable symbol, although I am not sure of what, for women are not permitted to enter McSorley's. A Village nymph who essayed it once, in fedora and trousers, was quickly ejected.

Here writers, artists, and laborers still meet on equal terms, without other distractions, to sluice down amber quarts in the abiding gloom. Said the man at the table next to mine to the chef, or sandwichmaker, who emerged briefly from his cubicle: "Hear about the girl who was raped on Rivington Street? She thought it was Grand." The chef didn't get it. There is still sawdust on the floor, but something new has been added: a TV. The bare table-tops are crisscrossed with names and initials; what must have been a jolly party is suggested by this vertical muster chiseled in wood:

> Lippi
> Joe
> Pot
> Tony
> Curti
> Chappy

Cummings also has recorded time spent in those pleasant environs:

> i was sitting in mcsorley's.    outside it was New York and beautifully snowing. . . .

### 2

Greenwich Village, of course, offered attractions of its own, restaurants not least. There was Romany Marie's, on the southeast corner of Washington Square and Thompson Street, a candle-lighted rendezvous in a pre-Revolutionary brick building whose walls bulged. It was said that Washington and Lafayette had reviewed troops there when the Square was a parade ground, but whether from a window or the roof was never made clear. The roof sloped steeply. The presiding genius of the place was Romany Marie herself, a handsome Romanian woman who read cards, hands, tea leaves, and was the mother confessor of Villagers in trouble; she was seldom idle or alone. I remember her "poets' table," where none durst sit except writers, whether established or not. She also had a special dinner, with a special price, for her Bohemian clientele: tasty coarse black bread, thick soups, Turkish coffee—rather sustaining fare, fifty cents, not always paid for. The uptowners who dined there, and made it possible for impecunious Bohemians to eat, were rewarded by Bohemian sneers. The building was torn down in 1928.

A block south, on Thompson Street, was the Grand Ticino, still a flourishing and pleasant place though long minus the huge pool table downstairs where old paysans played and two enormous mastiffs, somnolent with *ossi bucci* bones and *scaloppini* scraps, dozed in its shade.

There was also Polly's restaurant on West Fourth Street, rendezvous of prominent Bohemians, and the Lafayette on University Place, where dining may have been out of the question, but whose café with marble-topped tables was a pleasant and inexpensive place for coffee and rolls in the morning and coffee and liqueurs at night. In those days, the Brevoort on Fifth Avenue still had a noble staircase; staircase, Brevoort, Lafayette, have all been swept away in the inexorable march of progress, preceded by the depression that followed Prohibition.

And there were book shops—Albert and Charles Boni's book shop on Macdougal Street, where the Washington Square Players was born, and from which sprang the Provincetown and the Theatre Guild; and the Washington Square Book Shop on Eighth Street, still—surprisingly and agreeably—functioning under the original management on West Tenth Street, next to Patchin Place. Across the street from the Provincetown Playhouse was "The Black Knight," where liquor was always plentiful during Prohibition and the French cooking was first-rate and inexpensive.

Prohibition! There was Luke O'Conner's famous Columbian saloon—also known affectionately as the "Working Girls' Home" —on the corner of Christopher Street and Sixth Avenue, where beer flowed as copiously as when John Masefield worked there as a youth, and not only beer but stout and the best whiskey the mobs were purveying. There was also the *Golden Swan*, at the corner of West Fourth Street and Sixth, but better known as the "Hell Hole," probably with reason. Mobsters mingled there with actors from the Provincetown and drifters from the Bowery, but it was probably as safe as the Waldorf if you behaved yourself. The "Hell Hole" was the favorite resort of Eugene O'Neill. Gaunt, appearing underfed, he listened to everyone, saying little himself, sustained by whiskey and the plots leaping to life in his tortured brain. Here also were to be found the painters Charles Demuth, who has recorded the "Hell Hole's" sinister interior, and Marcel Duchamp.

In the Village, Cummings and Brown were soon joined by Edward Pierce Nagle, a sensitive, highly strung young man who was a painter, and M. R. Werner, afterwards well known for his biography of Barnum and a history of Tammany Hall. Werner, a native New Yorker, had been a classmate of Brown's at the Columbia School of Journalism.

Through Nagle, the son of Mrs. Lachaise by her first husband, Cummings met Gaston Lachaise, the French-born sculptor whose studio was on Eighth Street. Lachaise was twelve years older than Cummings. With his dark, unruly hair falling over his brow, his alive and brooding eyes, his scowl and sullen mouth, and his powerful build, he resembled Thomas Wolfe. His favorite word was "simple," as pronounced in French. He was romantic—he had seen Mrs. Nagle in Paris and followed her to America—and he was imbued with a feeling about art that can only be described as tender. Cummings has memorialized an incident that took place at the Society of Independent Artists during one of those catchall, hang-all exhibitions that provoked derision and occasionally riots in the early twenties.

"I was wrestling some peculiarly jovial mob of sightseers at possibly the least orthodox of all Independent 'openings,' when out of nowhere the sculptor Lachaise gently materialized," he wrote in the foreword to the catalogue of one of his own shows.[2]

" 'Hello Cumming' his serene voice (addressing me, as always, in the singular) sang above chaos 'have you seen one litel cat?' I shook my head. He beckoned—and shoulder-to-shoulder we gradually corkscrewed through several huge rooms; crammed with eccentricities of inspiration and teeming with miscalled humanity. Eventually we paused. He pointed. And I found myself face to face with a small canvas depicting a kitten.

" 'Dis ting' Lachaise reverently affirmed(in the course of what remotely resembled a lull) 'is paint with love.' "

[2] University of Rochester, May, 1957.

Lachaise's sculpture made a profound impression on Cummings, who was shortly to give it incomparable praise in *The Dial*.

The chief focus of the pattern earlier alluded to was the National Winter Garden Burlesque on Houston Street. This was literally as well as figuratively heaven to an old habitué of The Howard Athenaeum in Boston—literally because it was reached by elevators, it being on the roof of an old theater, once the home of Boris Thomashefsky's Yiddish troupe. Werner told me that over the proscenium arch were the startling words: "The Show's the Thing—W. Shakespeare." A runway, lighted from beneath, projected into the audience, and on it the girls paraded. Strip tease, of course, was the main feature, and to this American art the impassive Chinese in the audience responded with applause. They did not respond to the comedians.

"Every week," Werner said, "there was the same joke: 'Would you hit a woman with a child?' No, I'd hit her with a brick."

As for the American portion of the audience, Cummings was to write: "It was not only peculiarly demanding, it was extraordinarily well mannered. I have not sat, and I never hope to sit, with tougher or more courteous people."

The chief comedian at the National Winter Garden was Jack Shargel, of whom Cummings made a pen drawing that appeared in *The Dial*. He also wrote an article in praise of him, from which the above was taken, for *Vanity Fair*. Shargel had two roles that brought the roof down. One was downright earthy—as Anthony in a skit entitled "Anthony and Cleopatra." In a tin helmet, and, with a cigar as big as a guided missile, he is seen on a divan with Cleopatra, a strip-tease queen. Enter Caesar, who wallops him in the right place with the flat of a gigantic sword. Anthony jumps up and does a loping stagger around the stage.

Anthony: "I'm dying! I'm dying!"

Chorus: "He's dying! He's dying!"

Anthony: "I hear de voices of angels!"

Caesar: "What do they say?"

Anthony: "I don't know—I don't speak Polish!"

In the other role Shargel is handed a rose by a siren, who

promptly disappears. He looks longingly after her, enraptured; sniffs the rose, kisses it, sniffs it some more; then, as though his ecstasy is too great to bear, with an exquisite gesture of renunciation, he tosses the rose to the stage, where it falls with the noise of shattered glass.

"To sum up," Cummings wrote in *Vanity Fair*, "the creations of the National Winter Garden possess, in common with the sculpture of Gaston Lachaise, the painting of John Marin, and the music of Igor Stravinsky, the virtue of being intensely alive; whereas the productions of the conventional theatre, like academic sculpture and painting and music, are thoroughly dead—and since 'art,' if it means anything, means TO BE INTENSELY ALIVE, the former constitute art and the latter are balderdash. Furthermore, the fact that this highly stylized, inherently 'abstract,' positively 'futuristic' art known to its devotees as burlesk is indubitably *for the masses*, knocks into a cocked chapeau the complaint of many so-called 'critics' that 'modern art' is 'neurotic,' 'unhealthy,' 'insane,' 'arbitrary,' 'unessential,' 'superficial' and 'not for the masses.' "

Lachaise, with whom Cummings built a durable friendship, and for whom he sat, also fell in love with burlesque, and was soon sketching and casting Minsky belly dancers.

North and south stretched the limitless city. The Aquarium drew them—almost every day, Brown told me, he and Cummings walked to the Battery, stopping at Khouri's on Washington and Rector to eat delectable Syrian dishes. The Aquarium was one of the most delightful places, in a delightful setting, in New York; but the park commissioner had it torn down.[3] The Bronx Zoo drew them—and Cummings has left a record of a visit there. It was in the spring of 1919 that he, Brown, and Nagle squired Elizabeth Cummings and a Radcliffe classmate, a Miss Gay, to the Zoo.

---

[3] No one opposes
Commissioner Moses;
Even the fishes
Must do as he wishes.
                    —Francesco Bianco.

Cummings purchased "two bags of lukewarm peanuts" and gallantly offered one to Miss Gay, who declined in what must have been so polite a Cambridge fashion, saying, "No, thank you, I have one"—meaning a single peanut—that almost two score years later Brown could hardly tell the story for laughing. The incident is enshrined in a poem, which also states, "unhappily, the denizens of the zoo were that day inclined to be uncouthly erotic," with the result that "Miss Gay had nothing to say to the animals and the animals had nothing to say to Miss Gay."

A climax to the excursion came when they entered the alligator house. As they pressed eagerly forward to peer at the saurian, an unfortunate butterfly, innocently skimming the surface of the muddy tank, was instantaneously snapped up by ponderous jaws, which so upset Nagle that he had to make an abrupt exit.

Cummings has recorded his explorations of New York in an early sonnet,

"by god i want above fourteenth,"

which appeared in *Broom*, May, 1922. Professor Damon told me that it occasioned the first reference to Cummings in England—in *Punch*.

One other aspect of Cummings' discoveries during this period might be mentioned here. He said at Harvard:

"Last but most, I thank for my self-finding certain beautiful givers of illimitable gladness

>    whose any mystery makes every man's
>    flesh put space on; and his mind take off time."

### 3

In 1920 Cummings, Brown, Nagle, and Werner were joined on their tours of the city by Stewart Mitchell, in New York to take up his post as first managing editor of *The Dial*. Mitchell told me that two of his chief recollections of this period were of Second Avenue and the National Winter Garden. John Dos Passos was living at 3 Washington Square, at work on *Three Soldiers*. With the establishment of *The Dial*, Cummings became intimately associated with a number of men and women who were at the center of New York's literary and artistic life.

To begin with, there were the owners of the new publication, Scofield Thayer and James Sibley Watson, who not only encouraged Cummings as a writer, but had begun to purchase his pictures before the magazine appeared. There was Paul Rosenfeld, the music critic of the new publication, a brown-eyed, stocky, round-faced man with red hair and red mustache, who, wrote Edmund Wilson, "when I first knew him—in 1922, I think—was one of the most exciting critics of the 'American Renaissance.'" Rosenfeld, a bachelor, liked to give parties which were, says Mr. Wilson, "all the more agreeable for being of rather an old-fashioned kind." There was little liquor served, which was of course unusual during Prohibition. To these parties came writers, musicians, and poets. Mr. Wilson wrote: "One met Ornstein, Milhaud, Varèse; Cummings, Hart Crane, and Marianne Moore; the Stieglitzes and all their group; the Stettheimers, Mumford, Kreymborg. One of the images that remains with me most vividly is the bespectacled figure of Copland, at that period gray-faced and lean, long-nosed and rather unearthly, bending over the piano as he chanted in a high, cold, and passionate voice a poem of Ezra Pound's, for which he had written a setting." Van Wyck Brooks has recalled, in *Days of the Phoenix*, that "one met virtually all the contributors" to *The Dial* there. "There one saw E. E. Cummings, the last of the Yankee comeouters, who came out all the way in his poetry and drawings, and I remember Marianne Moore, on the long sofa by the fire, reading aloud some of her early poems. The mantel and the walls were covered with Marins, Doves, Hartleys and O'Keefes."

Rosenfeld's apartment was on Irving Place, a street afterwards memorable as the site of the Minsky Brothers' reborn burlesque in a rundown theater in which Gypsy Rose Lee stripped herself to everlasting renown.

In addition to the individual writing and other creative work that members of Cummings' circle were doing, they shared certain aesthetic views and enthusiasms. They looked askance at reputations, both recent and back-dated, and warred continually against "The Great God Bogus," Gilbert Seldes' phrase, afterwards incorporated in *The Seven Lively Arts*, where, under that heading, he listed the following beliefs:

That Al Jolson is more interesting to the intelligent mind than John Barrymore and Fanny Brice than Ethel;

That Ring Lardner and Mr. Dooley [Finley Peter Dunne's creation] in their best work are more entertaining and more important than James Branch Cabell and Joseph Hergesheimer in their best;

That the daily comic strip of George Herriman (Krazy Kat) is easily the most amusing and fantastic and satisfactory work of art produced in America today;

That Florenz Ziegfeld is a better producer than David Belasco;

That one film by Mack Sennett or Charlie Chaplin is worth the entire *oeuvre* of Cecil de Mille;

That *Alexander's Ragtime Band* and *I Love a Piano* are musically and emotionally sounder pieces of work than *Indian Love Lyrics* and *The Rosary*;

That the circus can be and often is more artistic than the Metropolitan Opera House in New York;

That Irene Castle is worth all the pseudo-classic dancing ever seen on the American stage; and

That the civic masque is not perceptibly superior to the Elk's Parade in Atlantic City.

Admiration for America's comic strips was not limited to natives. Gertrude Stein has told in her autobiography that as long ago as Picasso's Montmartre period—before World War I—she and her brother Leo used to give the painter their Sunday supplements from home so he could follow the Katzenjammer Kids. In *Civilization in the United States*, Harold E. Stearns declared that "Bringing Up Father" "symbolizes better than most of us appreciate the normal relation of American men and women to cultural and intellectual values." He also declared (in *The Freeman*) before rushing off to Paris: "There is something the matter with a culture whose youth is eager to desert it."

## 4

Still another member of the Cummings circle, who joined it early and stayed late, was Joseph Ferdinand Gould, afterwards better known as Joe Gould or Little Joe Gould, self-styled "Last of the Bohemians." He, too, was Harvard *magna cum laude*, a contemporary of T. S. Eliot, Walter Lippmann, Conrad Aiken, and Gluyas Williams. Joe was five feet four, bearded, and—with the passage of time—fringed on top with a frieze of hair like hoarfrost, which gave him the appearance—in cast-off clothing generally too large for him—of a gnome or pint-size, grubby Santa Claus. He weighed around a hundred pounds.

Joe had several legitimate claims to attention. He was a shrewd observer and a wit, his remarks gaining from the peculiarly slow, nasal manner in which he uttered them. He gave lectures, in Village dives, on the work of Cummings and Dos Passos. And he was the author of a mammoth (and unpublished) work entitled *An Oral History of Our Time*, which once reached the staggering total of eleven million words. At that point the manuscript towered seven feet high, which led him to boast that he was the only author in history who had written a book taller than himself. The *Oral History*, on which Joe worked daily for a quarter century, was at first a painstaking record of conversations overheard anywhere—saloons, streets, subways, and flophouses—plus the author's occasionally pithy observations.

"My general idea," he explained, "is that every human being is as much history as a ruler or a celebrity because he illustrates all the social forces."

Joe used to be a familiar sight in Greenwich Village streets with a battered, bespattered portfolio hugged to his bosom; but in his last years he no longer lugged portions of his work around with him and was evasive about the fate of his manuscript. (Cummings told me that he still remembered the start he got the first time he saw Gould without his portfolio.) Great chunks of the *Oral History* may have been left behind in abandoned rooms and in the clutches of irate landladies who were optimistic about his coming back to ransom his dearest possession. Homeless for decades, Joe slept on park benches, in hallways and subways, and was occasionally picked up for vagrancy. He had only fond recollections of his sojourns on Ward's and Riker's islands, however; when other inmates talked of getting out, he pondered how to stay in to continue eating three times a day and smoking cigarettes supplied by the city.

Joe also wrote poetry. His verse was terse, viz.—

> In winter I'm a Buddhist,
> And in summer I'm a nudist,

lines as often quoted, perhaps, as a couplet by Dorothy Parker or Ogden Nash. With this couplet, Joe became a member of the Raven Poetry Society of Greenwich Village, though not without opposition. He was accused of not being serious enough, whereupon he retorted that neither were most of its members, since they wrote only on such "trite themes as life, love and death." Supported enthusiastically by the late Maxwell Bodenheim, Joe was admitted. He immediately translated a poem by his sponsor into "seagull," a language Joe claimed to know. This offended everyone, especially Bodenheim. "Screek—squawk—screek," went the translation, with Joe making appropriate gestures to personate a gull, and he was ejected.

Newcomers to the dives where Joe hung out in Greenwich Village sometimes reacted to the thrill of meeting him by inviting him to dinner. He always had enough to drink; for like other cadgers he found that bar flies would buy him liquor to be amused, but turned their backs at the suggestion of food, which carried a hint of troubles. As a result, he too often settled for the liquor, which worked havoc with his system. In part it was his own fault, for he approached strangers with a gambit of his own. "I believe in democracy," he would say with a disingenuous, blue-eyed stare. "I believe everyone has the right to buy Joe Gould a drink." The

right was frequently exercised. After a while he resisted the harder
varieties, contenting himself with beer or ale. It sufficed, particularly on an empty stomach. "British beer," he told me, "has only
hops; American beer has hops, skips, and jumps."

Joe told me in 1952, just a few weeks before he was picked up in
the street and taken to a hospital for the mentally ill, that his last
square meal was in June, 1936, when he attended a class reunion
at Harvard. Classmates, who may have remembered him as a thin,
spectacled, serious-eyed fellow student, must have been jolted by
the bearded and soiled satyr in their midst stoking himself with
gusto. In any event, one sight of Joe Gould eating is forever
memorable. New England to the core, he preferred clams to cut-
lets, and after devouring a platter of them was so bespattered that
a paper napkin disintegrated on application, leaving his beard like
a hedgerow after a snow flurry. Having got that far with his ablu-
tions, Joe rested; and the rain of sauces and juices, dribbles of beer
and coffee, dried where they fell on his tie and suit, to merge
imperceptibly with the stains and smears of decades. "Give me a
cigarette," he would say to his host. "I feel naked without a
cigarette." He smoked with a holder.

Joe took a naive delight in his fame. "I find it natural," he said
of the attention paid him wherever he went—which was chiefly to
saloons. "It's like the home town I grew up in—everybody knows
me." He was born in Norwood, Massachusetts, the son of a doctor
and grandson and namesake of a professor in the Harvard Medical
School, and grew up among people who had known Hawthorne,
Emerson, and Thoreau. He once said of his father that he held
"the pessimistic belief that the Americans were the best people God
ever made." Joe ran away from home at the age of twelve, but was
recognized a few miles down the road by a neighbor, who hitched
up his horse and buggy and brought him back. A vagabond by
nature, Joe, surprisingly, had never been to Europe. "Why should
I go slumming?" he asked in mild surprise. "In the United States
I meet a better type of European. If I went abroad I would only
run into second-rate Americans."

In addition to hanging around saloons and cafeterias in the

lower depths of Greenwich Village, Joe was an indefatigable bell-ringer. His "route" included many famous residents. A quarter or half dollar brought him back in a day or two, a dollar kept him away for a week; and once M. R. Werner, unseasonably flush (after a movie sale), gave him twenty-five dollars. "Reckon this lets you out for quite a while," Joe said, and stayed away six months. He never mentioned *money*. The bell rang, and there he was, the shyest—and wittiest—of panhandlers. When money was finally passed, it was accepted like a light, without fuss.

Rain had a particular fascination for Joe. Everyone on his "route" knew when it rained that he was sure to turn up. Residents of the Village, huddled in doorways during a shower, watched with fascination as he trudged like an automaton through rain-swept streets, soaked to his socks, his battered hat running water like a spout.

Joe's portrait was painted by Cummings and other artists. Once, when Lachaise put him up for a night, Mrs. Lachaise suggested that Joe would make a good subject, but the sculptor demurred. "He is too formé," Lachaise said of Joe. "He is his own bust." Joe also posed for hundreds of beginners at the Art Students' League and Cooper Union, where he went often to pick up a slow buck. Cummings wrote about him in "little joe gould," and he is mentioned in the *Cantos* of Ezra Pound. In the *Oral History* he confessed: "I have delusions of grandeur; I believe myself to be Joe Gould."

Joe died at Pilgrim State Hospital in Brentwood, Long Island, August 18, 1957, aged sixty-eight. Everyone who did not know him was at his funeral, which was a little on the carnival side, courtesy of the Greenwich Village chamber of commerce and the cafeteria set.

He will reappear.

# VIII

## THE DIAL *and the Poet*

### 1

Although a good portion of Greenwich Village has begun
to look like Park Avenue, some of its streets have managed to
retain an almost unaltered appearance before the glacier-like
march of massive apartment houses. Such a street is Thirteenth,
between Sixth and Seventh avenues, with its three-story houses
and sidewalks thickly sown with flourishing plane trees. Its land-
mark is the Village Presbyterian Church, now shared with the
Brotherhood Synagogue, so that the Sabbath as well as Sunday
draws worshipers to its white-pillared, Greek Revival portico. Up
and down the street are restaurants—Felix's, Mario's, Little
Venice, the Mandarin House—long known to Villagers and uptowners. Next door to Felix's, at 152, is the three-story house that
was the home of *The Dial* for nine and a half years.

*The Dial* that is the subject of this chapter was not the publication founded in 1840 with Margaret Fuller and Ralph Waldo
Emerson as its first editors; that venture lasted only four years,
despite notable contributors and a market situated in the "Athens
of the West" and the "Hub of the Universe." In 1880 it was re-

established in Chicago, "hog-butcher to the world," and lasted longer; it was still going in 1917 when it moved to New York, where it became a fortnightly with advanced social and liberal views. Some of its editors and contributing editors were Robert Morss Lovett, Thorstein Veblen, Randolph Bourne, Van Wyck Brooks, Lewis Mumford, and Harold E. Stearns. But it was soon in financial difficulties, and two men, one of whom had been at Harvard with Cummings, decided to buy it. They were Scofield Thayer and James Sibley Watson. Dr. Watson, who could have practiced medicine but preferred editing, told me:

"Thayer said he would either start a magazine or set up a fund for artists. If he started a magazine, would I come in with him? The answer was 'yes.' Then came the question—should we start a new magazine or get hold of an old one? Because I had written for the fortnightly *Dial* I suggested we get hold of it. But we did not want to approach Martyn Johnson, the owner, directly. So Thayer wrote a check for ten thousand dollars, I wrote one for twenty-five hundred dollars, and we gave the money to Harold Stearns, who was to act as go-between. Time passed, and nothing happened. Harold simply disappeared. He afterwards returned the entire sum."

Stearns lives on as Harvey Stone in *The Sun Also Rises*. He told everyone that he had perfected a system for beating the horses.

"About a year later," Dr. Watson continued, "we heard that the magazine was on the point of suspending. This time we approached Johnson through our lawyers, and the deal was closed. We got *The Dial* in November, 1919, and let it continue as a bi-weekly for a couple of issues. In January, 1920, it became a monthly. We took with us Lewis Mumford, who did not stay long. Bruce Rogers, the Harvard typographer, designed the new format.

"We paid for contributions on acceptance—and had the usual tendency to stock up in advance. For prose, we paid two cents a word. Poetry was paid for at the rate of twenty dollars a page or any part of a page [the author of this book recalls with pleasure a check for twenty dollars for an eight-line poem].

"The more copies of the magazine we published, the more we lost. When the circulation went up to twenty-two thousand—the high watermark—we lost too much and let it sink back to four thousand, a normal run. Towards the end of the twenties this seemed a natural number. Our annual deficit was usually around thirty thousand dollars; but some years it was fifty thousand dollars."

Watson's munificence was not confined to *The Dial*. Margaret Anderson, the editor of the *Little Review*, tells in her autobiography of a visit to her office of this tall, spare, diffident American with his marked resemblance to Edwin Arlington Robinson. It was a Christmas day; she does not give the year, but it could not have been long after *The Dial* was purchased, so it was probably Christmas, 1919. She does not give the address, but it must have been in the basement of the "old Van Buren house" at 31 West Fourteenth Street, a four-story brownstone built by Abraham Van Buren in 1846. The brownstone, which was torn down in 1927, was next door to the loft building where Cummings and Brown lived. Miss Anderson wrote:

"At tea time a tall blond man arrived, introduced himself as J. S. Watson of the *Dial*, and said he wanted to buy a copy of Eliot's 'Prufrock.' We had published most of the poems in this collection and kept the book on sale. It cost seventy-five cents. Mr. Watson gave me a dollar bill, took the book and left, saying: 'Oh no, I don't want any change.' As I put the dollar away I chanced to look at it. It was a hundred-dollar bill. I ran after Mr. Watson to tell him he had made a mistake.

"'Oh no,' he said again, so embarrassed that he began falling down the stairs. 'I brought it for the *Little Review*. It's good, I assure you.'

"I made him come back and talk. We became friends and so remained during all our attacks on the *Dial* as 'a de-alcoholized version of the *Little Review*.' Watson came several times with his salutary hundred-dollar bill which kept the magazine alive when otherwise it would have succumbed" (from *My Thirty Years' War*).

2

The introduction of a new poet must be a memorable event to those who are present at the introduction, who respond to the poetry, and who live to see their original response generally confirmed. Such is probably the case as regards Cummings with some portion of the reading public old enough to have read *The Dial* and young enough to be alive today. His work appeared in it throughout its existence. Pound wrote a decade and a half later: "E. E. was undoubtedly the white-haired boy for that outfit." Dr. Watson told me that "it was always exciting when we had his poems or drawings in the office." He added that, so far as the editors were concerned, "a good thing had intensity; if not, 'it was not profoundly enough imagined,' in Thayer's phrase."

The first number—January, 1920—had for frontispiece a bas-relief of a female nude by Gaston Lachaise. The leading article was "An Autobiographic Chapter" by Randolph Bourne. This was followed by "Seven Poems" and four line drawings—of a comedian, hoofer, and ladies of the National Winter Garden—by E. E. Cummings. A contributor's note states that Cummings "has not previously published in any of the regular periodicals." He was then twenty-six years old. (Other contributors to the first number were Paul Rosenfeld, who wrote on music; Edwin Arlington Robinson, Maxwell Bodenheim, Carl Sandburg, Evelyn Scott, and Walter Pach.) The "Seven Poems" were "little tree," "the bigness of cannon," the poem about Buffalo Bill, "when god lets my body be," "why did you go," "when life is quite through with," and "O Distinct" (first lines: *Poems 1923-1954*).

The February number marked the appearance of Cummings as an art critic. His essay was entitled "Gaston Lachaise," and it was illustrated by Lachaise's drawings and sculpture. He did not appear again until the May number, this time with five poems: "into the strenuous briefness," "O sweet spontaneous," "but the other," "in Just-spring," and "spring omnipotent goddess," which he afterwards revised for book publication.

All the poems thus far referred to appeared either in *Tulips and Chimneys* (1923) or in *XLI Poems* (1925). Stewart Mitchell told me that, beginning in January, 1920, he took the original manuscript of *Tulips and Chimneys* to five publishers, all of whom declined it, including Cummings' present publisher. A glance at the group, particularly "little tree," will reveal an eye familiar with visual forms, for Cummings, being a painter, gave many of his lines structure as well as movement.

But his outstanding contribution is metaphor and simultaneity —plus, of course, music. In "cruelly, love," from *XLI Poems*, this combination results in a masterpiece. Here his invention encompasses divergent aspects of a single situation; all the strands of a mood, perhaps the deepest a poet can feel, are brought together, and single words—an example is "winter"—are made to serve the structure of the poem with all the weight of stanzas, as though the poet stood at a crossroads leading to simultaneous seasons:

> cruelly, love
> walk the autumn long;
> the last flower in whose hair,
> thy lips are cold with songs
>
> for which is
> first to wither, to pass?
> shallowness of sunlight
> falls and, cruelly,
> across the grass
> Comes the
> moon
>
> love, walk the
> autumn
> love, for the last
> flower in the hair withers;
> thy hair is acold with
> dreams,
> love thou art frail

—walk the longness of autumn
smile dustily to the people,
for winter
who crookedly care.

His poems offer few difficulties when read aloud, either to the reader or to the listener. This achievement is quite different from pictures formed out of type or calligraphy. Cummings was the first to introduce and develop those structural elements on the printed page that act as doors and passageways to ultimate effects. A simple test is to take any of his poems and note how his lines and divisions of lines help to establish meaning and accent as well as movement. In this respect, he was an innovator.[1]

## 3

In the June issue, Cummings reviewed Eliot's *Poems*, published that year. He unerringly chose not only the poems that were to become so familiar, but revealed Eliot's method. He wrote:
"Between the negative and flabby and ponderous and little bellowings of those multitudinous contemporaries who are obstinately always 'unconventional' or else 'modern' at the expense of being (what is most difficult) alive, Mr. T. S. Eliot inserts the positive and deep beauty of his skilful and immediate violins. . . . Some Notes on the Blank Verse of Christopher Marlowe are to a student of Mr. T. S., unnecessarily illuminating:

'. . . this style which secures its emphasis by always hesitating on the edge of caricature at the right moment . . .
'. . . this intense and serious and indubitably great poetry, which, like some great painting and sculpture, attains its effects by something not unlike caricature.'

---

[1] Cummings wrote me after reading the foregoing: "from my standpoint, not EEC but EP is the authentic 'innovator'; the true trailblazer of an epoch." Pound wrote me (November 20, 1957): "I do not think Mr. Cummings is indebted to me for any of the brilliance of his style, which is intensely personal."

Even without this somewhat mighty hint, this something which for all its slipperyness is after all a door-knob to be grasped by anyone who wishes to enter the 'some great' Art-Parlours, ourselves might have constructed a possibly logical development from Preludes and Rhapsody on a Windy Night along J. Alfred and Portrait up the two Sweeneys to let us say The Hippopotamus."

He praised Eliot's technique: "By technique we do not mean a great many things, including: anything static, a school, a noun, a slogan, a formula, These Three For Instant Beauty, Ars Est Celare, Hasn't Scratched Yet, Professor Woodbury, Grape Nuts. By technique we do mean one thing: the alert hatred of normality which, through the lips of a tactile and cohesive adventure, asserts that nobody in general and some one in particular is incorrigibly and actually alive. This some one is, it would seem, the extremely great artist: or, he who prefers above everything and within everything the unique dimension of intensity, which it amuses him to substitute in us for the comforting and comfortable furniture of reality. If we examine the means through which this substitution is allowed by Mr. Eliot to happen in his reader, we find that they include: a vocabulary almost brutally tuned to attain distinctness; an extraordinarily tight orchestration of the shapes of sound; the delicate and careful murderings—almost invariably interpreted, internally as well as terminally, through near-rhyme and rhyme—of established tempos by oral rhythms."

This was high and exact praise, delivered when it counted, and delivered through a medium in which everyone wanted to appear.[2] But two years later Cummings had other views, according to Malcolm Cowley: "When The Waste Land appeared, complete with notes [it had been published in The Dial without them], E. E. Cummings asked me why Eliot couldn't write his own lines instead of borrowing from dead poets. In his remarks I sensed a feeling almost of betrayal."

[2] In reply to a query, Mr. Eliot wrote me from London, September 13, 1957: "I do not know what I can say about E. E. Cummings which would be particularly suitable for your book, unless the book is to consist of encomiums by other authors. I have a very high opinion of Mr. Cummings as a poet, in spite of my dislike of his typography."

The June number of *The Dial* also carried "The Fourth Canto" of Ezra Pound, "Gavotte in D Minor" by Amy Lowell, and an appreciation of Rimbaud by "W. C. Blum," in reality James Sibley Watson, who also translated "A Season in Hell," which appeared in July. Cummings did not appear again until the January, 1921, issue, in which were published four of his drawings and the 290-line "Puella Mea," one of the most ambitious love poems of modern times. It afterwards appeared in *Tulips and Chimneys*, was unaccountably omitted from the *Collected Poems* of 1938, but is now back in its proper place in *Poems 1923-1954*.

4

I have mentioned a few of the other contributors to *The Dial* during the period under review. His friends appeared early in its pages: Slater Brown, S. Foster Damon, Malcolm Cowley, Edmund Wilson, John Dos Passos. Gilbert Seldes became an associate editor with the February issue, with a department to himself, "The Theatre." Soon another department was added, conducted by Henry McBride. Called "Modern Forms," it was devoted "to exposition and consideration of the less traditional types of art." The names that are at the heart of the literary twenties began to be familiar to readers of the magazine, and there were reproductions of the work of Picasso, Vlaminck, Redon, Marin, Stuart Davis, and Wyndham Lewis, Maillol, Jean Cocteau, and Matisse. To this bill-of-fare the owners of *The Dial* added an award of two thousand dollars, which, as they were careful to point out, was not a prize, since it was not to be competed for. In 1922 it went to T. S. Eliot for *The Waste Land*, in 1924 to Marianne Moore for her *Observations*, and in 1925 to E. E. Cummings. The issue containing the announcement of the award to him was embellished by three busts by Lachaise—of Cummings, Watson, and Thayer—photographed by Charles Sheeler. There was also a review, by Marianne Moore, of *XLI Poems* and &, both of which appeared in 1925, the latter privately printed. The announcement, written by Watson, states:

"*The Dial Award* for 1925 was offered to Edward Estlin Cummings and we are happy to announce that he has accepted it. His distinguished service to American letters will be obvious to all who have read either his story, *The Enormous Room* (1922), or any of his three books of verse, *Tulips and Chimneys* (1923), *XLI Poems* (1925), and & (1925).

"The two books of verse published this year are not as some think, made up of poems written more recently than those of his first volume. With the exception of a few poems written in 1915 and earlier, the whole lot is the result of six years of acute activity, 1917-1923, during which, to use his own expression, he wrote literally 'millions of poems.' & does indeed contain more stylistic experiments than the other volumes, but this is due not to any recent development of the poet's, but to the fact that he himself selected the contents of the book. These innovations could mean a great deal to some other poet but are not I think the key to any important change in his own quality or mood.

"Some of the younger writers, the writers under thirty, who may or may not yet be famous, but who belong after all to the only class who will or for that matter can read a new book of poems with insight, have preferred to see a new departure for Mr. Cummings in what they call his satirical verse. In spite of the excellence of some of those satirical poems, notably of the four poems published in *Secession* 1924,[3] nightmares of magnificent caricature, it seems to us that they close an epoch rather than begin one.

"And now let people chuckle all they have a mind to over the solemn way in which we speak of epochs and developments. One learns at school that much poetry called great has been written by very young men. As for the public's 'great poets' they are dead poets —or poets who have lived down to two or three generations. Meanwhile Mr. Cummings is one of this generation's great poets.

"*The Dial Award* therefore finds him when he has finished an epoch, and no matter how much difference it may make to *The Dial* to see no more of this poetry at once over-ripe and with the dangerous beauty of glare ice, it makes very little difference to Mr.

[3] Read 1922.

Cummings. He has become more and more absorbed in painting. If he has begun writing again by millions no doubt his new millions will be different."

The good blond poet had arrived.[4]

Marianne Moore, who was managing editor at the time of the award to Cummings, told me: "Winners of the *Dial Award* were supposed to contribute to the issue announcing the award. But instead of a poem, Cummings preferred to publish a painting. He invited me to his Patchin Place studio, on the top floor of No. 4, to help him choose one. It was not a very big piece of work. We let him choose it; *he* was to like that issue. He was very careful about the reproduction, its proportion and size."

She described for me Cummings' rare appearances in her office, "in a light tweed suit, an unequivocal person of convictions. He looked exactly like the Lachaise bust of him." She added: "There was nothing ambiguous or cowardly or vague about his views. And he was very witty; but of course one can deduce that from his verse."

Neither *Tulips and Chimneys* nor *XLI Poems* carried a dedication. & was dedicated to "E. O.," the former Elaine Orr, Cummings' first wife, by whom he had one child, a daughter. Her first husband was Scofield Thayer.

5

Little remains to be said here of the memorable publication launched in 1920 by Thayer and Watson. The July, 1929, issue—the last—had for frontispiece "Portrait of the Artist" by Picasso (the "property of Hugo von Hofmannsthal") and ended with the following "Anouncement" by Dr. Watson:

"Nine and a half years is a rather long time for one management in the present journalistic mêlée. On the edge of quitting we want to express our immense gratitude to the distinguished men and women who, with us, have edited and helped edit *The Dial* since

---

[4] Two more *Dial Awards* were to be made: to William Carlos Williams in 1926 and Ezra Pound, 1927.

1920. These are: Stewart Mitchell, Gilbert Seldes, Alyse Gregory, Kenneth Burke, Marianne Moore. We are also grateful to our readers, always bearing in mind that although a magazine can get along somehow without readers it cannot exist without contributors—who were, however indignantly, *The Dial*."

Thus did he pay tribute to all concerned in the great publishing venture of the twenties; and by use of a non-editorial "we" memorialized his absent partner, who retired because of illness in 1926. Dr. Watson now lives in Rochester, New York, where he is head of the Radiology Department of the University of Rochester's School of Medicine.

> Who killed *The Dial?*
> "I," said Joe Gould,
> "With my inimitable style,
> I killed *The Dial*."

Thus Joe, nasally, on his rounds of Greenwich Village after the magazine's end. He, too, had appeared in it, with an excerpt from the *Oral History*.

Miss Moore afterwards wrote in *Predilections:* "I recall a visiting editor's incredulity when I said, 'To me it's a revel,' after being asked if I did not find reading manuscripts tiresome—manuscripts meaning the requested, the volunteered, and the recommended; that third and sometimes uneasy entrant inducing a wish, not infrequently, that the roles of sponsor and author might be interchanged, as when in a letter of introduction a (Persian, I think) typographic neighbor wrote us, 'In the country where I came from, the people say: 'Ham Liyarat, ham Tújarat'—Both pilgrimage and business, and so it is. Miss Z would like to have you see some of her poems.' "

"Miss Z" eludes me; could it have been Marya Zaturenska? The Persian was S. A. Jacobs, "typographer for E. E. Cummings, a position that, I take it, has all the importance and weight of being camera man to Douglas Fairbanks," as Harry Hansen wrote in his column in the Sunday *World*.

One of my earliest impressions of him is, fittingly enough,

against the background of a printing press. It was in a building on Eighth Street. In the room with him and the press were a famous editor, Guy Holt, and a famous bibliographer and poet, Francesco Bianco. Also present was a young poet [5] with a sheaf of galleys in his hand. The young poet was upset. He had discovered, at the end of a stanza, a comma where a period should have been. The forms were locked, the book ready for printing. Mr. Jacobs smiled. He produced from somewhere a short-bladed knife with a round tip. He climbed into the press and almost disappeared from view. He was gone several minutes and emerged, unstained and triumphant. He had found the offending page, cut off the tail from the comma, and rounded what remained into a period like the others in the book. Everyone congratulated him.

His name in Persian was about a yard long—or so I judge from a reference to it in *Time*, viz.: "Jacobs is loth to give his full name in Persian, admits that part of it is Samuel Yakob Aivaz Sheraa-obode Azerbajode Muradkhan." He was dark-complexioned, and his skin seemed to glow. He was of average height, but full-fleshed, with an air of Eastern well-being. Not a man to lose his temper; gentle, understanding, and imbued with a passionate loyalty. He was not only Cummings' typographer—he was Cummings' friend, explainer, and defender. It was to him that interviewers went in the twenties to learn something about Cummings.

It seems almost a thing of fate that Jacobs and Cummings should have formed their triumphal partnership, and formed it so early. For Jacobs set up Cummings' first book of poems, *Tulips and Chimneys*, and discovered to his delight, among other beauties in that book, six poems, under the heading of "Orientale," that must have awakened racial memories. In them are emperors and elephants, incense, fountains, "a flutter of stars," a queen dancing, and the jealousy of the harem.

It was through Mr. Jacobs that I first met Cummings, in 1925, when he was thirty-one years old and renowned locally, not for *The Enormous Room* or *Tulips and Chimneys*, but for his appearances in *The Dial*, and for a curious book entitled &, privately

[5] The author.

printed in an edition of 111 copies on Vidalon handmade paper and 222 copies on De Coverly rag laid, the latter of which, if you were known to Josephine and Chase Horton of the Washington Square Book Shop, you could purchase for five dollars; but not if your name was John S. Sumner, secretary of the New York Society For the Suppression of Vice, who had a habit of dropping in. *The Enormous Room* was out of print, and was to remain so for three more years, when Lawrence of Arabia praised it and Robert Graves wrote an introduction to it. As for *Tulips and Chimneys*, I believe that, as of 1925, only the poets knew what had happened to American poetry as a result of its publication; some of them, of course, didn't like it—i.e., what had happened.

Mr. Jacobs, printer of &, introduced me with the remark that "poets should know each other," a view at odds with Dr. Johnson's. This was in the room on the top floor of the Patchin Place house, which was crowded with canvases. A bare expanse of floor bordered by burned-out kitchen matches in layers several inches thick made a path from the door to an easel. At that time Cummings smoked everything—cigarettes, cigars, and a pipe; in the last decade and a half of his life he did not smoke at all, on his doctor's orders. (Twelve years after he had stopped smoking, he told me: "I still miss it.") The burned-out matches were dropped in a pattern— perhaps to the left one time, and then the next one to the right as he stepped away from, or toward, his easel.

I was twenty-one, and bound for Paris. In honor of the occasion Cummings took me to dinner at Marta's, on Washington Place; it was during Prohibition, but I believe there was a bottle of wine on the table. No host could have been more charming; a better word for him, perhaps, is Horace Gregory's "courtly." He was very handsome—blond, with alive hazel eyes, quick gestures, and quicker repartee; he may have been wearing the light tweed suit that Marianne Moore recalled when she told me about his rare appearances in her office. It was only at the end of the meal, I think, when he drew out a checkbook, that I ventured to make a direct remark. I said: "If I were the proprietor [who was standing by], I would keep that check with your signature." He laughed heartily and said that he certainly hoped it would happen, but he "believed otherwise, alas."

The next time I saw him—the following year—it was in Paris; I was going past the Café des Deux Magots when we spotted each other. He was sitting at a table on the *terrasse* with Michael Larionov; the next moment he was up, and we were shaking hands. I said, "I am glad to see you," but instead of replying, he smiled and pointed. At the curb there was an automobile, and on the automobile a little pennant with the word *"Forever"* on it. And forever it was.

# 6

No one seems to know how the manuscript of Cummings' first book of poems found its publisher. Cummings was abroad when Thomas Seltzer, the head of a small, distinguished house, accepted *Tulips and Chimneys*. Mr. Seltzer is dead, his publishing house long defunct, its records gone. Albert and Charles Boni, nephews of Seltzer, who took over what remained of his business, and who became publishers in their own right, have no information on the subject. Dos Passos wrote me, "It's my recollection that Stewart Mitchell had something to do with getting the manuscript to Seltzer." Mr. Mitchell died in 1957 before I could ask him about this. Dos Passos himself once had the original manuscript in his possession, and his friend, John Peale Bishop, has left an account [6] of the excitement he felt when he read it:

"It is impossible for me as I reread the poems of E. E. Cummings not to recall the emotion with which I first read *Tulips and Chimneys*. Their freshness and grace have not been lost, but to these qualities there was then added a rare excitement of discovery. This was early in the summer of 1922; John Dos Passos had loaned me a copy of the manuscript which Cummings on going abroad had left in his hands that he might arrange, if he could, for its publication. The following year, Thomas Seltzer was persuaded to bring out *Tulips and Chimneys*, but only in a much shortened

[6] Review of *Collected Poems*, in *The Southern Review*, Summer, 1938.

form. About half the poems I had read in manuscript did not appear in print until much later and then scattered through volumes which wore other titles." [7]

*Tulips and Chimneys* appeared in 1923. One has only to examine the anthologies of that time, crowded with mediocrities now mercifully forgotten, to perceive the revolution the book wrought. How fresh, how lovely, was the new voice amid the "melancholy trillers":

> the hours rise up putting off stars and it is
> dawn
> into the street of the sky light walks scattering poems

It was a book of enormous surprises. The lower-case "i" and the typographical acrobatics—

                                        a tall

            wind
            is dragging
            the
            sea

            with

            dream

            -S

[7] In 1924, after selections had been made for *XLI Poems*, published by Lincoln MacVeagh:The Dial Press, Cummings sent Jacobs two lists—of MacVeagh's selections and "my own list (43 poems) of remaining material in the original T & C ms." He added: "On rereading, I was ever so pleased to discover that my most personal work had been carefully omitted by both Thomas&Lincoln. I hope that you will publish this,under your own coatofarms. Nobody else in the world can set what I like best of my own poems—for 1 thing...." A "PS" to this letter declares:

> I haven't,in the least,abandoned idea
> of an eventual publication of the
> original T & C ms as such— ....—
> my ancestors are hereditary optimists.

In 1925 Jacobs printed, in a limited edition, the volume entitled &, the major portion of which consists of the poems left out of the compilations by Seltzer and MacVeagh, and in 1937 he published the "Archetype Edition" of *Tulips and Chimneys* from the original manuscript.

—were the least of them. In it came to dwell forever "the Cambridge ladies who live in furnished souls"; in it appeared the now much-loved "All in green went my love riding," the (afterwards) much-anthologized "when god lets my body be," and "in Just-spring" with its magical ending. There was also the versification of a master:

> it is the autumn of a year:
> When through the thin air stooped with fear,
> across the harvest whitely peer
> empty of surprise
> death's faultless eyes

Above all, it was the book of a poet dealing from a fresh deck, who offered a way of writing that was peculiarly his own, and that his imitators, who have been legion, have never quite got the knack of; it said only what had to be said, while other poets were "busy stitching images together" (as Edmund Wilson remarked in his review of *Him*):

> into the strenuous briefness
> Life:
> handorgans and April
> darkness, friends
>
> i charge laughing.
> Into the hair-thin tints
> of yellow dawn,
> into the women-coloured twilight
>
> i smilingly
> glide. I
> into the big vermilion departure
> swim, sayingly;
>
> (Do you think?) the
> i do, world
> is probably made
> of roses & hello:
>
> (of solongs and, ashes)

In the light of contemporary reactions, it is interesting to note that the book opens with a poem—"Epithalamion"—of twenty-one eight-line rhymed stanzas, and ends with seventeen sonnets, including "it may not always be so." The book contains, as well, the long, rhymed, and beautifully cadenced "Puella Mea."

## 7

A poem is the culmination of a poet's experience, and is itself part of that experience. Cummings communicates his experience by means of language and forms that *dramatize* it, so that the experience is still taking place so far as the reader is concerned.

> since feeling is first
> who pays any attention
> to the syntax of things
> will never wholly kiss you;
>
> wholly to be a fool
> while Spring is in the world
>
> my blood approves,
> and kisses are a better fate
> than wisdom
> lady i swear by all flowers. Don't cry
> —the best gesture of my brain is less than
> your eyelids' flutter which says
>
> we are for each other: then
> laugh, leaning back in my arms
> for life's not a paragraph
>
> And death i think is no parenthesis

In miniature, "since feeling is first" is like the talk of the lovers in the play *Him*. Cummings' poem is different from Marvell's, and different from the kind of poem he wrote when he took Marvell's theme and tried persuasion by wit (Shakespeare's Sonnet 19— "Devouring Time blunt thou the lion's paws"—was also in his mind) in "(ponder,darling,these busted statues."

Another example of his dramatization is the poem about a mouse.[8] The mouse has not come and gone: we are in the room with the poet and his lady *and the mouse* (whose eyes peer out of a parenthesis). Abruptly:

here's a little mouse)and
what does he think about, i
wonder as over this
floor(quietly with

bright eyes)drifts(nobody
can tell because
Nobody knows, or why
jerks Here &, here,
gr(oo)ving the room's Silence)this like
a littlest
poem a
(with wee ears and see?

tail frisks)
                    (gonE)
"mouse",
          We are not the same you and

i, since here's a little he
or is
it It
?    (or was something we saw in the mirror)?

therefore we'll kiss; for maybe
what was Disappeared
into ourselves
who    (look).    ,startled

8 "All the arguments are of course on his side but E. E. Cummings's well-known poem on a mouse long since gave me a mouse I'll never forget and if literature has given me any other mice I don't remember them." (From a review of Max Eastman's *The Literary Mind* in the Tulsa (Okla.) *World*, Dec. 6, 1931.)

Cummings' love poems are devoid of literary devices, as opposed to technique. Only by an extraordinarily accomplished and controlled technique could he have communicated so much intensity. Everything is fresh, new, and deeply moving:

> i go to this window
>
> just as day dissolves
> when it is twilight(and
> looking up in fear
>
> i see the new moon
> thinner than a hair)
>
> making me feel
> how myself has been coarse and dull
> compared with you . . .

Twilight and the moon are very important and appear frequently in Cummings' poems, as do other natural phenomena. Is it because his background was suburban and country? [9] In another poem, twilight hesitates, the moon *emerges*, over the

> street
> where
> you will come,
>                 at twi li ght
> s(oon & there's
> a                    m oo
> )n.

---

[9] Max Eastman wrote in *Enjoyment of Poetry*: "Years ago, before Mr. Cummings was known as the inventor of the punctuational gymnastic, I sat with him and some others in a room where a cat was purring. In a pause of our conversation—which was a rather chilly one, he being a poet and I for the moment an editor—he suddenly exclaimed: 'I have it—it's milking the cow, it's the milk scudding into the foam in the pail!' The emotional incongruity of this remark to the prevailing atmosphere was so great that everybody, as I remember, was a trifle embarrassed. But as a pure matter of auditory sensation it was so accurate that it remained in my mind—John Stuart Mill to the contrary notwithstanding—as the sure proof of a poet."

It was logical for him, when he came to write a poem about a grasshopper, to make it *hop*; it hops out of the first line, grass-end first: [10]

<pre>
                    r-p-o-p-h-e-s-s-a-g-r
                who
        a)s w(e loo)k
        upnowgath
                PPEGORHRASS
                            eringint(o-
        aThe):l
            eA
                !p:
        S                                   a
                    (r
        rIvInG          .gRrEaPsPhOs)
                                    to
        rea(be)rran(com)gi(e)ngly
        ,grasshopper;
</pre>

This is the poem that traumatized Stanton A. Coblentz, publisher of *Wings* and head committeeman for the League for Sanity in Poetry. "No, we have not here the work of a drunken typesetter," he wrote in *The New York Times Magazine* in an article on modern poetry entitled "What Are They—Poems or Puzzles?" No, certainly not—it was by "E. E. Cummings, who has been widely credited with being one of our leading American poets—the author of 'Is 5,' '&,' 'CIOPW,' '1/20,' '1 x 1' and other volumes." An ingenious variation on *ad hominem*: if you can't attack the man, attack his titles.

Mr. Coblentz, in the article referred to, concludes that most of

---

[10] An example of *tmesis*—the separation of parts of a word by intervening words. Cummings told me: "The people who object to my way of writing have never read the classics. That has nothing to do with whether my work is good or bad." To add a text to this footnote, I quote Marlowe:

> Though some speake openly against my bookes,
> Yet will they reade me.

the modern poets are "(1) Sheer exhibitionists, never far from the 'lunatic fringe' and never better than literary clowns delighting in verbal acrobatics. (2) Tricksters who, having found the newer methods to pay dividends, prefer visible rewards to scruples." As for the first indictment, I rather like the idea of "literary clowns delighting in verbal acrobatics"; as for the second, Cummings once said to me: "I have been poor a long time but, you know, I have never gotten used to it."

The truth is that he cared very little whether an audience existed for him or not. He told me: "The relation of an artist to his audience is neither positive nor negative. It's at right angles. I'm not writing 'difficult' so that simple people won't understand me. I'm not writing 'difficult' for difficult people to understand. Insofar as I have any conception of my audience, it inhibits me. An audience directs things its own way."

His resistances were many and, like his language, special. An editor to whom he sent five poems returned two; Cummings returned the check and asked for the other three. (The editor used all five.) An anthologist wrote him: "If posterity could know your work only by one single brief poem, what poem of yours would you choose to represent you?" Cummings replied: "I do not know nor can I tell what I should care or not care to not have or have per(un)sist but my favorite poem is A Grave by Miss M. Moore."

What Cummings felt like publishing at this time was a drawing of an elephant, and he sent a drawing of an elephant. The anthologist reproduced it and also used Marianne Moore's poem.[11]

In addition to his instinct for drama, Cummings magically communicates atmosphere—

> when light fails and this sweet profound
> Paris moves with lovers, two and two
> bound for themselves

11 *Fifty Poets*, ed. by William Rose Benét.

—and constantly surprises by the *mot juste.* It is intensity that he is after.[12] I take two examples; one early, one late. The first occurs in the poem that begins

> beyond the brittle towns asleep
> i look where stealing needles of foam
> in the last light
>
> thread the creeping shores

Here, "stealing," "thread," and "creeping" are used with precision; but it is when he selects the word to describe what the sea itself does that he achieves a master stroke—the sea

> *pours* its eyeless miles

In the second, exegesis is superfluous:

> (did you kiss
> a girl with nipples
> like pink thimbles)

There is in his work a series of "private" poems that appear cryptic because they deal with persons unknown to his readers (I include myself). A simple example is the one about Miss Gay, previously cited. Another is:

> 2 boston
>
> Dolls;found
> with
> Holes in each other
>
> 's lullaby

---

[12] He once said to me in New Hampshire: "You know, I ought to like Frost. After all, we're both New Englanders. But I've never been able to read him. Why do you like him?" I tried to explain. He said: "I have four or five collections here; would you read me some of the poems you like?" He got the books down, and I read "My November Guest," the last stanza of "Reluctance," "To Earthward," and "Acquainted with the Night." He listened with eyes closed. There was a long pause. "Would you like to know what *I* think?" he asked. "They lack intensity."

No reader not familiar with the sensational "double suicide" of Harry Crosby and Mrs. Josephine Bigelow might be expected to understand this nevertheless vivid passage (there is an excellent account of the incident in *Exile's Return*).

Cummings' technical range has enabled him to write both light and dark, to compress a romance into three minuscule stanzas, as in "myself, walking in Dragon st," and to achieve the highest degree of excitement in a poem equally brief (conveyed in part by the extraordinary *caesura* that occurs between the first and second stanzas):

> no time ago
> or else a life
> walking in the dark
> i met christ
>
> jesus) my heart
> flopped over
> and lay still
> while he passed(as
>
> close as i'm to you
> yes closer
> made of nothing
> except loneliness

Cummings wrote this poem after a walk one night. He told me he started up West Tenth Street, and as he neared Greenwich Avenue he saw "a little person who now is dead and who lived by begging." He had known this man well; but now he suddenly saw him as "someone else."

It was Joe Gould.

# IX

## *The Twenties: Paris*

**1**

> Paris; this April sunset completely utters
> utters serenely silently a cathedral
> before whose upward lean magnificent face
> the streets turn young with rain....

"Thanks a million for the K Kats!" he wrote Slater Brown. "The batch which G. Seldes brought over he wanted to put with his own collection, so I let him—keeping the later arrivals myself, as you direct." In another letter to Brown: "thanks much for letters plus immeasurable KK!" A final accolade—thanks "for a Kat of indescribable beauty." [1]

---

[1] Years later, when a publisher decided to issue a selection of George Herriman's panels, Cummings was asked to write the Introduction. He wrote it with love, and love is his theme: "A lot of people 'love' because, and a lot of people 'love' although, and a few individuals love. Love is something illimitable; and a lot of people spend their limited lives trying to prevent anything illimitable from happening to them." Not Krazy Kat—she is overwhelmingly in love with Ignatz Mouse, and suffers ecstatically. "She has no fear—even of a mouse."

In Paris, and in his wanderings around Europe, Cummings followed his usual practice of painting in the daytime and writing at night. On December 28, 1922, he shipped fifty-nine water-colors to Slater Brown, who was then living on the top floor of *The Dial* building (by a coincidence of sorts Hart Crane lived on the top floor of the *Little Review* building). "By all means," he wrote Brown, "send for me to the Pittsburgh or other shows if convenient. Some of the 59 are amusing." He sent them registered but not insured, "with the idea that you won't have to pay duty."

Cummings went to Paris in March, 1921, and did not return until 1923. It was during this first of his many sojourns abroad that he met Pound. He thinks it was at the Hotel Meurice, where Scofield Thayer was staying. It was then that Mr. Thayer asked Pound to become the Paris correspondent of *The Dial*.

After the "Black Knight," after the "Hell Hole," after the Columbian saloon; after the whispered password in the half-opened door, after the metallic hooch, the needled beer, and the bathtub gin, the young men from Prohibition America slaked their thirsts in the open, at the round-topped tables with the carafes and the leaning-tower-of-Pisa saucers, the world in free and pleasant motion around them.

On a spring night in 1923 Cummings, with Gilbert Seldes and John Dos Passos, left the Café de la Paix and drove in a fiacre to the Left Bank. In the neighborhood of the rue Gît-le-Coeur, near the Place St. Michel, the fiacre stopped and the men got out. Cummings went to the rear of the fiacre, and Seldes began an oration on the advantages of pantheism over monotheism—how much more imaginative the Greeks were, if only because of this, while modern man has contented himself with only one deity, which showed up his dullness; and so forth. At that moment a gendarme seized Cummings and placed him under arrest.

For many years the story was that Cummings asked the gendarme why he was being arrested, and the gendarme replied, "For pissing on Paris." Cummings pointed out that he had merely pissed on the fiacre. "*Le fiacre—c'est Paris!*" exclaimed the gendarme, and took him along—Seldes and Dos Passos following.

Dos Passos wrote me: "Gilbert and EEC and I (was there somebody else? I don't remember) had had one of our long bibulous and conversational dinners and were walking, maybe noisily, through one of the dark little streets near the Place St. Michel when Cummings decided to take a leak in a corner. As I remember it he was set upon by a whole phalanx of gendarmes who carried him off to a *poste de police*. We followed protesting. I tried to get in to argue with the authorities in what I considered my very best French and was thrown out bodily a number of times. C. did some funny drawings of this scene. Gilbert went off to call up his acquaintance Paul Morand who, as a fellow literateur —he was fairly highly placed at the Quai d'Orsay—had Cummings sprung sometime before morning. It was an idiotic but fairly comic incident and much laughed over by all our friends."

Although the incident had its amusing aspects, there was a serious side to it: Cummings, with 1917 in mind, was naturally apprehensive that he would be thrown out of France. The same thought had occurred to his friends—Seldes told me that never in his life had he seen three men become sober so quickly. As they were being ejected, Seldes overheard this colloquy between the arresting gendarme and the officer behind the desk:

"*Un Américan qui pisse.*"

"*Quoi—encore un pisseur Américain?*"

Cummings told me the dialogue that took place inside.

"Would you do that in your country?" asked the officer behind the desk.

"Yes," replied Cummings.

"*Menteur!*" screamed the sergeant of police.

"Why do you call me a liar?" asked Cummings.

"Because I know about America—I have a relative there."

"Where?"

"In Brook-leen."

Cummings was asked where he lived, and a gendarme went outside to check with Seldes and Dos Passos. When it was found that he had told the truth, he was permitted to leave, but with

orders to report to a magistrate the next morning. This was alarm-
ing. It was then that Seldes decided to enlist Morand. He told
Cummings to come by on his way to the magistrate's court, and
the three men separated.

Seldes was living in Lewis Galantière's apartment on the Quai
de Béthune, Ile St. Louis, where he was writing *The Seven Lively
Arts*. When Cummings showed up, he was greeted by several
hastily drawn posters announcing, "Reprieve Pisseur Américain!"
Seldes had called Morand at the Quai d'Orsay and explained that,
whatever happened, it was essential that Cummings be permitted
to stay away from the magistrate's court. Morand, although naturally reluctant to involve the Foreign Office in a police matter,
gave Seldes his word that it would be arranged.

Stewart Mitchell, about to leave for Spain, called on Cummings
and was much struck by a self-portrait, the first his friend had
ever painted. The background of this oil is the tiny room in the
rue St. André des Arts, where Cummings was living. Mitchell told
me that when he expressed his admiration, Cummings gave him
the portrait, and when he sent a check from Spain to pay for it,
Cummings returned the check. Mitchell thought this the best
self-portrait Cummings ever made. Back in Boston, he showed it to
Dr. Cummings, who said:

"Well, Stewart, I'll never be known as anything but the father
of my son."

2

Cummings returned to New York and moved into a studio
on the top floor of 4 Patchin Place, in which he did most of his
writing and painting, and which his friend Watson had rented to
protect the occupant of the adjoining room, John Cowper Powys.
One of Cummings' most read, most marked-up books—sentences
copied out on flyleaves and underscored on pages—is Powys'
*Visions and Revisions: A Book of Literary Devotions*. On the
front flyleaf Cummings wrote "truth-joy," and directly beneath is a

quotation from Powys: "the truth of truth is not in labor and sorrow, but in joy and happiness," basic in Cummings' philosophy. The essay on Shakespeare is heavily scored by him. Powys termed Shakespeare "the perfectly natural man confronting the universe."

Shakespeare, of course, was *the* poet for Cummings. His favorite plays were the great cluster of tragedies—*Antony and Cleopatra, Lear, Hamlet, Macbeth, Othello,* and *Romeo and Juliet.* "Shakespeare's tragedies never end in gloom—there is always an upward surge, of life to be lived," he said. *Romeo and Juliet* he called "an incredible *tour de force,* the greatest love story ever written." In his notebook he wrote: "Of course Bacon wrote Shakespeare;but so did everybody else, including(luckily)Shakespeare."

The expatriates were also returning from their haunts abroad. Back and forth across the sick but for them joyful Continent they had shuttled, strangers in strange lands who had joined the "new race of tourists, the *Valutaschweine,* the parasites of the exchange," as Malcolm Cowley termed them in a new-fangled version of *ubi bene, ibi patria*—

> Following the dollar, ah, following the dollar, I
> learned three fashions of eating with the knife.

On a trip to Vienna Cowley had carried the material for the third issue of *Secession.* "Five hundred copies of the magazine could be printed in Vienna for twenty-five dollars." At Imst, in the Austrian Tyrol, he was asked if he knew "Herr Braun von Amerika." Yes, to be sure: William Slater Brown. In Berlin he was met at the station by Matthew Josephson and Harold Loeb (Robert Cohn in *The Sun Also Rises*); *Broom* was to be printed there—a dollar bought "two thousand paper marks or an all-wool overcoat."

"Farther than Atlantis is my land," Cowley wrote in his excellent poem,

> but I shall return to it never,
> never shall wed my pale Alaska virgin,
> in thine arms never lie, O Texas Rose.

Nevertheless, he returned, and the others returned, for they were never of Europe—the nostalgia in his poem alone would prove it—they were never really happy, they hankered after ham and eggs, and the checks stopped coming. Cowley and Josephson resumed publication of *Broom* on West Twelfth Street, William Slater Brown assisting.

Burton Rascoe, the first critic of reputation to hail *The Waste Land* as a great modern work, which he did immediately after its publication and was much belabored for it, published an interview with Josephson in his column, "A Bookman's Daybook," in the New York *Tribune*. Rascoe was a slender, eager (so eager that he seemed at times to be trembling), generous, and well-read columnist from Chicago, where he had tasted to the full the intoxication of the Midwestern renaissance. Now he had descended on New York, bringing with him his insatiable curiosity about writers and writing. His columns were liberally sprinkled with names, but it was not mere name dropping, as often the names he dropped were of unknowns.

"Matthew Josephson, one of the editors of the modern review, *Broom*, came to see me today and was kind enough to explain to me the aesthetic concepts formulated by him and his confrères in what is perhaps the youngest articulate generation.

"On one point I found it necessary mildly to reprove Mr. Josephson, or at all events to disillusion him. He, like Mr. Seldes, of *The Dial*, has just discovered the comic strip, the American vaudeville, Charlie Chaplin, Al Jolson, Fanny Brice, Eddie Cantor, Joe Cook, Ed Wynn, Paul Whiteman, Ring Lardner and the Ziegfeld Follies, and he thinks, like Mr. Seldes, that this is a brand-new discovery; he is in enthusiastic haste to familiarize the good people of America with these artists through the agency of *Broom*, which has a circulation, I believe, of 1,500. He thinks they have been neglected.

"I reminded him that, far from neglecting these artists, the appreciative American public has for ten years or more so roundly applauded their work and paid good money to enjoy it that some of these artists are millionaires."

At the time Rascoe published this, Seldes was writing his famous book on the Ile St. Louis.

## 3

In 1924 Cummings was again in Paris. In Lewis Galantière's apartment on the Quai de Béthune, talking with him and Louis Aragon, a leader of one of the two Dada factions of Paris, Cummings praised Cocteau's *Les Mariés de la Tour Eiffel*; as he wrote afterwards in *Vanity Fair*, "having been more amused by *Les Mariés* than by anything else in Paris—more, even, than by the police—I entertained a wish to meet the author of this excellent satire." Aragon, "a militant *superrealist* writer and one of the most charming of people," discouraged him. Aragon, in fact, "made several enormous assertions; the smallest of which was, that the renowned poet and author of such novels as *Thomas l'Imposteur*, *Le Grand Ecart*, etc., etc., did not know how to write French."

(According to Galantière, Aragon attacked, chiefly, the homosexual "tone" of Cocteau's prose.)

"My surprise," Cummings wrote, "when Aragon uttered this very superrealist statement was by no means negligible; but I was infinitely more surprised to learn that Jean Cocteau—doubtless overhearing, from the Eiffel Tower radio station, or in some even more obscure manner, those terrible words—had been moved to produce a volume, not of poems, nor yet of prose, but of drawings. My third surprise came when I opened this book and read the first words of the dedication to Picasso: 'Poets don't draw.'

"Cocteau continues: 'They untie writing and then tie it up again differently. Which is why I allow myself to dedicate to you a few strokes made on blotters, tablecloths and backs of envelopes. Without your advice I'd never have dared to put them together.'

"Judging by this profound and brittle bow to the greatest living draughtsman, and knowing Cocteau's predilection for satire, I anticipated a mass of imitative pretense. And once again I was

surprised. For *Desseins* (as this collection of more than 200 of
Cocteau's drawings is modestly entitled) reveals itself as a rather
lengthy and random concoction of portrait sketches, scenes, caricatures, scrawls, imaginings—or what you will—strictly by a 'poetic
ironist' of this day and time, and possessing so much originality
that if M. Picasso be to blame for its publication the world owes
him a new debt of gratitude."

Here Cummings, taking his cue from Cocteau's drawing, which
he termed "the person with the pipe, called *Picasso*," proceeded
to describe the Spaniard:

"Nobody, I am sure, will deny one thing: meeting him for the
first time, the flesh-and-blood Picasso is a troll who has just sprung
out of the ground. He is not a man. Picasso himself, I reiterate, is
a troll—tightly made, genial, clinched, eyeful, and moreover (as
E. O.[2] once remarked, descending the Elysées with me one fragile
and immortal evening) 'with little velvet feet such as dolls *should*
have.' Returning now, to what I shall call this portrait of Picasso
by Cocteau—let me assure any interested person who has not found
him- or herself face to face with the original, that what Cocteau's
drawing expresses, first of all, is an uncouth aliveness which
Picasso's actual presence emanates. In other words, this sketch
apprehends—in a spontaneous, acutely personal way—the tactile
stimulus which a glimpse of the Spaniard, creature, or genius,
called 'Picasso' involves: the feathery jolt or, so to speak, shock, of
confrontation."

He had been taken to Picasso's studio by Seldes; and later met
the "troll" *chez lui*, thanks to the painter Michael Larionov, of the
Ballet Russe. His admiration did not last.

On another day, on the Right Bank, at four o'clock in the afternoon, Cummings saw a Communist demonstration. The police
broke it up—"50(fifty)flics for every one(1)communist"—the
enormous room in little and in the open:

[2] Elaine Orr, afterwards his wife. Stewart Mitchell told me she had violet
eyes and was so breathtakingly beautiful that women as well as men turned to
look at her. The marriage did not last.

16 heures
l'Etoile

the communists have fine Eyes

some are young some old none
look alike

while on the other hand:

all the flics are very organically
arranged
and their nucleus(composed
of captains in freshly-creased
-uniforms with only-just-
shined buttons
tidiyum
before and behind)has a nucleolus:

the Prefect of Police

with the result that

the
communists pick
up themselves friends
& their hats legs &

arms brush dirt coats
smile looking hands
spit blood teeth

the Communists have(very)fine eyes
(which stroll hither and thither through the
evening in bruised narrow questioning faces)

It will be observed that Cummings pays his compliment typographically, too—that is, with a sudden capital letter. The Left-
wing literati in the United States liked it. But not for long.

4

Burton Rascoe was indefatigable. In Paris, on a chilly fall Sunday afternoon in 1924, he and his wife took a train at the Gare St. Lazare and rode to St. Cloud. As they stood on the ridge of St. Cloud in thick mist, three figures approached, and "There you are!" said a voice in the mist. "We won't take a cab, for the house is only up the road a step. Mrs. Rascoe, allow me to present Mr. Cummings and Mr. MacLeish. Mr. Rascoe, Mr. MacLeish; you've met Cummings."

The speaker was Lewis Galantière. He was referring to Mac-Leish's house, to which they now set forth, Cummings beside Mrs. Rascoe, who was suddenly heard remarking, "I like your *lyrical* poetry"; "which," commented her husband, "is like saying to a poet 'I like your *left* ear' and implying that his right ear leaves much to be desired."

But when Rascoe came to write an account of this visit,[3] he admitted: "Strange though, she said just what I feel, though perhaps less felicitously and more directly than I, in my brashest and most cock-sure mood, should be able to express it. Coming out on the train I had been counting up our lyric poets of the first order since Poe. . . ." They all get short shrift.

"Who remains? Who indeed, but the chap we're to meet this afternoon. If there is a finer lyricist since Keats and Swinburne (I include them both), forgetting Yeats, in the English language I wish you would introduce me to him. Uneven? Yes, I grant you! So was God—look at Ben Turpin and the Siamese Twins! Even He is always experimenting and sometimes turning out things more fascinating than tasteful. Even He is more radical and revolutionary and whimsical than that of printing the first person singular with a lower case 'i'—look at His turning out a man like Volstead. Take it all in all, or all in little, Cummings's poetry, the best of it, is beauty like a lark's song or the Ode on a Grecian Urn or any other danged thing you please."

[3] *A Bookman's Daybook*, 1929.

At this point, Rascoe began to soar like his lark:

"I won't argue the case any more. When our myopic literary birchmen finally gutter out in the grease of their own stupidities, when the geoffreys have left their parsonage and all the reeds are broken and the putnams have ceased to put—then milady, my dear lady, America will have discovered that it has some poets and Cummings will be highty-tighty among the lot."

In the MacLeish living room, in the mansion flamboyantly decorated by an ex-Russian prince for his former mistress, the six Americans conversed. Rascoe has described them: MacLeish, "a clear-eyed, deferential young man, with an extremely Nordic head, quiet manners . . . and a wife who is charming American 'quality' "; Galantière, wearing thick-lensed spectacles and plus-fours; Cummings, sitting by the fire. "His mouth was taut and sullen under a blond toothbrush mustache. His head was thrown back challengingly as always except when he is being courteous to a lady. There was the fire of passionate conviction in his eye." Cummings was about to talk, and Rascoe has done a pretty good job getting it down, all things considered; for Cummings' monologue lasted eight hours.

Cummings (according to Rascoe) "Poets and artists, especially in America, make me sick. What right has such a beggar to take on airs? I have no more interest in or respect for a man because he can write a poem or paint a picture that will hang in the Louvre than I have for a man because he can fix the plumbing or design a beautiful motor car. Crossing the Place de la Concorde this morning I saw a Rolls-Royce car with a body that was a thing of grace, beauty and utility. Someone designed it. Someone who is a genius, an artist, much more an artist than I am, because it is not only a beautiful thing, it runs, and not only does it run, but it is useful and in demand, and the man who designed it can make a living out of his design.

"I am a poet, true enough; but what right have I to be proud of my disease? It's such a shabby, idiotic disease. You know what I want? Money, comfort, love, ease, luxury, the price in my pocket for theatre tickets and good wine. What do I do to go about getting them? I sit up in a shabby room, shivering with the cold, and use my imagination to keep me warm, thinking about the South Sea Islands and the tropical swamps. Your plumber wouldn't do that. He has more sense. He would go out and get some coal and wood to make a fire. He wouldn't sit there and freeze and try to imagine he was warm. I make poems because it is the thing I know how to do best. In fact, it is about the only thing I know how to do. America doesn't want poems badly enough to make it a profitable business to be engaged in. That's America's privilege. If you don't need something you would be a fool to buy it. If a fellow comes to my door and tries to sell me a handmade butter churn, I send him away because I don't need a churn. What do I want with a churn? I haven't any cow or any milk and I buy my butter at the dairy store around the corner. I am in the position of a fellow trying to sell flat-dwellers butter churns which they have no need for.

"But I'd be a fool, a worse fool than I am, if I imagined that I was a superior and precious sort of being because I went around trying to peddle butter churns that nobody wanted. Poets and artists are unfortunate persons trying to capitalize their neuroses. They get a shabby sort of satisfaction out of thinking themselves superior to people who are able to adjust themselves to life. I know, because I used to be that way myself. Since I got hep to myself, I have seen what an ingrown, puny lot poets are. I'd rather listen to a group of paper-box manufacturers talk about their business than to hear poets talk about theirs—the box manufacturers at least know their business from the ground up."

"I have caught here only the gist of it," wrote Rascoe. "The monologue itself was brilliant, elaborated with the most startling images and the most laughable conceits. We roared with laughter."

Mrs. MacLeish suggested dinner "at a little restaurant about a quarter of a mile away. Cummings suggested another round of cognac." When they set forth, Rascoe and Cummings, arms linked, took the middle of the road. Over dinner Cummings "continued, a coruscating cascade of unrelated or only slightly related images, poetic tags, remembered lines in Greek, French, Latin, German, and English. At one point he convulsed us with a recital of a whole episode from 'Hiawatha,' with a sententiousness which made the banality of that banal poem insupportable."

After quoting Sappho's "Ode to Aphrodite," says Rascoe, Cummings remarked: "Noblest poem, messieurs, noblest poem ever written." He quoted Laforgue, Verlaine, Catullus, Amy Lowell, and Shakespeare, and resumed his monologue: "It is not snowing snow, you know; it's snowing but-ter-cups! [4] And there we were, the crew of us, sailing through the air at the rate of 300 miles or the equivalent in parasangs and kilometers per hour in the good ship 'Galapogos' on our way to the Canary Islands. And there was poor old Wilson pounding the table at Versailles without a chance of being heard. He couldn't talk French, you know, not a single word of French. What chance did he have? Poor soul and I knew Mrs. Peck—charming woman; don't believe all the stories you hear about her—and our rations getting lower and lower all the time until we were living on pemmican and unicorns, one tablespoon full every three hours. It relieves the congestion in the lungs and tones up the body, and be sure to open your windows at night. When without a word of warning what should happen but the whole hulk burst in flames and David Wark Griffith not standing by the shores of Gitchee-gumme, by the shining big sea waters, where he used to paddle his own canoe, a birch bark canoe, guaranteed not to rust, leak or upset, children cry for it, women die for it, going going gone, did I hear seventy-five soixante-quinze, sold to the gentleman in the corner over there . . ."

"Again," wrote Rascoe, "again I must plead my inability to

[4] It may be that Rascoe was imperfectly recalling a poem by Cummings—

> than(by yon sunset's wintry glow
> revealed)this tall strong stalwart youth,
> what sight shall human optics know
> more quite ennobling forsooth?

which ends:

> with all his hearty soul aglow)
> his nightly supper sups
> it isn't snowing snow you know
> it's snowing buttercups

convey, and my hope to suggest, the quality of this fantastic rigmarole. Eight solid hours of it, to my hearing, and never a repetition, scarcely ever a break in the flow of unconnected images, all like the dissolving lights of a kaleidoscope. And MacLeish said he had kept it up all afternoon."

MacLeish told Rascoe: "His memory is astounding. I've heard about Swinburne memorizing and declaiming whole Greek tragedies and Hugo knowing the Iliad by heart and all that. What a bore it must have been to listen to them! I'll bet there was a rush for the exits at the Savage Club whenever Swinburne looked as if he might burst into a recital of Oedipus Rex in the original any moment. But Cummings is different. I have never been so royally entertained in my life. His mood changes. One melts into the other, tenderness into comicality, burlesque into profundity, snatches of Heine alternating with Rimbaud, advertising catchlines tied up with Catullus and Longfellow. Funny thing—he knows yards and yards of Tennyson and Longfellow by heart."

Monologue, dialogue, and dinner came to an end, and the Rascoes, Galantière, and Cummings returned to Paris. The hands of the clock in the tower of the Gare St. Lazare semaphored one-thirty. "I was a rag from listening," Rascoe commented; "but Cummings wanted to go somewhere and dance."

"Count me out!" said Galantière. "I have to be at work at nine in the morning. Paris for you fellows is a pleasure resort. For me it's where I earn my living." Galantière was employed by the International Chamber of Commerce, and worked six days a week. He was also translating Cocteau.

They all got into a cab.

"It's funny I never thought of that," said Cummings. "Somehow you never seem to associate Paris and a job. Think of having a job in Paris! What a quaint idea! But having a job anywhere would be a quaint idea for me, least of all in Paris. Did I say an idea? Why, it would be a godsend! Do you know where I can get a job, any little job—in Paris, Andalusia, New York, or Hong Kong? I hereby apply for any little job that may be floating around. All I require of the job is that it shall not be eleemosynary. It must pay me enough for a bed, cognac and cheese—and, oh yes! a ticket fortnightly for the Bal Tabarin and two sous for the vestiare. Vestiares must live. Two sous for the vestiare. That's all I ask."

Rascoe has also recounted[5] that the night before he left Paris, "Cummings, Galantière, Morris Gilbert, Morris Bishop, my wife, and I had dinner at the Café de Paris and, having consumed much champagne, we made a night of it, going from one bar to another and landing up finally at a restaurant in the market amusingly named *Aux Pères Tranquilles*."

This restaurant in Les Halles afterwards became the setting for Act III, Scene III, of Cummings' play, *Him*.

## 5

According to the announcement of *The Dial Award* for 1925, Cummings had been living in France "for reasons of economy." He now returned to New York and got a job. It was not, however, one for which he had to report at nine in the morning or six days a week. He began to write for *Vanity Fair*, which left him free to go abroad again. All he remembers about this roving assignment is, "I talked with Frank Crowninshield." It sufficed.

One of his pieces was entitled "How I Do Not Love Italy." He had made three trips there at the time he wrote it. He did not care for it the other times, either. "Shocks, however, cannot discourage really inquisitive people," he wrote. But he begs to opine "(1) that the ceiling of the Sistine Chapel is worth all the rest of *Italia* dead and undead (2) that we love Venice much but that we love Coney Island more (3) that one small church at San Tomé (Spain), which contains El Greco's *The Burial of Count Orgáz*, houses more aesthetic intensity than does the whole *Galleria degli Uffizi* and (4) that the world is still looking for an unidentified man who disappeared after partially expressing a desire to show us the coliseum by moonlight."

Of the country, he wrote: "*Italia*, without any doubt the most overestimated country in this world, consists of a peninsula which

[5] In *We Were Interrupted*, 1947.

is shaped like a leg that has been caught in the act of kicking Sicily. This naughty leg, whose chief industries are ruins, religion and automobiles, is technically a monarchy ruled over by a king (S.M. Il Re) but he is actually a pawn in the hands of the *onorevole* Benito Mussolini. The king nevertheless retains two extremely important functions, which are (a) to be photographed with Mussolini and (b) to pose for postage-stamps."

And of Mussolini: "He could not possibly be satisfied with being merely Caesar. He also wanted to be Napoleon. This was easily arranged. A photographer 'shot' him in Napoleonic costume, the photograph was printed on thousands of postcards and the post-cards were circulated all over *Italia*."

It is as Napoleon that Mussolini appears in Cummings' play.

Cummings was back in Paris in 1926, when John Carroll made a drawing of him. Cummings kept up a rapid-fire of talk while posing; "he was a witty sonofabitch," said Carroll admiringly. He told me that he drank champagne with Cummings at the Rotonde while Cummings talked about "the significance of Was," [such was Carroll's recollection after thirty-one years; I suspect is] and when they tired of the Rotonde they went to a place on the Right Bank where they continued to drink champagne, and finally re-turned to the Rotonde, but it was "too early for us to be served, the sun was just coming up."

# 6

It was Morrie Werner who called my attention to Cum-mings' humorous articles in *Vanity Fair*, many of which appeared under pseudonyms. He dwelt with particular pleasure on the one about Edna St. Vincent Millay, a good-natured piece of spoofing, which also contained imitations of her verse style. The piece about Miss Millay, entitled "Helen Whiffletree, American Poetess," was signed "P. H. Dunkels, N. G." and appeared November, 1925:

"Her mother, Gertrude Magee, was descended from a long line of brewers. Giusseppi Paladini, her father, rose to the position of first assistant dish-washer in the local automat restaurant, but apparently failed to make good." This, enshrined in his first paragraph, triggers the salvo in the last, in which Professor Dunkels describes his first glimpse of Miss Whiffletree, which took place as she alighted from a taxicab in Montmartre: "The poetess (for it was indeed she) was attired in a red tamashanta, a white *cache-nez* and sky-blue pyjamas. True to her ancestry, she carried under one arm the *Decameron* and under the other a nearly empty quart bottle labelled *Hennessy Three Star*."

This is what he wrote about her verse: "Early in her career, in fact while still in her teens at college, Helen Whiffletree wrote verse in which *naiveté* is carried to a pitch of unheard of poignancy. As an example, I can do no better than quote eight lovely lines which appeared, over the signature 'H. W.', in the literary magazine of her *alma mater*, and which are entitled 'Conversation':

> Quoth a busy bee,
> To a butterfly
> "Honey make I
> And what maketh thee?"
> "Go ask a lily,"
> Was the sage reply
> Of the silly
> Butterfly.

"To this, her collegiate period, belong also such lilting lyrics as 'Sodom and Gomorrah,' 'A Sparrow's Christmas,' 'Under the Mistletoe,' and the inimitable 'Day-Dream'—her first experiment in the Petrarchan sonnet form; which, beside showing the influence of Keats, caused three leading New York critics to compare her to Mrs. Browning, Shakespeare, and Sappho, respectively. Readers of *Vanity Fair* will doubtless pardon me for reminding them of the exquisite sextet:

> I ope my windows to this April eve,
> Letting sweet twilight whisper o'er my soul
> Its wondrous secrets without more ado.
> Night from day's sentence now doth seek reprieve,
> While—from the summit of yon wooded knoll—
> A final whippoorwill the ear doth woo.

"Alexander Woollcott is said to have remarked, when the last line was recited to him for the first time by a friend in the course of a camping trip in the Canadian Rockies: "It hurts, it is so fine.' "

Perhaps Mr. Woollcott remembered this for a later occasion.

Cummings' *Vanity Fair* pieces, whether serious or spoofing, appear now like kaleidoscopic views of the twenties. His own stance is everywhere expressed.

Item: "That the recent exhibition of abstract sculpture by Ivan Narb proved the big aesthetic event of 1926 is far from surprising —given the overwhelming originality of the sculptor's conceptions and the bewildering variety of the media employed (tin cans, sealing wax, hay wire, candlegrease, birchbark, bottle glass, gingerbread, chewing-gum etc.) as well as the quite preposterous mastery of his materials which Narb displays at every turn" (from "Ivan Narb: Abstract Sculptor of the Cosmic, by Gwendolyn Orloff").

In addition to a piece on tabloids, he did one on sex and confession magazines, signing it "John F. Rutter," which sounds suspiciously like John S. Sumner, onetime Secretary of the New York Society for the Suppression of Vice and the terror of booksellers who had long ago decided—I think in the infancy of the trade— that a little pornography don't hurt none; but Mr. Sumner disagreed, sometimes very efficiently. The byline of the piece—entitled "I Confess!"—is adorned with an asterisk that, when collated below, reveals that Mr. Rutter "was formerly President of the Society for the Contraception of Vice." He discovers the pleasures of sex magazines, if not of sex, and concludes "they are one of the three greatest blessings which our civilization has produced, the other two being the playerpiano and the radio." Mr. Rutter, in his more militant phase or role, reappears in Cummings' play.

Cummings wrote for *Vanity Fair* for approximately two years.[6] He also wrote occasional pieces for other magazines. One of these, "Mr. X," appeared in *The Bookman*—edited by Burton Rascoe— for September, 1927. It seems, on a rereading, to have suggested, as it preceded, Chaplin's *Modern Times*. Mr. X works for Drof,

---

[6] His pieces, together with others hitherto uncollected, were published as *A Miscellany*, 1958.

"the greatest industrial genius of the twentieth century." He works in a Wheel Mine. Cummings explains: "If you can imagine wheels, and if you can imagine but, and if you can imagine nothing, then you certainly ought to be able to stand on your head and imagine nothing but wheels; and if you can do that, you can get some idea of what Model Wheel Mines are like. In my opinion, they are like a novel by Mr. Dos Passos, only different." Cummings returned to the subject of Wheel Mines in his morality, *Santa Claus,* described in "The Poet as Playwright."

# X

## *The Poet as Playwright*

### 1

"The poet who is both lyrical and dramatic usually turns to drama." Thus Edna St. Vincent Millay to the present writer. "The best plot is a man," said John Galsworthy, not to the present writer.

Cummings turned to drama in 1927. His play, *Him*, is about a man and a woman. He tells her: "I am an Artist, I am a Man, I am a Failure." He also tells her—and shows the audience—by means of the play he is writing everything else that is of consequence to him: everything that is low-down and earthy, everything that is lyric and magical; circus, burlesque, and vaudeville; love, and the anarchy and pathos of the modern world. Him, in "reality," gives Me (and you) a thorough self-analysis. But she does not understand, because she feels. The woman Me is at once indefinable, being beautiful and tender; and more rooted in life, the victim of emotions and experiences she cannot share.

ME: You mean I'm no good to you and that we should have ended everything long ago; because—not being interested in all the ideas you're interested in—it's obviously silly of me to pretend.

HIM: To pretend?

ME: —because with part of you I think I'm in love. What can I do?

HIM: Well now let's see ... here's a bright idea; you can advertise in the Paris edition of the New York Herald for a new lover, thus—"By a freckled fragile petite brunette incapable of loneliness and cooking, wanted: a tall strong handsome blond capable of indigestion and death (signed) Cinderalla Van Winkle."

ME (*Involuntarily*): Who's she?

The idea for his play must have germinated swiftly in Cummings' mind. He had taken over the theater department of *The Dial* for two issues, April and May, 1926. In August, 1927, *The Dial* published six scenes from *Him*, and it appeared in book form the same year.

As a writer on the theater, Cummings had his own views of what constituted entertainment. Writing in April, he gave high praise to the Moscow Art Theatre Musical Studio performances at the Lyric: "as in the case of any authentic experiment, there is not much failure and much invincibility." In May he reviewed three productions—*Little Eyolf*, at the Guild; the International Theatre Exposition "occupying two floors of the Steinway Building"; and the Harry Greb-Tiger Flowers middleweight championship fight at Madison Square Garden. The first had "a more than creditable performance; a performance far more than creditable, or even than excellent, in so far as Clare Eames was concerned." Of the third, he wrote:

"On February 26, '26, in a circus-theatre bulging with incredible thousands of human and nonhuman unbeings and beings, a negro deacon named Tiger Flowers won the middleweight championship of the world. Mr. Flowers (who moves pleasantly, fights cleanly, and plays the violin) said: 'Harry stuck his thumb in my eye once, but it may have been an accident for he fought a clean fight after that. The only thing I didn't like was that he used some profane language at times. But I guess he was a little excited.'" (Cummings also made an oil painting of the fight.)

Of the International Theatre Exposition, Cummings quoted with approval from the program note by Friedrich Kiesler, who criticized the contemporary theater as "a peep-show stage... appended to an assembly room. This box owes its form to technical considerations; it is not the result of deliberate artistic purpose." From Kiesler's note, as quoted in *The Dial*, I take a passage that appears to me to have been significant for Cummings: "The elements of the new dramatic style are still to be worked out. They are not yet classified. Drama, poetry, and scenic formation have no natural milieu. Public, space, and players are artificially assembled. The new aesthetic has not yet attained unity of expression. Communication lasts two hours; the pauses are the social event. We have no contemporary theatre."

So far as Cummings was concerned, the real contemporary theater was what he had been viewing unofficially and writing about for years: burlesque, vaudeville, the circus. From this came his basic concept: a writer for hero—or as Cummings prefers to term him, "nonhero"—who is writing a play in which elements from the "lively arts" would appear. Instead of a "peep-show stage," the static space in which actors act out their roles, Cummings visualized a room for his lovers to converse in which has three visible walls; the fourth is invisible—that is, it faces the audience, although for the occupants of the room it is a real wall, solid and functional. In successive scenes, the room turns clockwise, so that the invisible wall is different each time. For the scenes from the play Him is writing, Cummings utilized either depth or the "flats" of vaudeville and burlesque. The least that can be said for his conception is that he introduced some dynamism to the "peep-show."

I have said that Him shows Me—and the audience—what he believes in; but it is Him seen through the mind of Me, who, when the play opens, is being anaesthetized for an abortion. It is interesting to note that Cummings made use of a vaudeville device for the scene: "A flat surface on which is painted a DOCTOR anaesthetising a WOMAN. In this picture there are two holes corresponding to the heads of the physician and of the patient, and through these holes protrude the living heads of a man and of a woman." In this crisis of her life Me reviews her relationship with Him, projecting in the ensuing scenes all that has meaning for her lover, but not always for herself. Him reads from his notebook: "I do not stroke edges and I do not feel music but only metaphors. Metaphors are what comfort and astonish us, which are the projected brightness of ourselves—a million metaphors times or divided by a million metaphors constitute a moment or a coatsleeve—here is what we call smells and flavours, the difference between this face and another, god, never, tomorrow, love, yesterday, death or whatever yourself and myself agree to entitle that minute indestructible doll which only the artist possibly may endow with a carefully passionate gesture." She comments: "Maybe you mean something, I don't know."

HIM: Lips, which touched—at first how lightly! What were lips distinctly slowly coming against more than lips; mouths, firmly living upon each other: the focussed Ourselves (alive proud deep bewildered) approaching gradually. Nearing, exquisitely and scarcely. Touching. And then—heartily announced by miles, by years, of strutting light—the minute instant, the enormous Now.... (*Pauses; smiles*) Only think, dear, of you and of me gone, like two kites when the string breaks, positively into nowhere. Shut like umbrellas. Folded like napkins.

ME (*Looking at him and away, speaks softly*): Only think, dear, that you and I have never been really in love. Think that I am not a bit the sort of person you think. Think that you fell in love with someone you invented—someone who wasn't me at all. Now you are trying to feel things; but that doesn't work, because the nicest things happen by themselves. You can't make them happen. I can't either, but I don't want to. And when you try to make them happen, you don't really fool yourself and certainly you don't fool me. That's one thing about me. I'm not clever and I don't try to make things happen.—Well, you made a mistake about me and I know that. But the fact is, you know you made a mistake. Everybody knows it. . . . Think what is: think that you are now talking very beautifully through your hat.

*Him* was written partly in Paris and "chiefly" in New York City, Cummings recollected, and added that "the book was probably published soon after the play had finished itself." On the inside flap of the jacket was printed the now well-known *Imaginary Dialogue Between an Author and a Public as Imagined by E. E. Cummings*. The entire back of the jacket was given over to Colonel Lawrence's praise of *The Enormous Room*. The title page carries the following epigraph:

> looking forward into the past or looking
> backward into the future I
> walk on the highest
> hills and
> I laugh
> about
> it
> all
> the way
>
> ANNE BARTON

Anne Barton was Cummings' second wife. There were no children. Her first husband was Ralph Barton, a famous caricaturist of the twenties, by whom she had a daughter. It was Edward Pierce Nagle who first brought her to the upstairs studio in Patchin Place to meet Cummings, she told me. She used to bring him bouquets of flowers and paints to paint them; and she also posed for him—his portraits of her are among the most joyous of his creations, and her loveliness glows in them. She was a most beautiful and gallant lady. She afterwards married a doctor and had two sons.

2

Playwriting is a profession in which it is possible to achieve success without being a writer—that is, it is possible to be a very successful playwright without being a very good writer. In April, 1928, the following were the "current attractions" that had achieved the longest runs: *The Ladder, The Ivory Door, The Trial of Mary Dugan, Command to Love,* and *The Shannons of Broadway.* This was the situation that confronted Cummings when *Him* was offered for production, and produced. It was not produced on Broadway.

Henry G. Alsberg, an associate director of the Provincetown Playhouse, afterwards National Director of the WPA Writers' Project, told me that he took a number of play scripts with him when he went to Europe in the summer of 1927. Among them was *Him.* When he returned, he said, he told his fellow directors, James Light, M. Eleanor Fitzgerald, and Eugene O'Neill, that "whatever they did or did not produce the next season, *Him* had to be done." (One wonders what O'Neill thought of the take-off on *The Great God Brown* that occurs in Cummings' play.) Cummings, however, affirmed in writing: "Him was only produced by the Provincetown Playhouse because Fitzi (Eleanor Fitzgerald) insisted it should be;she thought 'twas humanitarian;& sent the Ladies Garment Woikuz down to see. Boy were they bawd!" What is certain, in any case, was that Alsberg had an immediate ally in Miss Fitzgerald; or perhaps it was the other way around.

Neither was blind to the difficulties involved—the script was long, staging presented many problems, and the expense, they foresaw, would be greater than for any previous production. An average of two thousand dollars had been spent on Provincetown plays, including O'Neill's; *Him* called for an estimated expenditure of six thousand dollars which was raised; [1] but even this sum, as it turned out, did not suffice, and there was a constant scurrying for more money, chiefly on the part of Miss Fitzgerald.

---

[1] Among the important contributors were Mrs. Harry Payne Whitney, Felix Warburg, and James Sibley Watson.

There were also technical problems.

The play consists of 21 scenes. There are 72 roles, not counting "crowds, cripples, beggars, black figures, jazz dancers, shapes," which raised the total cast to an estimated 105. By means of charts that were the joint work of Cummings, Light—who directed the play—and Eugene Fitsch, who designed the sets—it was found that the multitudinous roles could be played by 30 actors. There still remained the problem of scene-shifting. The Provincetown stage had no wings and no overhead flies. As Light recounted later: "The problem was to rig the stage. Cummings had a designer's sense; by his direction, the room was turned out—a really magical thing." Cummings repaid the compliment: "Only the ultramagic of Jimmie Light could have persuaded Him's 21 scenes to chase each other smoothly over the infradiminutive Province-town Playhouse stage." Ben Shahn designed the sets.

It was magic, and something more mundane. The cast assisted the stagehands in lowering scenery "flats" through a trap door to the cellar. The slot through which the scenery was lowered was a narrow one, but finally shifting was down to a flat ten seconds. Alsberg recalled: "The actors rehearsed scene-changing like a military drill." He told me: "The self-sacrifice of the kids in the cast was something to remember. Some of them were married, most of them were broke; yet no one withdrew, even after salaries were pared down to keep the production going." The actors' budget was "frozen" at length at eight hundred dollars a week, but emergencies kept occurring. "When the play closed because of budget difficulties, it closed to full houses," Alsberg said.

It was at first thought that the play would be done in two install-ments, on successive evenings. When it was decided that that was not practicable, the suggestion was made that some of the scenes be eliminated. Cummings, however, would not agree to this; he had a reason for the succession of scenes, all of which were im-portant in the projection of Him's character. He agreed to cut; Alsberg thinks that as a result "a few scenes lost something of their richness." Cummings, he recalled, "was around all the time, but didn't interfere with the rehearsals." They all ate in "The Black

Knight," the speak-easy across the street from the Provincetown, where Cummings entertained his companions with his talk. He once complained that he couldn't keep it up, that the excitement of the theater and all the talk was preventing him from getting anything new written, but he found it impossible to stay away.

A comparatively unknown actress, Erin O'Brien-Moore, a former model known as "the Benda Girl," from her portraits by W. T. Benda, got the feminine lead. She told me that Light was desperate, as all the uptown actresses had turned the role down. She thought she got eighty dollars a week. She said she suggested a young actor friend, whose name was Franchot Tone, for the male lead, but Light had already decided on William S. Johnstone.

Johnstone was only twenty years old when he was cast for the role of Him. Previous to that he had played as an extra in Theatre Guild productions. Five feet ten and a half inches tall, and weighing only 135, he portrayed the part with an intensity that he afterwards admitted he did not always quite understand. He had gray-green eyes, dark brown hair with some gray in it, and a "broken" aquiline nose ("I fell as a child, and the doctor just gave it a twist"). Like Cummings, he was Scottish.

"I read for Light and Cummings," he told me. "I have often wondered why they cast me in the part. I wasn't prepared to meet the challenge of this play. The experiences in it were very foreign to me. I can't say I completely knew what Cummings meant. I was trying to get to know my own part without troubling too much about the play. I guess I was too young to appreciate any of the values. But I soaked up some of Cummings' character to some extent by listening to him. And I began to think in symbols rather than words.

"Light and Cummings were wonderful to me. They were spending as much time with me as they could, taking me to the places where they went and where I listened to them talking. I have never done anything since that has given me quite the same satisfaction as an actor. It required all your concentration. As a consequence, you felt you had accomplished something every time you got through a performance."

I asked him what he thought of Miss O'Brien-Moore. He said: "She was voluptuous, she was sultry; I have no reason to believe she wasn't just right. Maybe she brought out in me the innocence and immaturity that I myself had at that time and that the character of Him felt in his relationship to Me." I asked him what he thought of the reviews. "The critics felt the power of it," he told me, "but didn't understand it. It was very depressing, because I would have liked to play the part longer. It wasn't a question of money."

The doctor was played by Lawrence Bolton, who told me that Cummings had given him "long, detailed information" about the part. But sometimes, he confessed, he had to ask himself: "What am I doing here—what is it all about? To this day, frankly, I am baffled." Nevertheless, "It was a romp."

Cummings wrote me from New Hampshire: "William Johnstone made a marvellously attractive unhero,&lovely Erin O'Brien-Moore proved an absolutely perfect Me; while the vivid versatilities of Lawrence Bolton as The Doctor more than amazed everyone (including perhaps himself). Let me only add that Lionel Stander's gargantuan impersonation of a Fairy in Act II, Scene 8 brought the house to its ankles."

Stander, croaking swish talk with his concrete-mixer voice amid the short togas, was indeed memorable. Stander was six foot one, and had played football. He had never acted. He was nineteen. He had just been fired from his job. A minor member of the cast, Stanley Zipser, brought him to the Provincetown during a rehearsal. The rehearsal was going badly—it was the crap-shooting scene with which Act II, Scene VIII opens. The actor rolling the dice did so without conviction; he had never shot craps before. Light kept shouting, "No! No! No!" but the rolling got no better. At this point Zipser leaned over and whispered to Light that by sheer chance and happenstance "an actor friend" of his was in the house. Stander was introduced. He told Light: "I am a crap-shooter by training, environment, and tradition." He was not lying. He picked up those dice and rolled, and Light said: "The job is yours." But higher things were in store for him: he became the First Fairy. Picture this man speaking *soprano*, for such is the stage direction.

When he said, "O dear O dear—I could just cry," there was not a dry eye in the house; it was, in fact, simply divine. Stander afterwards played the role of the poet Maxwell Bodenheim in *The Scoundrel,* the memorable film about Horace Liveright. In this, as in his many Hollywood roles, his voice and his scowl were his fortune.

Act II, Scene VIII, is sheer, delicious nonsense; I might have said "pure nonsense," except for its bawdry. Its ingredients are simple and basic:

"The Old Howard's conception of a luxurious Roman villa, columns 'n' everything."

Crap-shooters.

Fairies.

Mussolini caricatured.

A final ingredient: a pun, drawn out and lingering, on the name of a famous and unabashed homosexual comedian, recently struck dead by lightning, an event much discussed at the time, which gave Cummings the opportunity for a happy invention: lightning rods for fairies. The scene opens with two centurions shooting craps in front of the "villa"; an Ethiopian joins the game. Enter two Fairies "in scarlet togas, with lightningrods." The centurions and Ethiopian exit, the latter remarking:

"If daze anything worse dan Christians, it certainly am peddy-rasts."

Two more Fairies with lightning rods join the other two, after which trumpets sound, and "enter majestically the onorevole BENITO MUSSOLINI, more or less in the costume of Napoleon and with the traditional pose of that hero—'hands locked behind, As if to balance the prone brow Oppressive with its mind' (Browning) —but also wearing, at the end of a lightningrod, a halo, probably in token of his Christlike role in raising Italia from the dead."

Despite the "honorable" before his name, his costume, and his pose, he is as queer as the others.

VOICE OF HIM: On the whole, how did that scene strike you?
VOICE OF ME: Not very favourably.
VOICE OF HIM: Really?

VOICE OF ME: You can see for yourself how silly it is to try to make a critic out of me.

VOICE OF HIM: I shall confine myself, however, to stating that your disapproval comes as a surprise; considering the all-pervading atmosphere of inherent spiritual nobility—not to mention the profound, deepspread, underlying religious significance of the thing. Possibly you didn't realize that those lads in the passionate nighties were Ecce Homos: the only lineal descendants of the ancient and honourable house of Savoy?

VOICE OF ME: I hate history.

Cummings wrote me in reply to my "queery" (his word) anent the lightning rods:

(1) the great comedian killed by lightning was Bert Savoy; of the Savoy & Brennan team, which appeared in B'way musicals at e.g. The Winter Garden uptown (not the National Winter Garden, 2nd Ave & Houston St).

(2) a favorite fascist slogan in the "onorevole BENITO's" early days was *sempre avanti Savoia* i.e. forever onward (& upward with) the house of Savoy.

(3) Him Act II Scene 8 is thus built on a pun—SAVOY equals (a) Italian royalty, temporarily rescued from soidisant socialism by Mussolini; & (z) the unbelievably hideous incomparably obscene & excruciatingly funny Female (pour ainsi dire) Impersonator Bert S.

(4) that's why the fairies have lightningrods. It's also why Him talking with Me on page 73,[2] describes these "Ecce Homos" as "the only lineal descendants of the ancient and honourable house of Savoy."

(5) But, in my experience, enthusiastic advocates of any form of totalitarianism are inclined to be nothing-if-not-queer, mentally if not otherwise (Henry Wadsworth Longfellow Dana, the Virgil of EIMI, is a good illustration of the otherwise).

[2] Of the published text.

There is a good picture of Savoy, female impersonator extraordinary, in Gilbert Seldes' *The Seven Lively Arts*. Savoy is dressed as a demimonde, one black-slippered foot on a stool, and a froth of petticoat rippling like ocean in a cove. Out of a puffed sleeve one white-gloved hand rests on his hip, the other nestles coquettishly under his chin. A bird on a rakish hat is falling as the sparrow falls, nose downward over his left eye. Only his right can be seen, but that one is all leer stuck in a chubby face on which an eager grin floats lasciviously.

Cummings' attitude toward homosexuals was frankly "against." He simply did not like them. For him life was a totality—men, women, and children; it is significant that he always wrote this phrase as "children, women and men." But this is not to say that he was not often amused by homosexuals, which kept him from being openly hostile. To a friend who wrote him in alarm from an artists' colony, after finding himself surrounded by men in shorts in vibrant pursuit of the arts and each other, he replied: "let me suggest that you purchase(don't rent)a *made-to-measure* chastitygirdle from your local blacksmith;& be sure to throw away the key when same arrives."

## 3

*Him* opened at the Provincetown Playhouse on Wednesday night, April 18, 1928. Copies of the play were on sale in the "lobby." Just before curtain time William Johnstone managed to get off a telegram to the author, care of the playhouse:

AS ONE FATHER TO ANOTHER I CLAIM THE HONOR OF
WISHING YOUR OFFSPRING A PROSPEROUS CAREER.

To this, Cummings replied (after seeing the show):

MY PLAY RECIPROCALLY SALUTES YOURSELF BEGGING
THAT YOU WILL ALLOW MYSELF SINCERELY TO CON-
GRATULATE YOU ON ITS HERO.

In contrast to other openings, Alsberg says the performance was smooth from the start. Miss O'Brien-Moore told me: "I felt the first night was right, so I was shocked by the reviews the next day. You got an exaltation from the play. Cummings created a great poignancy without begging for it. And it was the audience that did it; he did not set a trap for them."

In the audience were the drama critics.

Perhaps it was unfortunate that the long handbill, which served for program, and on which both the title and the author's name were printed in lower case, contained the following note, written by Cummings:

"WARNING: *him* isn't a comedy or a tragedy or a farce or a melodrama or a revue or an operetta or a moving picture or any other convenient excuse for 'going to the theatre'—in fact, it's a PLAY, so let it PLAY; and because you are here, let it PLAY with you. Let it dart off and beckon to you from the distance, let it tiptoe back and snap its fingers under your nose, let it sweep up at you from below or pounce down on you from above, let it creep cautiously behind you and tap you on the back of the neck, let it go all around and over and under you and inside you and through you. Relax, and give this PLAY a chance to strut its stuff—relax, don't worry because it's not like something else—relax, stop wondering what it's all 'about'—like many strange and familiar things, Life included, this PLAY isn't 'about,' it simply is. Don't try to despise it, let it try to despise you. Don't try to enjoy it, let it try to enjoy you. DON'T TRY TO UNDERSTAND IT, LET IT TRY TO UNDERSTAND YOU."

But strange, strange and pitiful, were the attempts to turn this back on the author and the production. One can only wonder why the effort proved so irresistible to the majority of the drama critics, except that in quoting it, they filled up space that otherwise would have required thought to fill. But I have no wish to be entirely ungenerous, for it should be borne in mind, as I have noted elsewhere, that everyone was young in those days.

Alexander Woollcott wrote in the *World*:

"Fatiguing, pretentious and empty, a play called 'him' was un-furled last evening on the patient stage of the Provincetown Play-house. It is the work of that intermittent poet named E. E. Cummings, who once wrote a war book called 'The Enormous Room'—a malign and fascinating narrative, with curious overtones.

"It was somehow characteristic of his contribution to the drama that the management should have been at such pains to print both the title of the play and the name of the author in lower case type —should, with one bold and splendid gesture, have flung off for-ever the debasing tyranny of capital letters.

"The author of 'him' is one of those playwrights south of the deadline [3]—cousins to the surgeon who needs no knowledge of anatomy and to the architect who really couldn't be bothered with anything so Victorian as specific gravity.

"I have a suspicion that the author of a piece like 'him' spends a good deal of leisure idly thinking what odds and ends would be nice to have in a play some time and even, on great occasions, jotting them down. Then some fine day someone asks him just once too often how he is getting along with that play he is sup-posed to be writing, and in a burst of bravado he says it is finished. The next thing he knows it is being taken seriously in Macdougal Street."

At this point Mr. Woollcott quotes the program note up to "let it go all around and over and under you and inside you and through you." It was, of course, made to order for someone absorbed in his own prose:

"Well, friends, I did just that. I let mr. cummings's drama sit on my knee and tickle my ear and play paddycakes with me, but the result was only an inexpressible boredom except for that all too brief interval when, for reasons which escaped me even at the time, a great many people seemed to be up there on the stage sing-ing 'Franky and Johnny' at the top of their lungs.

"That was the only bright moment up to 10:30, when, as second

[3] The "deadline," established by the Police Department in the nineteenth century, and past which known criminals could not go, was far to the south of Greenwich Village, since New York City did not extend very far north.

watch, I was relieved by Alison Smith, who was settling down to let the piece play peek-a-boo with her as I fled into the night."

Walter Winchell wrote in the *Graphic*: "Perhaps the playbill's own confession that *him* is an experiment at incoherency will suffice to keep the reader informed. It follows."

Alan Dale wrote in the *American*: "To quote the programme is all that is necessary, and I herewith educe this chuck entitled 'Warning.'" He educed it.

Robert Littell of the *Post* was disgusted: "Every now and then it is exactly like stepping on something extremely nasty in the dark."

*Variety* summed up:

"'Him' is the most incoherent play ever mounted. Under the mantle of hobohemian art, the Provincetowners are getting away with murder at their converted Macdougal street stable theatre.

"The tip-off on the program sums it up as follows:—

"WARNING"

(and the expected followed).

## 4

Although the Provincetown, in its 1928-1929 announcement, stated that "E. E. Cummings is now writing his second play," and scheduled it unseen, Cummings did not deliver. In December, 1929, it closed its doors. I do not think that the "critical" reception of *Him* had any influence on his theatrical thinking or ambitions, whatever effect it may have had on his feelings at the time. He worked for many years on a play about Joan of Arc, speeches from which have appeared in various publications. In 1930 he contributed a one-act play to a symposium entitled *Whither, Whither*. The play, *Anthropos: The Future of Art*, was afterwards printed in a limited edition by Jacobs at the Golden Eagle Press. In 1935 Cummings published *Tom*, a poetic choreography. It will be recalled that a ballet about Uncle Tom was one of the most enchanting episodes in the Broadway success,

*The King and I*, some fifteen years later. A complete score for *Tom* exists, the work of the composer David Diamond.

*Santa Claus*,[4] published in 1946, is subtitled "*A Morality*" and reveals Cummings in a didactic vein. It is a one-act play in five scenes, its basic line being iambic pentameter, but so varied for the purpose—presumably—of dramatic speech that it loses some of the intensity of blank verse. This defect, if defect it be, applies of course only to reading; in the presentation everything would depend on the speaking. The idea is ingenious—Death and Santa Claus, who is a young man under his mask, exchange appearances; nevertheless, a child knows Santa Claus even with his death's head disguise:

> *Santa Claus.*          Do you like me this way?
> *Child.* I guess . . . I like you any way—if you're you.

The didactic vein, to which I have referred, appears with greater force in this play than in individual poems, for its entire motivation, or reason, springs from Cummings' view that love and individuality are scarce commodities in the modern world. Santa Claus complains to Death that he has "so much to give; and nobody will take." Death knows why:

> You're speaking of a true or actual world.
> Imagine, if you can, a world so blurred
> that its inhabitants are one another. . . .

Cummings also equates Science with Death which, considering the times we live in, is far from an odd concept. Death advises Santa Claus to become a Scientist. "Or, in plain English, a knowledge-salesman":

> once people hear the magic name of "Science"
> you can sell people anything—except understanding.

and

> the less something exists, the more people want it.

---

[4] A careful analysis of this verse play by its author occurs in *i* ("Nonlecture Six").

Santa Claus thereupon sets forth to sell people "preferred stock in a giltedged wheelmine." A wheelmine, it will be recalled, is what Mr. X worked in. It is, of course, nonexistent; but after buying stock, the people are persuaded that there has been a disaster in the wheelmine, and are looking for the promoter to wreak vengeance on him. Their cry is now "Down with Science!" To save himself from lynching, Santa Claus has to prove he is not Science, although he looks like Death, because they have exchanged masks:

> Santa Claus.  all men and every woman may be wrong;
> but nobody who lives can fool a child.
> —Now I'll abide by the verdict of that little girl
> over there, with the yellow hair and the blue eyes.
> I'll simply ask her who I am; and whoever
> she says I am, I am. . . .
>
> Child.  You are Santa Claus.

The final scene deals with the reunion of Santa Claus, the mother of the child, and the child. In his notebook Cummings wrote: "it takes three to make a child." *Santa Claus* is dedicated to Fritz Wittels, the eminent analyst. The drawing of Santa Claus removing his mask in the first edition of this play is a self-portrait.

# XI

## *The Poet as Painter*

### 1

"To a large extent," wrote Wallace Stevens, "the problems of poets are the problems of painters, and poets must often turn to the literature of painting for a discussion of their own problems." [1]

In our time, the overriding concept that the new masters have assimilated, and that is reflected in their best work, stems from Cézanne: a picture is a self-contained organism—that is, it exists as itself alone and is not a "picture" of something else, or "about" something else that it approximates. Thus the good painter, like the poet, is a man of metaphors. He presents an image—not, as some suppose and many desire, an object.

Not all images are easily perceived or felt, and most collections reflect the subjective feelings of the collector. It is a simple trick to "see" all kinds of "things" and "symbols" in a work, but this being subjective, and therefore vague, can be all things to all men or become "fixed" by means of the most authoritative or most

[1] *Opus Posthumous,* 1957.

persuasive expositor. This is never the artist, and should suffice as warning.

Eugène Delacroix, a painter whom Cummings admired, and from whose *Journal* I have heard him quote, noted on Tuesday, April 27, 1824: "At Leblond's. Interesting discussion about genius and unusual men. Dimier thought that great passions were the source of genius. I think that it is imagination alone, or better still, what amounts to the same thing, that delicacy of the organs that makes one see what others do not see, and which makes one see in a different way. I was saying that even great passions joined to imagination lead most often to disorder in the mind, etc. Dufresne said a very true thing: what made a man unusual was, fundamentally, a way utterly peculiar to himself of seeing things." [2]

I happen to be one of those—Cummings said "one of five"— who like his pictures. I think he underestimated his audience; or perhaps it was a figure of speech to signify that the audience was a small one. I like his pictures for the reason Dufresne gave, plus ability; but perhaps ability may be taken for granted. We know from Cummings' poetry that he had "a way utterly peculiar to himself of seeing things." I shall attempt in this chapter to show that this applies to his pictures as well, and is the reason why they are important. I am speaking here, of course, of his best pictures; it is by them that he will be judged. Yet it seems proper to add that the unrealized or incomplete works of a good artist are infinitely more interesting than the best works of second-rate men. Cummings' studio in Patchin Place—like his house in New Hampshire—was stacked with pictures that form a text, and there are innumerable sketches that provide the footnotes. He once showed me eighteen such sketches, in oil, of a single subject. "Every aspect of a beautiful woman is interesting," he remarked; yet what struck me at once was that he had made no effort to catch merely beautiful effects, but only what he saw, which included angles of the face no woman would see—or perhaps care to see—in her mirror.

His best pictures and portraits are the result of intense applica-

[2] *Journal of Eugène Delacroix*, trans. by Walter Pach.

tion beforehand. These pictures seem to me to have that mingling of concept, texture, and form that has always pleased and probably will always please. Despite this, however, as a painter he has suffered from his fame as a poet, for a man who paints as well as writes is usually written off as a man who "also paints." Cummings' habit of referring to his writings in catalogue forewords also has contributed its mite to misunderstanding. They are quite different from the forewords of other artists. I give one of them here, for the light it throws on him and on his approach to painting. It is in dialogue, a favorite literary device with him:

Why do you paint?
For exactly the same reason I breathe.
That's not an answer.
There isn't any answer.
How long hasn't there been any answer?
As long as I can remember.
And how long have you written?
As long as I can remember.
I mean poetry.
So do I.
Tell me, doesn't your painting interfere with your writing?
Quite the contrary: they love each other dearly.
They're very different.
Very: one is painting and one is writing.
But your poems are rather hard to understand, whereas your
     paintings are so easy.
Easy?
Of course—you paint flowers and girls and sunsets; things that
     everybody understands.
I never met him.
Who?
Everybody.
Did you ever hear of nonrepresentational painting?
I am.
Pardon me?

I am a painter, and painting is nonrepresentational.
Not all painting.
No: housepainting is representational.
And what does a housepainter represent?
Ten dollars an hour.
In other words, you don't want to be serious—
It takes two to be serious.
Well, let's see . . . oh yes, one more question: where will you
    live after this war is over?
In China; as usual.
China?
Of course.
Whereabouts in China?
Where a painter is a poet.[3]


2

Cummings drew and painted from childhood. He was early encouraged to do so in that remarkable household on Irving Street. His father supplied him at first with large sheets of brown paper on which he drew in pencil and crayon. Many of these drawings are still in existence; one is an elephant a yard long. From drawing Cummings went on to watercolor and oil, a transition facilitated by his father who worked in those mediums. It is clear, then, that Cummings' pictures are not the result of idle hours of daubing. The truth is otherwise: he painted more than he wrote, and he painted—for more than half a century—with an intense, undeviating passion. His mastery in one medium has undoubtedly helped him in the other. Just as his painter's eye helped his poetry, his poetry helped his vision as a painter.

Many present-day painters can paint like anybody; which of course raises the question whether they can paint like themselves. Cummings' handling of his medium, whether in line or color, has made for individuality of style. His line drawings are different from Picasso's or Cocteau's, for example, in that they stop abruptly

[3] Foreword to catalogue, Rochester Memorial Art Gallery, 1945.

at the point where movement has been caught. In his drawings of hoofers and comedians, it is their characteristic stance that he was after. Thus, in the drawing of Jack Shargel, the National Winter Garden comedian, which appeared in *The Dial*, and that of Charlie Chaplin, which appeared in *The Dial* and in Seldes' *The Seven Lively Arts*, he achieves their stance with a few flowing lines, and the stance is the design.

In watercolor, which he used profusely, he achieves—again with a minimum of strokes—an Oriental simplicity. His watercolors are deceptive, because Cummings was after an impression, some-times so fleeting as to be gone with a change of light; but having caught what he wished, the picture remained without embellish-ment. For a moment it looks as though anyone could do it; but let anyone try. His trees squirm into sunlight, his leaves are like light or birds taking off joyously into blue latitudes. Delacroix noted in his journal: "The fleeting instant of gaiety throughout nature. Those so fresh leaves, those lilacs, that rejuvenated sun. Melan-choly takes flight during these brief moments." Cummings never forgot his first encounter with "that mystery who is Nature" in Norton's Woods.

In his watercolors Cummings was not so much painting a pic-ture as capturing a poetic metaphor in paint; that is to say, he was celebrating Nature, as he does so often in his poetry. Loren MacIver, who owns several examples of Cummings' work, told me: "He celebrates events, because he believes in honoring things. He is a celebrant; his works revere." Nevertheless, either because of their swift execution, or the limitations of the medium itself, Cummings' watercolors—with very notable exceptions—fail to satisfy western eyes used to projections of mass instead of space. In this, as I have suggested, he is more Oriental than occidental, as though he really had been an inhabitant of China "where a painter is a poet."

It is with his oils that Cummings calls for consideration as a painter wholly apart from his other, writing self. His oils reveal a mastery of his medium in which the tactile and the sensory com-bine, and in this combination, faces, landscapes, and flowers no longer celebrate life, but are a part of it. They are felt, skillfully projected, and more than skillfully executed.[4] The best of them have an existence of their own, being caught in timelessness. I venture to suggest that only those who have examined the mass of his work in New York and New Hampshire, and the collection of Hildegarde Watson in Rochester can appreciate his industry, let alone his achievement. Reproductions in black and white are a poor substitute, and even reproductions in color do less than justice, because of their reduced size. And yet it is possible to feel the impact of discovery by seeing the reproductions of Cummings' work in CIOPW. Not surprisingly, the impact is cumulative.

CIOPW is a cloth-bound volume measuring 9½ by 12½ inches. The letters stand for the mediums in which he has worked, examples of which are included: charcoal, ink, oil, pencil, and watercolor. It was published in 1931 by Covici, Friede in an edition limited to 391 copies, each signed by the artist on the title page. To sign them, Cummings used a brush. It is in the foreword to this volume that he referred to himself as "An author of pictures, a draughtsman of words." The foreword begins:

"Like many,the undersigned was found to write spontaneously or pictures before finding oneself compelled to draw or words: unlike some who are threatened with knowledge,he encouraged himself by to be. While the portraiture progressed—while a painfully hand achieved likenesses of even polysyllabic sitters,the gradually fingers overcame perspective, his clumsily wrist contrived verses—child spinning on a point of chalk emits boy who rides the squirmings of a crayon,legarms begin inhabiting bodies who are not faces,sidewalks cohabit with notebooks and joyously always writing continues

"—for once-upon-a-time read, neither life nor living, but originally infinitive cooling through participle into compulsion; therefore once-upon-a-now equals 'art',When to live is."

He pays his respects to "his distinguished audience(J. S. Watson,

---

[4] His palette was Cézanne's: flake white, Naples yellow, raw Sienna, burnt Sienna, Chinese vermilion, rose madder, viridian, terre verte, cerulean blue, cobalt blue, ultramarine blue, and ivory black, with additions of lemon yellow and cadmium yellow.

Jr., and Scofield Thayer)" and to S. A. Jacobs: "persianly poem-printer predicated picturebook." (He also printed it.) Reproduced are forty-nine oils and twenty-three watercolors, as well as drawings in charcoal, ink, and pencil. The pictures range from portraits, which include the artist and his friends—Joe Gould, M. R. Werner, Gilbert Seldes, Thayer, Watson; and Anne Barton, the painter's second wife—to landscapes in New Hampshire and Europe; there are several still lifes and several nudes, and a line drawing of an elephant. The drawings of Shargel and Chaplin, previously mentioned, are also reproduced.

What strikes one at once in CIOPW is Cummings' ability as a draughtsman and his gift for expressive portraiture. One of the charcoal drawings, "Larionov dessine," shows the famous designer of the Ballet Russe making a sketch as he is himself being sketched by Cummings. The Russian's face is intense in its concentration on his own sketch; but this, by itself, would be mere reporting, like a photograph in a newspaper. Cummings depicts Larionov's inner radiance, that warmth and wit that his friends knew and that he put at the service of the greatest ballets of modern times. This ability to capture both the "portrait" and the essence of the person portrayed is everywhere evident in the section devoted to oil paintings. Among the best are the self-portraits, particularly the one with Anne Barton and her daughter Diana (whose father was Ralph Barton) in the background. Here, everything is luminous and fresh, and everyone is young. (A later self-portrait—1938—with notebook, pencil, and pipe, is at the University of Texas.)

There is something else that Cummings did in his paintings that has the enchantment of certain of his poems. Just as he was able to see with the eyes of a child, he could also draw with a child's hand (see, for example, the two locked, dancing figures of children in the picture entitled "merrygoround"). This kind of verve is entirely different from imitation of children's drawings, which remains imitation. On this subject, Cummings wrote in his article on Lachaise:

"To analyze child art in a sentence is to say that houses, trees, smoke, people, etc., are depicted not as nouns but as verbs. The more genuine child art is, the more it is, contrary to the belief of those incapable persons who are content merely to admire it, purely depictive. In denying that the child 'represents' and substituting for 'representation' some desperately overworked word like 'expression,' these people are only showing their hostility to the academies, just as when they tell us (which is true) that the bad artist is the representational artist. But, as has been sometimes pointed out, the artist who represents is bad not because he represents: he is bad because he represents something which a camera can represent better. This means that he is depicting something that is second, or rather nth, hand, which a child most distinctly is not. Consequently to appreciate child art we are compelled to undress one by one the soggy nouns whose agglomeration constitutes the mechanism of Normality, and finally to liberate the actual crisp organic squirm—the is." [5]

3

Cummings exhibited, either by himself, or in group shows, on only a few occasions. The earliest showings I have been able to trace were in 1925 and 1926 at the Society of Independent Artists, and at the Spring Salon of the Salons of America, May, 1928. In 1931 and 1932 he exhibited at the Society of Painters, Sculptors and Gravers.

Two comprehensive shows were held at the American British Art Center, New York City, in March, 1944 (the month that also saw the publication of his 1 x 1.), and May 1949. In the latter show were thirty-eight oils, eleven watercolors, and two drawings. Asked

[5] There is an interesting glimpse of Cummings as painter in the Paris edition of the Chicago *Tribune*, May 30, 1933: "Far from the bang of the bistros, in a retreat off the Parc Montsouris, the Guggenheimed poet E. E. Cummings lives. 'I'll be here a couple of weeks and then the south for me,' he said cheerfully." [His "retreat" was in the rue du Douanier.] Cummings invited the reporter to "Come on up on the roof." He went. "The sun was shining on the roof when we got there. 'This is my workshop,' said Cummings. 'I do my painting here.' I saw easels, canvases and two or three models fast asleep. 'I paint in the afternoons and write the poetry at night.' " The reporter asked him what he did in the mornings, and Cummings replied: "That's when I do my shopping. You see, I have to economize and do my own cooking."

for a comment to accompany reproductions of a self-portrait and "Portrait in Shadow" from this show, he wrote in *Art News* for May:

Perhaps a few individuals may enjoy my pictures. Possibly a few may enjoy my poems.

And if yes, what could be better?

Equidistant from such wonderful luck—with a distance not reckonable by mere lightyears—are the naying and the yeaing of numberless televisionary unindividuals: movieloving each blinder than radioactive any is deaf.

Were I a critic, should probably add that "academic" (i.e. un-) art resembles every good coin, which it isn't, in having two sides. One side can be called "photographic realism" or even "naturalism"; the other, "nonrepresentational" or "abstract" sic "painting." And your stupid wiseguy doing his worst to deny Nature equals your clever fool who did his best to possess Her.

XAIPE.[6]

Cummings also exhibited in Chicago, Cleveland, Baltimore, and Rochester. In the last-named city he had shows in 1945, 1950 (when he combined his two professions by giving a reading at the opening of his one-man show in the Rochester Memorial Art Gallery), 1954, and again in 1957. The biggest privately owned collection of his pictures is also in Rochester, the property of Hildegarde Watson (Mrs. James Sibley Watson), to whom XAIPE: *Seventy-One Poems* is dedicated. This truly representative collection includes examples of every medium in which Cummings has worked and from each of his periods, even the abstract (which, he told me, "leads nowhere," and this is why he gave it up). Here are the large New Hampshire landscapes in oil, a rage of color in the foliage; the delicate watercolors, the vivid portraits and caricatures, the poetic nudes in color or ink. They are all unmistakably the work of one man, and do not resemble another's.

[6] Literally "rejoice!"—a Greek mode of greeting; also, title of book of poems by Cummings, published the following year.

# XII

## *The Pilgrim and the Commissars*

1

Cummings went to the Soviet Union in the spring of 1931. He went there from Paris. He went as himself—"peesahtel y hoodozhnik," writer and painter. To do this he needed a special passport ("byez-parteenee"—i.e., without political affiliations), which eventually arrived but was reputed to be unobtainable. Foreign visitors were not allowed to enter Russia except as members of some organization or as tourists, "since otherwise they could not easily be controlled and might discover that the real ruler of 'Karl Marx's paradise' was the universally feared and immemorially loathed—once Tzarist, now Socialist, but always inhumanly pitiless —'Gay-Pay-Oo' or Secret Police."

"When Russia was interesting," wrote Ezra Pound in a review of *Eimi*, "Mr. Cummings got up and went there. When one of us wants to know about Russia to the extent that Mr. Cummings once wanted to, we might perhaps show like activity." Paul Rosenfeld thought "the mirage had been drawn for him by members of the circle of his friend Louis Aragon."

It was at the request of Mme Aragon that Cummings took to Moscow "an extraordinary assortment of indubitably capitalist literature and trinkets" (which, to his astonishment, were passed by the Soviet customs officials) and "presented them to the lady's radiantly grateful sister" ("Madame Potiphar" in *Eimi*). Later, when the Revolutionary Literature Bureau suggested that he translate Aragon's "ecstatically marxist poem 'Le Front Rouge,'" Cummings—who by this time abominated everything marxist—undertook the task as "a friendly gesture of farewell." Its movement, its sparsely placed fresh images, its harsh novelties, and, above all, its fierce contempt (so close to Cummings' own) of the advertisement product with "tissue paper around the packages" and "paper around the tissue paper," struck a responsive chord. Although Aragon wrote with revolutionary fervor—

Fire on Leon Blum
Fire on Boncour Frossard Deat
Fire on the trained bears of the social-democracy
Fire Fire I hear pass by
the death which throws itself on Garchery—

and was afterwards arraigned on a charge of inciting to murder, he could also write with a poet's art. The force of his pistoned verse remains (with a bow to Honegger's *Pacific 231*):

The red train starts and nothing shall stop it
UR
SS
UR
SS
UR
SS
No one remains behind
waving handkerchiefs Everyone is going
UR
SS
UR
SS....

> The past dies the moment is thrown into gear
> SSSR SSSR
> The roads spring the rail warms SSSR
> The train plunges toward tomorrow—

and so forth. But now the world would rather have yesterday or today, without benefit of commissars.

Having translated the poem, which he may have regretted, Cummings proceeded to analyze certain lines and ideas in it. The analysis went into *Eimi*, and is interesting on many counts but chiefly in showing Cummings' indestructible consistency:

"how sweet is the groan which comes from ruins"—. Bullshit

"the bursting of gunfire adds a hitherto unknown gaiety to the landscape"—. If you're not within range. If you are,you'll be apt to accept even communism rather than endure that same gaiety.

"hail to materialistic dialectic and its incarnation,the red army"—. Anciently, de gustibus;or as(anent "modern art") Professor Bliss Perry of Harvard used to chuckle "it's all right if you like it"

"spare nothing"—. Nyet. Hardboiledness is dull

dressez-vous contre vos mères—. See complex, Oedipus

"the most beautiful structure isn't worth the splendid and chaotic heap which is easily produced by a church and some dynamite"— Untrue. Dynamite, however, is an easier vocation than poetry

"abandon night pestilence and the family . . . you are holding in your hands a laughing child . . . a child such as has never been seen . . . he knows beforehand how to speak,all the songs of the new life"—. And let's hope he also knows that all the microtelescopically rhetorical optipessimism of any premeditatedly Un (or possible)world may not katalyze 1 spontaneously singular impossibility or(shall we say)workof art

"a star is born on earth"—. Very neat;the "star" being Russia's cross

"dawn rises over the salles de bain"—. Fact. And over a great

many other things,cher maître;for wonderfully dawn,unlike the
propagandist,and like the poet,is no snob
  "history led on leash by the third international"—. Also, muz-
zled

Nevertheless, when the poem appeared in translation, the Left-
wing literati again thought they had an ally, and again turned out
to be badly mistaken—which was resented.


2

  Cummings spent "a fabulous month" in Russia before
"reentering the world" at Istanbul. Back in Paris, he said:
  "Are the Russian people happy? They struck me like this: they
just love to suffer and they're suffering like hell, so they must be
happy. You know, Dostoievsky.
  "They couldn't seem to understand my visit.
  "They said, 'Why are you here?'
  "I said, 'I don't know.'
  "They are very serious. According to their point of view they are
engaged in the greatest work of all time.
  "They asked: 'What do you want to see?' I didn't know exactly.
They suggested the theatre; I said 'Fine.' They suggested five or six
other things. I said 'Fine.' They said: 'You won't have time to see
them all in three weeks.' I said 'Fine.'
  "I kept a regular old-fashioned diary. Getting it through was just
a matter of graft. Just like in the United States. Only in the United
States it would be a matter of dropping $200 here or there while
in Russia it was small graft.
  "You can't compare Russia with anything else. There is nothing
sufficiently like it. I wouldn't dream of making any thesis. Nobody
should shoot his face off about Russia. They themselves admit the
present state of affairs is temporary.
  "According to their own formula Russia is like a beleaguered city;
traitors within and besieged without. This is no time to form any
judgment of them.

"There are three worlds in Russia. The first world consists in the tourists for whom everything is fixed up. The second world is composed of sympathetic pilgrims from abroad. Naive bozos go roaring in there and see nude bathing carried on in complete modesty and think it is due to the system. It's not. It's just the character and temperament of the people. They are marvelous people. These people are the third world.

"On my way to Odessa a Russian gave up his berth in the train to me. I had been talking to him in German for four hours. At midnight I was awakened by a G.P.U., a handsome man with a revolver. I asked him why, but he made no reply. I asked my German-speaking Russian friend who said: 'I don't know, but you had better hurry.' I tried to find my shoes. I found one. The friend said, 'Keep quiet.' Then the G.P.U. changed his mind and left me alone. I asked my friend again, 'Why?' He said, 'I don't know.' 'I don't know' is the greatest phrase in Russia. You hear it everywhere.

"The foreigner who doesn't come in as a sort of official tourist is isolated. No foreigner is expected to be found in a third-class carriage talking to Russians. The amazing thing is that no one can tell you anything. Try living a month without finding anyone that you can trust.

"I went on to Odessa. It is a beautiful place. I was walking along breathing in the free air and feeling good when I saw my G.P.U. friend, still tagging along. In other words, the Soviet Government went to considerable expense on my trip through Russia.

"Their propaganda system is great. They've got the goods on everybody. It is silly to rave about Russia if you don't know anything about it.

"People talk about the strain and tension of life in the United States. It is nothing to that in Moscow. If you said 'boo' to some of those people they might drop dead. If they are supposed to work 24 hours a day, they try to work 25. If it's 36 they try to make it 37. They are in a peculiarly nervous condition.

"The generalizers go there. Life is so soft outside Russia and so hard there. The generalizers go there and spout platitudes.

"An idealistic girl friend of mine went there to help them and work with them. She never dreamed of the fact that when you apply an ideal you may get very strange consequences. She went crazy." [1]

The references to the diary gave party members and the Left-wing generally the tip-off. When the book was published, one of them—a poet—said at a literary gathering that it was not an accurate account of Russia. M. R. Werner overheard him. Twenty-five years later, when he told me about his retort, he was still indignant. He told the poet: "If there is one thing you *can* count on, it's that Cummings is accurate."

Cummings told me: "When the book appeared, some of my 'best friends' crossed the street to avoid speaking to me."

He worked on *Eimi* in Patchin Place. Chiefly his labors consisted in transferring his diary notes in the preparation of his manuscript, and he refrained from expanding in recollection what he had put down on the spot. Covici, Friede, a firm which had previously published Cummings' book without a title (1930) and CIOPW (1931), announced *Eimi* as a novel, possibly because it was thought the book would sell better that way; and the preliminary notices in the press took up that designation, which was unfortunate. The first edition was printed from type and was limited to 1,381 copies, representing the number of orders received up to February 15, 1933. These copies were numbered in ink and signed by Cummings. The book carries no dedication. Instead, there is a tribute:

The author joins the publishers in congratulating S. A. Jacobs; who designed the format of EIMI, solved all the technical problems connected with the typesetting and printing, and from start to finish personally supervised this book's production.

Mr. Pascal Covici, who is now with Viking, told me that whenever Jacobs was in charge of setting up a book he, as a publisher, ceased to worry about it. Cummings told me that Jacobs, having seen what other linotypers were making of the copy, snatched the manuscript away, sat down before his own machine in the base-

[1] From a front-page interview in the Paris edition of the Chicago *Tribune*, June 29, 1931.

ment at 48 Charles Street, and set up the entire book himself in seventy-two hours, working almost without stopping, on a diet of coffee.

### 3

I have said that Cummings has only one style, and that it suffices because of its range and flexibility. Thus, to the interest in his achievements as a writer must be added a factor, or different interest, which exists independently: the development of a personality. For Cummings has only one subject: himself *vis-à-vis* the world or people.

Henry Wadsworth Longfellow Dana, "the Virgil of *Eimi*," was a dyspeptic "improper" Bostonian with deep-set eyes and sagging jowls. He has been described as "a combination of Baron Charlus and The Village Blacksmith." Cummings had met him in Paris, and ran into him again at the Hotel Metropole in Moscow.

"I like it here so much!" lyrically explains Virgil "have you noticed a particular feeling in the air—a tension?"

"Have I!"

and Dante has. Apparently one cubic inch of Moscow is to all the metropolis of New York—so far as "tension" goes—as all the metropolis of New York is to tensionless Silver Lake,New Hampshire:around,through,under,behind,over myself do amazingly not physical vibrations contract,expand,collide,mesh,and murderfully procreate:each fraction,every particle,of the atmosphere in which moving moves,of my moving,of me,of cityless city,of peopleless people,actually is charged to a literally prodigious degree with what might faintly be described as compulsory psychic promiscuity. Whereby(if in no other respect)Moscow of the inexorably obsessing mentality, and merely mad NewYork(not to mention most complacent Cambridge Mass and proudly peaceful New Hampshire)belong to different universes ... verily,verily have I entered a new realm,whose inhabitants are made of each other; proudly I swear that they shall not fail to note my shadow and the moving of the leaves.

Another talk with Dana (the "Q" of this dialogue may stand for "Question," but it may also represent "Queer"):

Q: The whole trouble with you is that,like so many people who were brought up on religion,you can't bear the idea of anything doing away with it.

A: Can't bear the idea of any what doing away with which?

Q: Of science doing away with religion.

A: I see:we're supposed to suppose that the new religion, science,does away with religion,the old religion—tahk.

Q (snorts): How can you be so perverse!

A: I?

Q: As if religion and science weren't direct opposites!

A: Right you are,colonel:every coin has two sides.

Q: Odear. There you go,utterly confusing the issue—

A: Issue? We've all tried paying with one side and keeping the other side for ourselves, haven't we?

Q: But, my dear chap—can't you possibly be serious?

A: I'm afraid I'm being much too serious,comrade.

Q: No you're not—you're being extremely trivial and very childish and rather cheaply amusing.

A: And I'm quoting Emerson.

Q: Emerson?

A: "When me you fly,I am the wings".

Q: Who said that?

A: Brahma,[2] the sage of Concord;who(inconsiderately)went to Rome and found—

Q: O,of course ... but to return to our muttons. What you can't seem to realise is this:religion imprisons the human mind, whereas science makes people free.

A: What I can seem to realise is that I'd just as soon be imprisoned in freedom as free in a jail—if that's any help.

Q: You simply won't be serious,will you.

---

[2] The title of Emerson's poem of which Cummings (mis) quotes a line.

*Eimi*, like *The Enormous Room*, is full of vivid portraits. But foremost, and chiefly, Cummings portrays himself. On "Mon. 25 Mai," at Moscow's Museum of Western Art, having waded through "much bourgeoise merde" plus "certainties & uncertainties" plus "ponderous(wouldbe proletarian)unvisions of amorphous 'workers'—and may Marx help the cause of labour if ever these should come to life," Cummings stood in a room completely filled with paintings by Picasso and Matisse; "painted when these artists were in their prime, before 'Jehovah's anaesthetic commandment' dehumanized a world." Here was "oasis"; now our pilgrim could actually feel not merely "why comradeless Kem-min-kz made pilgrimage to socialist soviet Russia" but "why socialist soviet Russia made pilgrimage to Is."

He sailed from the "incredible but real unworld" on an "unbig" Soviet steamer, bound for Istanbul. This is an impression of Kiev:

> The churches are drowning with stars,everywhere stars blossom, frank and gold and keen. Among these starry miracles time stops,lives a silence which thought cannot capture. Now(touched by a resonance of sexually celestial forms)the little murdered adventure called Humanity becomes a selfless symbol(the doomed assertion of impermanence recoils;falters the loud insignificant intrusion)whereas these stars eternally and all their cathedrals march to some harmony beyond themselves(here the lone star of socialism dies;defeated by all stars)

## 4

Pound wrote Cummings from Rapallo:

Thank you or Covici for *Eimi*.

I dunno whether I rank as them wot finds it painful to read; and if I said anything about obscurity, it wd. fare ridere polli—in view of my recent pubctns. Also I don't think *Eimi* is obscure, or not very; BUT, the longer a work is, the more and longer shd. be the passages that are perfectly clear and simple to read. Matter of scale, matter of how long you can cause the reader to stay immobile or nearly so on a given number of pages. (Obviously

NOT to the Edgar Wallace virtue (?) of the opposite hurry scurry.)

Also, despite the wreaths upon the Jacobean brow,[3] a page two or three, or two and one half centimetres *narrower* (at least a column of type that much narrower) might solve all the difficulties. That has, I think, been tested optically, etc. The normal or average eye sees a certain width without heaving from side to side. May be hygienic for it to exercise its wobble, but I dunno that the orfer shd. sacrifice himself on that altar.

At any rate, I can see
    *"he adds, unhatting and becoming his raven mane,"*
but I don't see the rest of the line until I *look specially at it.* Multiply that 40 times per page for 400 pages. . . .

Mebbe there is wide-angle eyes. But chew gotter count on a cert. no. ov yr. readers bein at least as dumb as I am. Even in Bitch and Bugle [4] I found it difficult to read the stuff consecutively. Which probab. annoys me a lot more than it will you.

At any rate, damn glad to have the book and shall presumably continue taken er chaw now here n naow there.

One gets the impression that Pound had merely dipped into the book. But one day he read it; and then he reviewed it. His review is valuable for the light it throws on himself at the time he wrote it, as well as on Cummings. It appeared in the December 20, 1934, issue of the *New English Weekly*, with the heading,

"E. E. CUMMINGS ALIVE."

Cummings seems a unique exception to the law that America tries to kill her own litter when ever it produces anything more than a hoglet. Cummings undoubtedly crashed through with "The Enormous Room." There was a war, and a preface, and there was the massed force of the Dial's approval, for E.E. was undoubtedly the white-haired boy for that outfit, although never quite of it.

---

[3] For S. A. Jacobs.
[4] Read *Hound & Horn*, in which some sections of *Eimi* appeared.

There was also the mistaken idea of the New York hair-oil contingent, who boomed E. E. C. as a funny man, because of his sense of humour.

They missed his being a slow man, a man who needs four hundred pages. That wouldn't have suited 'em. A decade ago someone discovered that Cummings "wasn't very obliging."

That was good news in the Rue Notre Dame des Champs. And New York didn't discover it, or rather, didn't uncover it. New York heard he was clever, oh crushingly clever, and sat round hoping for funniness. Some men are born snobs, others occasion snobisms in others. Cummings did and survived it.

Cummings had almost a decade to himself. Certainly in New York for a decade there can have been little other writing that would have stood foreign inspection. Hemingway and McAlmon appeared later in Paris, post war in outlook. Until the publication of "Eimi," "The Enormous Room" stood as an isolated performance, which might have been either an end, a man's one book, or a beginning of something wholly unindicated and undetermined.

My more intelligent correspondents "in them partibus" write me of the pest of pinks now blowing through small streets of the wilderness. It being 17 years after 1917, after the no longer so recent events in Russia, after the Tarasov-Rodianov's "February 1917"; the half-baked little American pip-squeak has heard about communism, and has been told it is the thing to wear, and that he ought to dress it up with a "literature," the result being, mostly, deplorable.

In so far as any of 'em can be defined as *histoire morale contemporaine,*" they are modelled on the European tradition as filtered through McAlmon and Mr. Hemingway. "Ghees! ain't it hell to be poor," or "How Mamie slept in a sewer." As necessary reports on the filthy conditions of a hypocritical country in the last staggers of liberal capitalism they are necessary. Many of them are excellent. At least six good writers are writing them. At least ten or twenty volumes of them are worth reading, though they offer almost nothing that requires any discussion by literary critics.

But all this can be very dull. Carlos Williams almost unfailingly succeeds in finding new subject matter; Farrell, Caldwell, succeed quite often, others now and again. Cummings has taken no part in this action. . . .

That either Mr. Joyce of the regression or Miss Stein have said anything that will be of any interest in itself, apart from their varieties of galimatias, I doubt without any great diffidence. Mr. Cummings on the other hand, has presented a subject. When Russia was interesting, Mr. Cummings got up and went there.

When one of us wants to know about Russia to the extent that Mr. Cummings once wanted to, we might perhaps show like activity. Most parlour Bolsheviks were not so much interested in Russia. Few of them were sufficiently interested to subscribe to that really instructive and highly stimulating periodical, "U.S.S.R. en Construction." That really did tell about Russia—Russia awake to MATERIAL civilization, to all the paraphernalia that boasting America has carried to a higher degree of bathtubbedness, of telephonedness, of nickelplatedness, of meat-cannedness than even Europe.

Cummings went to see what else there might be. "EIMI." Had you or I, kind reader, gone to Russia, somewhere or other they would have got us, I mean an IDEA would have got us—for it or against it—the noble aspiration, the worthy perspiration, something would have got us. We would have forgot to be writers. We would have forgotten to take it in at the pores. . . .

It is not a specifically Douglasite volume. It belongs to the Cultural Heritage. It is a *pièce justificative*, it is I should say The *pièce justificative*. The reader who will take it slowly (no Englishman can do otherwise if he take it in at all) will find out why civilized Europe cannot sit down and wait for Russia to show her.

5

At the time Pound wrote this, the latest collection of poems by the author of *Eimi* was going the rounds without coming to rest anywhere, and at last Cummings decided to issue the book himself. He called it *No Thanks*.

*No Thanks* was published April 1, 1935, by S. A. Jacobs at the Golden Eagle Press, 48 Charles Street, in Greenwich Village. There were three editions of the book, all of them limited, including the trade edition. An advertisement before publication stated that there would be nine copies of a "holograph edition" priced at ninety-nine dollars; these were quickly subscribed. The subscribers were assured that a poem in holograph, No. 44, would never be printed; hence, the autograph and unsigned editions have a blank page where this poem should be, and there is a blank page in the *Collected Poems* of 1938 and in *Poems 1923-1954*. The poem is perhaps the starkest example of coprology in English verse. It is saved from complete coarseness by its logical structure and verve. Readers who will never see it need not repine, however, for *No Thanks* contains several poems, notably "may i feel said he," which can shock or please—or both—as the case may be.

There are two dedications in this handsome, ledger-shaped volume. The "Initial Dedication" is to

Farrar & Rinehart
Simon & Schuster
Coward-McCann
Limited Editions
Harcourt, Brace
Random House
Equinox Press
Smith & Haas
Viking Presss
Knopf
Dutton
Harper's
Scribner's
Covici, Friede

This is a formidable list. It raises a moral question.

The judgment of poetry—and indeed of any of the arts—has

become one of the most difficult exercises of the aesthetic faculty. This is so because the "modern" artist is not only a creator; he also creates the laws by which his art can be judged. Cummings' view, that his anti-Communist position was not welcome, fits the thirties; but this is conjecture.

The question whether *No Thanks* was a good book or not has nothing to do with the moral issue involved. The issue is whether a poet with the achievements of Cummings should have been denied an audience—denied, that is, the opportunity to function completely as a poet by being published. But the book happens to be a good book. The bawdry aside, it is full of inventions—for example, the grasshopper, neither intaglio nor cameo, which *hopped* so agilely into the consciousness of Stanton A. Coblentz. It contains several portraits of unpeople—

> çi gît 1 Foetus(unborn to not die
> safely whose epoch fits him like a grave)

and another who

> does not have to feel because he thinks
> (the thoughts of others, be it understood)

and a variety of "muckers pimps and tratesmen" and "mischief-hatchers," with the Communists prominent:

> kumrads die because they're told)
> kumrads die before they're old
> (kumrads aren't afraid to die
> kumrads don't
> and kumrads won't
> believe in life)and death knows whie

The book also contains "little joe gould," "what does little Ernest croon," and the tender

> little man
> (in a hurry
> full of an
> important worry)

the incomparable

> at dusk
>> just when
> the Light is filled with birds

and

>> be of love(a little)
>> More careful
>> Than of everything

The "Terminal Dedication" of *No Thanks* reads:

AND

THANKS

TO

R.H.C.

—Cummings' mother, who provided the money for the publication.

# 6

In 1937 a young editor at Harcourt, Brace thought the time had come to bring together all of Cummings' volumes of verse in a collected edition. Charles A. Pearce, afterwards of the publishing firm of Duell, Sloan & Pearce, told me that he first broached the idea over lunch with Bernice Baumgarten (Mrs. James Gould Cozzens), Cummings' agent. In answer to specific queries, Pearce wrote me:

> I proposed a COMPLETE book, but e.e.c. made the decision to limit it, I believe. There *may* have been other factors in this, but I don't remember them and I doubt they existed.
>
> It must have been Cummings, not I, who omitted 'Puella Mea,' because that was one of my favorites and I was (am?) all too ready to read it aloud to anyone willing to listen. You can consult my wife on that one. Fact is that the final selection was completely in the hands of Cummings.

One by-product of the venture always pleased me, too: the recording we made to publicize and promote the book, especially with booksellers to whom about 200 samples went at the time of publication. This was one of the first and remains one of the best of its kind.

Pearce told me that the idea for the book "met with somewhat reluctant approval" at Harcourt, Brace, "but turned out well in the long run." His proposal was made some time in the spring of 1937, and by the end of May, on the eve of Cummings' departure for London with his third wife, a tentative contents had been put together. There was, of course, some sparring. Before leaving the country, Cummings wrote Pearce:

> thanks to your extremely sporting suggestion,the enclosed
> list represents what I like,irrespective of whether it's
> obscene or unsetupable. What I don't like is,naturally,
> whatever I don't feel to be myself.

The list that Cummings forwarded with this letter specified the number of poems to be retained and omitted from each of his six previously published books. & contained seventy-nine poems; twenty-five were marked for omission. *XLI Poems* contained forty-one; omissions, sixteen. *is* 5 contained eighty-four, omissions six. *ViVa* contained seventy; no omissions. *No Thanks*, seventy-one, no omissions, but minus the one in holograph. There was additional sparring:

> concerning format:our hero,being poorbuthonest and(some-
> times) wearing clothes,he is very naturally partial to some-
> thing will fit his pocket after he's been able to pay the price.
> But what I care infinitely is that each poempicture should
> remain intact. Why? Possibly because,with a few exceptions,
> my poems are essentially pictures. And(in my naif way)I
> believe that you're one of the few people in America who can
> work out such a combination of typesize and papersize as will
> allow every picture to breathe its particular life(no "runover"
> lines) in its own private world. A vous le dummy!

shall send, as suggested,the new poems and the introduction along with corrected galleyproofs.

When proofs arrived, Marion Cummings discovered two poems had been set twice—"impossibly" and "Paris; this April sunset completely utters." Pearce wrote: "I am not surprised that two of my favorites got repeated."

Cummings and his wife returned to the United States "for autumn in New Hampshire," and afterwards spent the winter in Patchin Place, where copies of *Collected Poems* reached them in February. Cummings wrote Pearce:

> being a thorow felleau,have taken my socalled
> time & space over new arrival. Verdict:
> congratulations. Marion's:ditto,Et Comment.
> A singularly perspicuous(she considers
> catalogueannouncement of CPs "a decent
> sensible straightforward account")New England-
> ess's:"I think it's your best book since The
> Enormous Room" adding proudly "they're a
> dignified lot,that Harcourt Brace". As one
> unaffiliated with headgear industry,je
> pause

To this, Pearce replied February 17, 1938:

> You are a fine fellow, and your letter of Sunday about the book was mighty good to have. We tried to do a decent job. We usually do, but in this case, I think we tried to do the very best we could. You wouldn't believe it, but there are authors who never bother to pat us on the head. In fact, they think it is a good thing to insult us regularly, and the arrival of a finished book is often the occasion for attempted assault.

The final total was 315, including 22 new poems. Despite the fact that "Puella Mea" and other favorites were missing, the collection had continuity. The last poem in the book, and the last

of the new group, is a sonnet. It is one of the most beautiful of all
his poems:

> you shall above all things be glad and young.
> For if you're young,whatever life you wear
>
> it will become you; and if you are glad
> whatever's living will yourself become.
> Girlboys may nothing more than boygirls need:
> i can entirely her only love
>
> whose any mystery makes every man's
> flesh put space on;and his mind take off time
>
> that you should ever think,may god forbid
> and(in his mercy)your true lover spare:
> for that way knowledge lies,the foetal grave
> called progress,and negation's dead undoom.
>
> I'd rather learn from one bird how to sing
> than teach ten thousand stars how not to dance

## 7

The revived interest in Cummings resulted in several interesting letters. The first was from Selden Rodman, who wrote
Cummings that he was editing an anthology, "but I now find
myself up against the prices, which are higher than any other prices
quoted on any other poet living or dead. I wonder whether you
will be kind enough to intervene on my behalf, and at least give
me a lower rate on a few of them?" Cummings replied:

> may I somewhat tardily but most sincerely
> salute your generosity and ask it to believe
> that the present writer is as sorry to dis-
> appoint you as he is delighted to learn that
> just for a change I'm expensive?
>                                          —yours for living
> P.S. no poet is dead

Pearce wrote Cummings: "I had a pleasant interview with Carl Sandburg yesterday, and he tells me that he has written you a long letter that was practically a sentence about the COLLECTED POEMS. I am very keen to have a copy of this letter. Won't you send me one, or won't you send me the original so that I can have a copy made?" Sandburg's letter follows:

Dear E E Cummings

Quite a few months ago when your Collected Poems came out and for the first time I got at the sequence I said I would write you a fan letter and the days and weeks passed by and I didn't get around to it and nevertheless I reread some of the high spots and said again I must get around to telling this fellow he has much on the ball and I like to watch him pitch in his own chosen world series and he has grand blue sky and stinking prison flowers and fine lovemaking madrigals and a compassionate identification with conscientious objectors and the dust of very common streets and a capacity for exquisite clowning and inexplicable effrontery and somehow he owns what is under his hat and at some moments he himself does not know whether he is kidding us or himself or Jesse James or the American flag the Murrican flag extra extry uxtra mister and he has had a rich life and is one of those isolationists requiring no fan letters a sort of a czechoslovak who can take it with dry tears and merge himself with twilight and darkness and never be completely divested of his songcraft or his clowning or his adumbrant quaker speculations and some finality of holiness that he would deny and deny

Carl Sandburg

Marianne Moore also wrote Cummings, after receiving *Collected Poems*:

Dear Mr. Cummings—
blasphemous, inexorable, disrespectful, sinful author though you are—

you received a cordial welcome at my door today. I remarked to my mother not long ago, "I wish I could write something that people would regard with the anticipatory confidence with which I hear of any new book by E. E. Cummings." The Introduction to this one makes me blush for the moderateness of the above statement. The more I study the equivalences here of "mostpeople's" language, the formidable use of nursery lore, and the further unfortuities,—known to you as technique but never known to lookers-on,—the better, live-er, more undimmed and undiminished they seem. Those who are deaf to the sublime, have to be without it; that is their honorarium. So, *no thanks*; in the sense that thanks are too trivial.

Sincerely yours,

Marianne Moore

On March 10, 1938, Werner wrote, enclosing a review:

The attached I clipped from the Daily Worker today. I send it to you because I thought you might be pleased. When the Daily Worker attacks one it is a badge of righteousness, for the poor, pusillanimous, doped failures who inject themselves with a watered hate supplied in the laboratories of the Communist International never can be on the right side of any issue—except by accident of juxtaposition. Look out for the day when they praise you! I have confidence that that will never happen.

Best of luck!

Morrie

P.S. I have to get the Daily Worker these days, because it prints the full transcript of the testimony at the Russian trials, and the idiots are so dumb that they don't realize that the full transcript is more damaging than any reports in the capitalist press.

The *Daily Worker* review of *Collected Poems* began without sparring: "Of E. E. Cummings it might be said that he sold his poetic birthright for a mess of punctuation marks. Unlike Keats, who feared that his name might be writ in water, Mr. Cummings probably wants his epitaph to read: Here lies one whose name was writ in lower case. At any rate, some bright Ph.D. might write a thesis on the Relation between Punctuation Marks and Reaction in the Poetry of E. E. Cummings."

8

Ezra Pound came to New York on the liner *Rex* April 30, 1939. It was his first visit to his native land in a quarter century. The tall man with the pointed red beard, who had corrected the poems of Yeats and the poetry of Eliot, talked of strange things: "I regard the literature of social significance as of no significance. It is pseudo pink blah. The men who are worth anything today are definitely down on money—writing about money, the problem of money, exchange, gold and silver. I have yet to find a Bolshevik who has written of it." Asked if he thought there would be a war, he replied: "Nothing but devilment can start a new war west of the Vistula. I'm not making any accusation against anyone. But the bankers and the munitions interests, whoever and wherever they may be, are more responsible for the present talk of war than are the intentions of Mussolini or anyone else."

Cummings was in bed with grippe when Pound knocked at Patchin Place, but sat up to welcome his visitor, whose views he found disturbing.

The story of Pound's broadcasts from Rome has been too often told for more than a brief mention here. A charitable view—and I think the correct one—is that he was already sick when he began to make them. He gave himself up on May 5, 1945, near Genoa, and was confined in a U.S. Army prison camp near Pisa. On November 18 he was flown from Italy and placed in the District of Columbia jail to await trial. He was then sixty years old.

A fairly comprehensive account of his life, work, and influence, together with the views of several eminent writers, appeared in *PM*, New York's short-lived afternoon tabloid newspaper. Its author attempted to be fair, and by and large wrote objectively. He gave full expression to his admiration for Pound's achievements in the realm of literature, and quoted excerpts from his poetry and letters. He also quoted excerpts from his broadcasts. He was afterwards attacked for "defending" Pound, and attacked for "attacking" him. In the former category was the *New Masses*, which followed the *PM* article with a symposium of its own, in which all the contributors declared Pound should be executed forthwith, some favoring hanging, some shooting, although he had not yet been tried, and consequently had not been found guilty of anything. So much for their claim that "Communism is twentieth century Americanism."

To the symposium in *PM* Cummings contributed the following:

Re Ezra Pound—poetry happens to be an art;and artists happen to be human beings.

An artist doesn't live in some geographical abstraction,superimposed on a part of this beautiful earth by the nonimagination of unanimals and dedicated to the proposition that massacre is a social virtue because murder is an individual vice. Nor does an artist live in some soi-disant world,nor does he live in some so-called universe,nor does he live in any number of "worlds" or in any number of "universes". As for a few trifling delusions like the "past" and "present" and "future" of quote mankind unquote, they may be big enough for a couple of billion supermechanized submorons but they're much too small for one human being.

Every artist's strictly illimitable country is himself.

An artist who plays that country false has committed suicide; and even a good lawyer cannot kill the dead. But a human being who's true to himself—whoever himself may be—is immortal; and all the atomic bombs of all the antiartists in spacetime will never civilize immortality.

Cummings' generosity was not limited to this or other expressions (see also "Nonlecture Four"). Julien Cornell, Pound's counsel, wrote me:

In the course of preparing to prove that Ezra Pound was mentally unfit to stand trial, I sought information concerning him from a number of his friends, among them E. E. Cummings. For this purpose I went to Cummings' home on Patchin Place, New York, in November 1945. He and his wife, Marion, were in their living room. They expressed concern over Pound's condition which I described to them as a physical and mental breakdown brought about by his imprisonment. I also told them of my plan to have him examined by a leading psychiatrist, and to secure hospital treatment for him.

Although nothing had been said about a contribution, Cummings went over to a desk [5] in a corner of the room and came back with a check, which he handed to me, saying, "I recently sold a painting and I don't need the money. Please use this for Ezra."

I was, of course, much surprised and moved by this spontaneous generosity, and by the large amount of the gift. I told Cummings that the money would be used to secure psychiatric and medical treatment for Pound.

Although this was an outright gift, with no thought of repayment, Mrs. Pound repaid it a year or so later after she had succeeded in obtaining the release of personal funds which had been blocked in England.

## 9

In 1940 appeared 50 Poems, in which Cummings continued to express his own stance, which was and is that of an individual who happened to be a poet. He was his own position, which of course was and is anathema to those who "take sides." I am tempted to use Powys' forceful phrase, "the perfectly natural man confronting the universe," for if there is a better definition that can fit Cummings, I do not know it. In 50 Poems he wrote:

[5] For "desk" read "table," described in the first chapter. No portrait of Cummings can be even remotely a likeness which does not include his many generous acts. At the time of this visit the check represented the only money he had.

wherelings whenlings
(daughters of ifbut offspring of hopefear
sons of unless and children of almost)
never shall guess the dimension of

him whose
each
foot likes the
here of this earth

whose both
eyes
love
this now of the sky

This is the volume that contains "my father moved through dooms of love," "a pretty a day," "anyone lived in a pretty how town," "these children singing in stone," "(sitting in a tree-)," among other enchantments, and a sonnet that expresses his undeviating, undeviated view, whether we look backward to *Tulips and Chimneys* or forward to *Poems 1923-1954*:

there are possibly 2 ½ or impossibly 3
individuals every several fat
thousand years. . . .

But now, with the beginning certainty that the United States would be drawn into the war, there was much soul-searching among the intellectuals. The Communists had no such difficulty. They saw the war as a conflict that did not concern America—because it did not concern Russia—and were scathing in their denunciations of Great Britain and France as well as Germany. Their tune changed when Russia was invaded, thus fulfilling Cummings' observation, "moscow pipes good kumrads dance," for when this happened, they wanted everything to go to Stalin, regardless of other fronts. The embryo commissars had become generalissimos.

On June 10, 1940, *The New Republic* published an article by Archibald MacLeish entitled "Post-war Writers and Pre-war

Readers." The writers were "men like Barbusse, Latzko, Dos Passos, Ford Madox Ford, Ernest Hemingway, Erich Maria Remarque and Richard Aldington"—all of them authors of war books. But, added MacLeish: "They were also books filled with passionate contempt for the statements of conviction, of purpose and of belief on which the war of 1914-1918 was fought. And they left behind them in many minds the conclusion that not only the war and the war issues but *all* issues, all moral issues, were false —were fraudulent—were intended to deceive." He concluded that these books were "disastrous as education for a generation which would be obliged to face the threat of fascism in its adult years."

The gist of what I have thus far presented was incorporated in a wire by the editors of LIFE and sent to a number of writers, including some not named by MacLeish, with the additional comment, "The moral and spiritual unpreparedness in arms he blamed squarely upon writers like himself and like you," and the request to "rewire fifty or a hundred words of comment."

Cummings told me that when he received the telegram from LIFE he went walking in the Square. When he returned to Patchin Place he replied: "If you will stand in the supposed fountain at Washington Square, New York City, and look up at the so called arch, you will find yourself reading 22 words by a man now living." The words,[6] engraved across the back of the Arch, are:

> LET US RAISE A STANDARD TO WHICH THE WISE
> AND THE HONEST CAN REPAIR     THE EVENT
> IS IN THE HAND OF GOD     WASHINGTON

[6] To the Constitutional Convention of 1787.

# XIII

## *Portrait: More Views*

### 1

Cummings at forty-six, Christmas, 1941: the same spare
and supple figure, thinning blond hair, and alive eyes laughing—
was it at me as well as the world? He lounged in a sweater and
unpressed trousers—his painting costume—sucked on a pipe, puffed
a cigarette, ended up with a cigar. Somebody gave him a box of
cigars for Christmas—probably not for Christmas but because
somebody liked him. I thought of half a dozen books and a play
that had delighted me; I saw his paintings on the walls; I heard his
talk full of laughter and images; and still there was something
about the man that eluded me. His wife was in the room, she
listened intently to all he said, and I felt that she, too, sensed that
elusive quality. (She once told Hildegarde Watson: "He keeps me
interested all the time.")

The talk turned to newspapers. He didn't mind when newspapers
printed his name in lower-case letters, but she did. Someone, she
explained, would tell her there was a story about her husband; she
was unable to find it "because I'm looking for his name."

"Why don't you look for a couple of dots in the middle of a line?" he asked her.

The talk turned serious.

"You ask me what I think about this war. Well, let's see. The word *war* reminds me of a poet named Hart Crane. He said there had always been three kinds of people—warriors, priests, merchants. Not just one kind; not just merchants. And I think he was right.

"As for this particular war, I think that if the totalitarians think they can destroy our culture, they're crazy. Do you know why? Because we have no culture.

"To be accurate, we have nothing even remotely approaching culture. Quite the contrary. What we have is a very expensive system for compelling things to mean whatever they aren't.

"Take anything. Labor, for example.

"What is labor?

"Labor is a miracle. When this miracle happens, a girl or an earth or a poet begins to sing: that's labor. That's not what labor means, that's what labor is.

"But what does labor mean, according to the idiotic system of compulsions which we playfully call ours?

"Labor means this—ever so many people do what they don't want to do in order to be compensated for the loss of their self-respect. I refer to money. In other words, a laborer and a slave both do what they don't want to do; but a laborer gets paid for doing it, whereas a slave does it freely.

"What a fine specimen of our heap-big sub-moronic super-mechanized hyper-unworld's non-mind!

"Now take the millennium. The millennium, my friends, will automatically arrive when and if some few supposedly lucky and laborless s.o.b.s. are totally eliminated—when and if that slavish vice called free will is a mere bit of Disney twaddle—when and if (are you still with me?) not almost everybody, but everybody absolutely without exception, is being paid and paid for unluckily doing what he or she (or preferably it) doesn't want to do.

"Peace!—it's war.

"But I have an idea. Maybe, just before the millennium, we might listen.

"Do you hear a sound? No? Try again. Yes?

"That sound isn't Mr. Woman and Mrs. Man sleeping the sleep of the secure. It isn't a couple of billion ignoble confused inhuman semi-quadrupeds. It isn't any theory of economics or mathematical-physics or good government or bad biology. It isn't promising anything or proving anything or explaining anything or excusing anything or meaning anything or—pardon me for speaking frankly —selling or buying anything. Truth doesn't sell or buy: truth sings.

"I hear singing.

"Am I crazy? Sure. So were a few perfectly amazed individuals, standing bolt-upright in pitch-darkness among a lot of sheep." [1]

## 2

In the din of the slogans and slaughter Cummings went on quietly celebrating the things that endure, there where "yes is a pleasant country," and

—tomorrow is our permanent address

and there they'll scarcely find us(if they do,
we'll move away still further:into now

In that country and the new book he was compiling

the red and the round
(they're gravensteins)fall
with kind of a blind
big sound on the ground

and

we're wonderful one times one

[1] This appeared in *PM's Weekly*, Feb. 16, 1941. Marianne Moore praised it, adding: "But, then, to be sure, you had help." I thank her for her praise, I acknowledge the help.

The book was 1 x 1. The war was very much on his mind, and many of the poems in that book reflect his preoccupation with the world's ills, which, as he foresaw, the war would not resolve:

> plato told
>
> him:he couldn't
> believe it(jesus
>
> told him;he
> wouldn't believe
> it)lao
>
> tsze
> certainly told
> him,and general
> (yes
>
> mam)
> sherman;
> and even
> (believe it
> or
>
> not)you
> told him:i told
> him;we told him
> (he didn't believe it,no
>
> sir)it took
> a nipponized bit of
> the old sixth
>
> avenue
>
> el;in the top of his head:to tell
> him [2]

[2] The Harris Structural Steel Co., Inc., wrote the Committee to Investigate Contract for Demolition of 6th Ave. "L," April 7, 1939: "1. 98% of the wrought iron and structural steel—sold to the Bethlehem Steel Co. with

*1 x 1* contains, among its many delights, Cummings' continuous incantation to spring—

> Hills jump with brooks:
> trees tumble out of twigs and sticks;

and

> until and i heard
> a certain a bird
> i dreamed i could sing

and

> such was a poet and shall be and is

> —who'll solve the depths of horror to defend
> a sunbeam's architecture with his life:
> and carve immortal jungles of despair
> to hold a mountain's heartbeat in his hand

The book also contains a poem of more than special significance for the student of his work.

New Hampshire was important to Cummings. It was not only because his father was a native of that state; it was there that he met Sam Ward, caretaker of Joy Farm, whose epistolary style, by Cummings' own admission,[3] influenced the poet.

"I remember once he wrote: 'we had a Big snow,'" Cummings said. "He'd write 'i'—not 'I'—because 'I' wasn't important to him.

"Sam Ward's way is the only way. Instead of being artificial and affected, it is the conventional way that is artificial and affected. I am not a scholar, but I believe only in English is the 'I' capitalized."

Sam Ward, New Hampshire farmer, shares with the Greeks, Elizabethans, and Jacobeans the honor of influencing his neighbor Cummings. *They* have their own mighty monuments, and it is a

principal offices at South Bethlehem, Pa., under a contract dated January 11, 1939." The Bethlehem Steel Company wrote me: "We would have no way of knowing whether the City of New York sold any scrap from the Sixth Avenue Elevated to a Japanese Firm. We buy scrap, not sell it."

[3] Interview with Harvey Breit, *Times Book Review*, Dec. 31, 1950.

pleasure to record that Cummings has memorialized his friend
with this poem in *1 x 1:*

> rain or hail
> sam done
> the best he kin
> till they digged his hole
>
> :sam was a man
>
> stout as a bridge
> rugged as a bear
> slickern a weazel
> how be you
>
> (sun or snow)
>
> gone into what
> like all them kings
> you read about
> and on him sings
>
> a whippoorwill;
>
> heart as big
> as the world aint square
> with room for the devil
> and his angels too
>
> yes,sir
>
> what may be better
> or what may be worse
> and what may be clover
> clover clover
>
> (nobody'll know)
>
> sam was a man
> grinned his grin
> done his chores
> laid him down.
>
> Sleep well

3

XAIPE: *Seventy-One Poems*, published in 1950, is the last separate volume before the monumental *Poems*, of which it is the last section. It thus offers an opportunity for discussion of Cummings' achievement as well as those "oddities" on which certain critics have harped. Even without further evidence, it must be apparent that Cummings is the author of a large body of work that, by its individuality and range, its power and influence, wears a major aspect, certainly for our time. His originality is all the more remarkable because he has functioned in an age of eclectics—Pound, Eliot, Joyce, and other synthesists (painters above all).

I have earlier referred to his experiments, and particularly to his use of *tmesis*—the separation of the parts of a word or words—to achieve simultaneity. Like Picasso in painting, Cummings has continued to probe the syntactical barriers of language in a search for effects often yielded, and perhaps equally as often with results bewildering to the ordinary reader. Picasso said: "I do not seek—I find"; Cummings, with equal candor, might have said: "I do not find—I seek." His search for the secret of emotion and movement that lies at the heart of words has had, and will continue to have, an incalculable impact on his contemporaries, as the experiments of Picasso have had on the painters of our time. To complete the parallel: both the painter and the poet have created their masterpieces, but perhaps have found their greatest impetus and joy in constant experimentation to push back the frontiers of language and line, poetry and paint.

As for the "oddities," while many poems are cryptic, and some mere *jeux d'esprits*, one or two have led to persistent mischief:

> a kike is the most dangerous
> machine as yet invented
> by even yankee ingenu
> ity(out of a jew a few
> dead dollars and some twisted laws)
> it comes both prigged and canted

This poem, on its first appearance in the *Quarterly Review of Literature* and afterwards on page 46 of XAIPE, dampened the ardor of some of Cummings' admirers, although it was not long before a different kind of explanation than the seemingly obvious one began to appear. A writer in *Congress Weekly*, a Jewish publication, stated unequivocally: "Even a cursory examination of Exhibit 46 should prove that, far from being anti-Semitic in intent, the lines are pointedly and effectively anti anti-Semitic." I asked Cummings: "What is the real meaning of poem 46 in XAIPE? Is it reaction to a particular individual?" He replied:

"I feel that a poem 'means' differently for each individual who encounters it;but which(if any)of its 'meanings' deserves to be called the 'real' one,I don't know. All I can even try to tell you is what this poem means so far as I'm concerned.

"Whereas in unpopular parlance 'a kike' equals a jew,for me 'a kike' equals an UNjew. Why? Because for me a jew is a human being;whereas 'a kike' is a machine—the product of that miscalled Americanization,alias standardization(id est dehumanization)which, from my viewpoint,makes out&out murder a relatively respectable undertaking."

An examination of Cummings' successive volumes—except the first three, which were mere samplings from a large general stock— reveals a progressive growth in depth, force, and invention, until single lines are almost painfully concentrated, and subtleties of texture and movement occur that sight-readers can easily overlook. An obvious comparison is suggested by the sonnet in XAIPE about the Canterbury pilgrims and the passage about Chaucer in "Puella Mea." More relevant, however, are the "facts" of such a poem as "no time ago," and the sonnet beginning

> so many selves(so many fiends and gods
> each greedier than every)is a man
> (so easily one in another hides;
> yet man can,being all,escape from none)

which reveal growth on all levels, not excluding the poet as human being as well as the poet as craftsman. In addition XAIPE, like his other books, is one more testament of "the perfectly natural man confronting the universe." For once again Cummings has celebrated earth and people—or, more properly, persons. There is also a general:

> (five foot five)
> neither dead
> nor alive
> (in real the rain)

a statue:

> why must itself up every of a park
>
> anus stick some quote statue unquote to
> prove that a hero equals any jerk
> who was afraid to dare to answer "no"?

the mob:

> (as
>
> the boodle's bent is the
> crowd inclined it's
> freedom from freedom
> the common man wants)

and an individual:

> o
>
> the round
> little man we
> loved so isn't
>
> no!w
>
> a gay of a
> brave and
> a true of a
>
> who have
>
> r
> olle
> d i

nt

o

n

o

w(he)re

The "round little man" was Paul Rosenfeld; an exclamation point and parenthesis express the surprise and pathos of his death. In a book of tributes [4] to this much loved man, Allen Tate wrote:

"One Sunday he was to come to us for dinner. After we had waited until about nine thirty we decided that he had forgotten it. My wife thought it considerate not to remind him; so she decided not to telephone him but to invite him again in a few days; for even the appearance of discourtesy in his behavior distressed him. Two days later Marion Cummings telephoned us from New Hampshire to ask us to send flowers, for her and Estlin, to Paul's funeral. That was how, in New York, in 1946, one heard about the death of one's old friend and new neighbor." (Rosenfeld had recently moved from Irving Place to the Village.)

It was Allen Tate who brought T. S. Eliot to Patchin Place. John Malcolm Brinnin brought Dylan Thomas. Around the corner from Patchin Place, and a short walk up Greenwich Avenue, is St. Vincent's Hospital, where three years later Thomas died. To the *Yale Literary Magazine*, which published a memorial issue, Cummings contributed the following wire:

FROM MY DOUBTLESS LIMITED POINT OF VIEW THE ONLY THING TO SAY ABOUT DYLAN THOMAS IS THAT BEING A TRUE POET HE'S ALIVE

To me he said, returning Georges Blond's *The Great Migrations*: "I knew a couple of lemmings once. Nobody could stop them. On they rushed—straight ahead—and plunged in." He paused, gesturing. "Hart Crane and Dylan Thomas."

[4] *Paul Rosenfeld: Voyager in the Arts*, 1948.

# XIV

## *The Poet as Reader*

**1**

Public appearances by writers are not new, but the vast number of readings by contemporary poets is a modern phenomenon. A recent study [1] divides them into three categories: performer, personality, and public speaker. In the first were Dylan Thomas, Dame Edith Sitwell, W. H. Auden, Ogden Nash, and E. E. Cummings; in the second, Marianne Moore, Wallace Stevens, T. S. Eliot, Robert Frost, and William Carlos Williams; in the third, Louis MacNeice, Archibald MacLeish, and Stephen Spender. "If success is measured by the size of the crowds that flock to hear him, the performer is the matinee idol of the poetic circuit," the author wrote.

Cummings was the first poet to read at the Poetry Center of the Y.M.H.A., which he termed "the best audience in New York." Despite his popularity, he never liked having to read in public, and he did it for the same reason that everyone else does. He did not like the preparation that was involved—he was conscientious

[1] "The Poet as Player," *New World Writing* No. 11, 1957.

about it—because it took him away from his work. (The care with which he prepared his readings may be exemplified in a tape recording he made for the National Association of Educational Broadcasters. A studio engineer suggested a run-through. Cummings said he was ready to record, no run-through was necessary. His allotted time was twenty-nine minutes thirty seconds. He finished reading on the thirtieth second. The engineer insisted on buying him a drink, and in fact bought him two.) He did not like the travel that was often involved, because it took him away from home as well as from work. But once arrived at his destination, and once fairly launched on the platform, he was a showman to his fingertips, establishing an instant rapport with his audience. He read at most of the major centers of learning.

He set out for Loyola University, Chicago, in the dead of winter and arrived in a blizzard, certain that no one would come to hear him. The hall was nevertheless full, and there were standees in the back. He was so surprised that he mentioned it to a Jesuit brother, who replied: "Don't you know our motto? 'Discipline above all else'?"

The second surprise occurred just as he was being introduced.

"Here I was, all ready to give my reading," he related at Patchin Place, "when at the very last minute a group of nuns trooped solemnly in and sat down in the first row, right under my nose. You can be sure I made a quick change in the program."

"What change?" asked Allen Tate.

"I had to cut out several poems I had been planning to read." [2]

"Oh, but you needn't have, Cummings," said Tate, amused. "Those nuns can take it, you know."

"Yes, but I couldn't," was the reply. "I was well brought up."

The third surprise occurred when, to prevent a rush for autographs, two husky Jesuits virtually lifted him by the shoulders and bore him down the aisle to safety. Cummings did not autograph for strangers (indeed, the only books he ever signed were those he gave to friends). After a reading in Rochester he was surrounded

[2] "A salesman is an it that stinks Excuse" and "a politician is an arse upon."

by suppliants with copies of his books. A woman, thrusting *Poems 1923-1954* at him, pleaded that she was going back to India and wished to show a famous signature there.

"Get Elvis Presley's," said Cummings, and moved on.

Winfield Townley Scott, poet and onetime literary editor of the Providence *Journal*, introduced Cummings at Brown University. He told me that Cummings had liked his remarks, particularly a reference to Thoreau: "I said we New Englanders should claim Cummings as a regional poet," Scott wrote me. "Not in the accustomed sense, but in an intellectual sense. I quoted Emerson, 'Give all to love,' and Thoreau, 'Institutions are like snowdrifts: they occur where there is a lull in the wind.' There, I said, if I understand Cummings's poetry at all, are the two sides of his coin: love and rebellion. He is a direct heir and descendant of the great New Englanders; and where we have fixed in our firmament the stars of Emerson, Thoreau, Dickinson, and Robinson,[3] he too belongs and will remain there."

Mr. Scott also told me that at Professor Damon's house after the reading Cummings, on being praised by Mrs. Damon, pointed to her husband, and said: "I owe everything to him."

2

On February 5, 1957, David McCord, poet and executive secretary of the Harvard Fund, wrote to Cummings from 4 Wadsworth House, Cambridge: "As chairman of the Poetry Committee of the Boston Arts Festival—of which both Archibald MacLeish and Jack Sweeney [4] at Harvard are members—I have the honor to invite you to be the Festival Poet in June of this year. Your predecessors have been successively Robert Frost, Carl Sandburg, and Archie himself.... We ask only that you write a poem for the occasion—which need not be long—perhaps 100 lines more or less.... If you accept, the Festival Committee will be more than

[3] I have heard Cummings praise Robinson as "the last of the craftsmen."
[4] John L. Sweeney, Librarian, Houghton Library, Harvard.

delighted. There is an honorarium of $500 plus traveling expenses, and you would receive the Festival Medal which goes each year to the poet of our choice."

This invitation from Mr. McCord touched off a prolonged correspondence, in the course of which Cummings withdrew his consent twice, was twice prevailed upon to reconsider, reconsidered, and at length made perhaps his most triumphant appearance as a reader. He replied on February 9:

> it's a fact(is it not)that nothing but an hour's reading is expected of the "festival poet":and that in "the occasional poem" he can say whatever he likes?

This was clairvoyance. Mr. McCord wrote back: "Yes, an hour's reading, with such comment as you care to make on each poem (or on poetry in general) is all that is expected. You can choose your own subject for the occasional poem. I enclose what Archie MacLeish wrote last summer—chiefly to guide you in length. There is no tradition about this since his was the first of the occasional poems in a series of three. For my own part, I should like to think that a Boston or New England subject might become a tradition since this is a New England festival."

> many thanks for your enlightening
> second letter and the copy of Archie's
> expert opus. Studying these documents,
> I realize what a "festival poem" should
> be;something quite(as it happens)foreign
> to my own feeling. Let me only add that
> am sorry I've wasted your time,and wish
> you may have much better luck with your
> next candidate

McCord asked him to "reconsider and agree simply to read one new poem of any length whatever, on any subject whatever, and then read from and comment on some of your published poems." Cummings now replied:

am delighted that "a new poem"
will suffice;partly on general
principles;partly because I've
two new poems and should enjoy
reading either of them.

Peter Temple, manager of the Festival, came to Patchin Place
to discuss the ceremonies and reading. Mr. Temple suggested that
when Cummings had decided which of his new poems would be
the "principal" one, a copy be forwarded for release to Boston
newspapers. The poem finally chosen was inspired by the Hungarian uprising. Cummings told me: "I was so frantic and sick, I
felt I would die if I couldn't do something in this situation. Then
the poem came."
This was the poem:

THANKSGIVING
(1956)

a monstering horror swallows
this unworld me by you
as the god of our fathers' fathers bows
to a which that walks like a who

but the voice-with-a-smile of democracy
announces night and day
"all poor little peoples that want to be free
just trust in the u s a"

suddenly uprose hungary
and she gave a terrible cry
"no slave's unlife shall murder me
for i will freely die"

she cried so high thermopylae
heard her and marathon
and all prehuman history
and finally The Un

"be quiet little hungary
and do as you are bid
a good kind bear is angary
we fear for the quo pro quid"

uncle sam shrugs his pretty
pink shoulders you know how
and he twitches a liberal titty
and lisps "i'm busy right now"

so rah-rah-rah democracy
let's all be as thankful as hell
and bury the statue of liberty
(because it begins to smell)

## 3

A long silence descended on Boston. Like Sandburg's fog, it moved on little cat feet from the Festival offices on Newbury Street and over the Public Gardens. And in New York, Cummings waited for word. The word that came was not from McCord. At noon on Tuesday, May 21, Cummings dispatched the following wire to 4 Wadsworth House, Cambridge:

RUMORS HAVE REACHED ME WHICH comma FOLLOWING YOUR FAILURE TO ACKNOWLEDGE MY LETTER OF APRIL THIRTEENTH ENCLOSING A POEM ENTITLED THANKSGIVING 1956 comma MAKE ANY CONNECTION WITH THE BOSTON ARTS FESTIVAL COMPLETELY UNDESIRABLE FROM MY STANDPOINT semicolon KINDLY THEREFORE CONSIDER OUR ASSOCIATION TERMINATED UPON RECEIPT OF THIS TELEGRAM

E. E. CUMMINGS

McCord replied by wire, and Mr. Temple came a second time to Patchin Place. But when he left, Cummings was still perturbed. Should he read "Thanksgiving (1956)" and then explain that the Festival committee had rejected it? For read it he would, if he went to Boston. His wife's view, which he afterwards adopted, was

that he should either decline the invitation, or read the poem—
along with the others he had selected—without comment. He
thereupon wrote Temple:

> I've a feeling that what's needed
> now & here is a completely generous
> gesture;& since you are in no position
> to make one,let me try to do so
>
> please treat the enclosed POEM as
> "occasional";with the understanding
> that my 40minute "reading" will
> most certainly include *Thanksgiving*
> (1956)

He enclosed "i am a little church(no great cathedral)." There
was rejoicing in Boston. The gesture was acknowledged. Later
than usual that May, Cummings and his wife went to New Hampshire. Preparing for the Festival, Cummings made the following
notes, to serve as introductory material and to guide him in reading:

31 years ago, appeared a book of poems called IS FIVE; whose
foreword contained these words:
    "If a poet is anybody, he is somebody to whom things made
    matter very little—somebody who is obsessed by Making...
    ...whereas nonmakers must content themselves with the
    merely undeniable fact that twice two is four, he rejoices in
    an irresistible truth(to be found,in abbreviated costume,upon
    the titlepage of the present volume)."
Such was,& still is,my conviction—that twice two IS FIVE. Does
my conviction strike you as crazy? Well,perhaps it is. But from
it have already come over 9 books of poetry;which are now collected in one large volume, entitled POEMS 1923-1954.
And, in all that time, I have never made a single atom-bomb.
This evening,I shall try to read you 15 or 16 poems—some early,
some recent;some satyrical,some lyrical—dealing with a variety
of subjects:

science,death—the socalled world—war,peace—religion—life—
love, and Spring

Only one of these poems has a title:it is called THANKSGIVING
(1956). Except for this poem—& the socalled festival poem,
which will come first—all my poems are taken from the collection beforementioned.

One thing more.

Since I feel that poetry is not to be explained, but *to be enjoyed*,
I shall make no comments whatever on my poems;but simply
read them one after another,as well as I can, slowly; with a
slight pause at the end of each poem.

At 8:30 on the evening of June 23 Archibald MacLeish introduced Cummings to his vast audience in the Public Gardens.
"With wicked mimicry he caught the intonations of a fatuous
politician; with delicacy and sentiment he recalled his parents;
with unalloyed disdain he read a poem (called 'thanksgiving')
denouncing official apathy during the Hungarian revolt. Expressing a strong point of view with Swiftian savagery, it caused gasps
among the audience, but was received most warmly." [5]

A week after the reading Marion Cummings wrote me from
New Hampshire:

> The Festival reading was a great strain. An audience of 7000
> & a background of traffic noises, dogs barking, children scream-
> ing in the gardens & air planes overhead. Cummings did an
> extraordinary job & held the audience & was a great success.
>
> Unfortunately it was in the 90's & between that & the air con-
> ditioned restaurants etc. C. came back here with his medal &
> a dreadful grippe. He's had fever all week & has been very
> wretched. As soon as he is better I'll write a proper letter—just
> now I haven't time or energy. Cummings is a terrible invalid.
> Even with a high fever I can't keep him in bed.

[5] Boston *Herald*, June 24.

# XV

## *Harvard Revisited*

*suddenly it lies in the air like fame.*
    —RILKE'S "ROSE"

1

"I don't know how it all started, but it seems that everyone was in favor of seeing the return of the native. I think the lectures were useful to him, too, to lay the ghosts of his Cambridge revolt."

The speaker was John H. Finley, Jr., Eliot Professor of Greek Literature and Master of Eliot House, who talked with familiarity and ease about modern poetry, although he thinks a text of Aeschylus sufficient to occupy him contentedly for the rest of his life. We were discussing Cummings' appointment as the Charles Eliot Norton Professor of Poetry at Harvard, in which Dr. Finley had played an important role. From talk of the appointment we turned to talk about the appointee.

"Cummings," he said, "is closer to the modern world of abstraction and physics than other poets. He knows there is no return to a primitive world and primitivist images, as in Yeats, for example. Cummings's achievement is his mind as much—if not more—as his sensibilities. That is, he grasps things quickly, much in the manner of modern scientists and physicists."

It would appear, also, that the scientist and physicist see the earth whole, with a comprehension of nature found only as a rule in naturalists and poets. Dr. Finley did not overlook the naturalist side of Cummings; I am especially grateful to him for telling me about the poet's view of the woodchuck, an animal that farmers dislike and shoot on sight.

"The farmer," Cummings had told Dr. Finley, "only sees two per cent of the woodchuck, comprising that part which nibbles a few leaves in his vegetable garden. He doesn't see the other ninety-eight per cent, the dignified animal who lives in his own world and has his own business to attend to, which he does very well."

## 2

The first word about the Harvard appointment came from Paul H. Buck, University Provost, who wrote Cummings on February 18, 1952: "On behalf of Harvard University, I have the honor to extend to you a cordial invitation to accept a one-year appointment as Charles Eliot Norton Professor of Poetry for the academic year 1952-53 with a salary of $15,000. The Norton Professor must be in residence in the University from October 1 to Christmas, and from February 1 to May 1, and is expected to deliver not less than six lectures with obligation to publish these lectures through the Harvard University Press."

Dr. Finley also wrote: "I have so far left unexpressed all the more important things: our admiration for your life and writings, our hope that the return of the native to changed scenes would be stimulating and perhaps even encouraging, and our simple eagerness to have you here. The professorship best fulfills itself if it gives a spur to a man's doing what for want of such a clear interval he might never get around to. If it can perform some such function for you, it will fulfill our highest hopes."

Cummings thought it over. On February 23 he replied to Mr. Buck from Patchin Place:

your excellent letter(magnificently
seconded by Professor Finley's)has
arrived. May I ask for a little time
to consider this most generous invitation
with the careful seriousness which it
more than merits?

perhaps you'll be so very kind as to
tell me exactly when(and if possible
where)the six lectures are delivered;
how long each lecture is presumed to last;
whether or no a lecturer may say whatever
he likes in whatever way he chooses; and
(finally)if the appointee could postpone
his appearance until October 15

There were more letters. The last in the series was brief:

> 4 Patchin Place
> New York City
> 11
>
> March 11, 1952
>
> Dear Mr Buck—
>
> I've decided to accept the
> appointment. Thank you for
> giving me so much time
>
> —sincerely
> E. E. Cummings

Cummings rented a house at 6 Wyman Road, Cambridge,
where he and his wife lived during the time he held the Norton
professorship. He told me that the reason he inquired about the
October 15 date—in his letter to Mr. Buck—was that he wanted
to be in New Hampshire "when the trees turned red," for him a
never-missed event. The first lecture was delivered to "a packed
Sanders Theatre audience" the night of October 28. By the third
lecture it was standing room only. Between the third and fourth

lectures—the latter delivered on February 16—Cummings and his wife left Cambridge for Patchin Place. The last lecture was delivered on March 16, after which they left Cambridge for good, returning to New York only to prepare for their sojourn in New Hampshire.

The lectures were written during the summer of 1952. The predominantly autobiographical tone was the suggestion of Norman Friedman, a young instructor at the University of Connecticut, who told Cummings that nothing would be more interesting to his audiences than hearing from him about the world he grew up in, and the other formative influences of his life. They are also a little anthology of his work, prose as well as poetry, and the poems of others, some of them surprising in this context: Wordsworth, Keats, Shelley, Nashe, Chaucer, Swinburne, Robert Burns, Charles d'Orléans, Dante, Donne, Walter von der Vogelweide, and several ballads. Rossetti was not included. They were published by Harvard University Press, 1953, under the title *i: Six Nonlectures*. The book was dedicated to Dr. Finley. The jacket photograph, by Marion Morehouse, is a superb portrait of Cummings, tanned from his summer in New Hampshire—in an open white shirt the bronzed neck is powerfully cylindrical, the face is full, the eyes, as in life, thoughtful and piercing. He was then fifty-eight years old.

Alfred Kazin reviewed *i: Six Nonlectures* in *The New Yorker*: "one reads a book like this with disappointment at hearing so many familiar jokes told over again, while the poet escapes into a fairyland of his fathers and points with a shudder to all who are not, equally with him, his father's son."

## 3

In 1954 Harcourt, Brace published a large volume—468 pages—which contained all of Cummings' poetry then in book form, from *Tulips and Chimneys* (1923) through xaipe (1950). The volume was called *Poems 1923-1954*. As no poems written after 1950 were included, the title was, to say the least, ambiguous. It was not Cummings' title. He wrote Bernice Baumgarten, of Brandt and Brandt, his literary agents, March 11, 1954:

> Am sure that what I intended to suggest was a volume entitled, not COMPLETE POEMS, but POEMS 1923-1950; & comprising
> 1) an index of first lines
> 2) the full text of each of the following books
>      as originally published:
>        Tulips and Chimneys
>        & (AND)
>        XLI Poems
>        is 5
>        VV (ViVa)
>        No Thanks
> —selections from which constitute poems 1-293 of Collected Poems
> 3) introduction & poems 294-315 of Collected Poems
> 4) the full text of each of the following books as originally published:
>        50 Poems
>        One Times One
>        XAIPE
> —nothing less & nothing more.
>
> At all events, & whatever my earlier letter suggested, I wish to make perfectly clear that the preceding paragraph expresses my present wishes with regard to any collection of my poems published in the immediate future.

Work on the book had already started, and for a time it even looked as though it might be ready for publication on Cummings' birthday. By midsummer the immense labor of proofreading was well advanced. In charge of this phase of the operation was Catharine Carver of the Harcourt, Brace staff. The operation was involved, and required extraordinary patience and care, for Cummings continued to send in corrections, and to ask for corrected pages. He also wired:

> PLEASE CORRECT PAGE 243 POEM 29 STOP THE SECOND
> WORD OF THE FIRST LINE SHOULD BE A NOT THE STOP
> THUS THE FIRST LINE SHOULD READ QUOTE IN A MIDDLE
> OF A ROOM UNQUOTE

Western Union was somewhat baffled, and repeated "SHOULD BE A NOT THE." This was on August 25; the same day he wrote Miss Carver: "I like the titlepage VERY MUCH. The dedication is ok as set. In the typographically excellent Contents—& you certainly deserve a diamond croix-de-guerre for typing it or them—please make these additional corrections (besides those already marked in redink)."

By September there were clean pages, and Cummings realized with a start that the title of the book, which he had admired, was not what he had had in mind. He protested. As a result, on September 20 Robert Giroux, editor-in-chief at Harcourt, wrote Cummings in New Hampshire:

> I am very sorry that there is a misunderstanding between us about the dates and the title. It appeared "1923-1954" in the original contract. Since you changed it from *The Poems of E. E. Cummings: 1923-1954* to Poems 1923-1954, it appears that way in the present contract. It also appears in the catalogue copy which we sent you, and on the title-page proof which you approved. We therefore thought that it had your OK and, when Catharine Carver received (as we thought) your OK'd final revisions on September 7th, I released the book for the press. We were extremely distressed to learn on September 10th that you took exception to the dates and we hope that you will understand that we acted in good faith.
>
> If you feel that the dates, 1923-1954, imply that there are poems later than 1950 in the book, I can only answer that the

very full table of contents, and the blurb, belie this.... What we have always meant by the 1954 in the title, and assumed you agreed with, was the date of *this* book....

To this Cummings replied on September 26:

> re the misunderstanding about "1950":
> if our non(even more than usual)hero
> signed a contract reading "1954",it's
> obvious that noone's at fault but
> himself

Although bound copies were ready by Cummings' birthday, October 14, review copies had not been distributed in time to make that day the date of publication. Instead, October 25 was chosen. On October 31, Randall Jarrell reviewed *Poems 1923-1954* in *The New York Times Book Review*. He wrote: "What I like least about Cummings's poems is their pride in Cummings and their contempt for most other people; the difference between the I and you of the poems, and other people, is the poems' favorite subject. All his work thanks God that he is not as other men."

In "Nonlecture One" Cummings said at Harvard:

"During my six fifteen minute poetry readings, I shall only try to read poetry as well as I don't know how. If you object 'but why not criticize as well?' I shall quote very briefly from a wonderful book, whose acquaintance I first made through a wonderful friend named Hildegarde Watson—a book whose English title is Letters To A Young Poet, and whose author is the German Poet Rainer Maria Rilke:

> Works of art are of an infinite loneliness and with nothing to be so little reached as with criticism. Only love can grasp and hold and fairly judge them.

In my proud and humble opinion, those two sentences are worth all the soi-disant criticism of the arts which has ever existed or will ever exist."

*Poems 1923-1954* was followed by *95 Poems,* which contains "Thanksgiving (1956)" and "i am a little church(no great cathedral)." The volume was another affirmation:

> in time of all sweet things beyond
> whatever mind may comprehend
> remember seek(forgetting find)
>
> and in a mystery to be
> (when time from time shall set us free)
> forgetting me, remember me

## 4

Nature and the universe held him in profound awe; any manifestation from either meant more to him than works of man. With this reminder, for such it is, the following may fit the pattern of his life and thoughts.

On a visit to the farm, as I was reading by the light of a kerosene lamp, Cummings suddenly appeared in the doorway of my room. He said quietly: "Would you like to see a flying saucer?" I leaped up, and in pajamas and slippers followed him to the roof.

It was a flat roof with a railing around it, like a captain's walk. Mrs. Cummings was peering through a telescope. Cummings pointed to a bright point in the sky and handed me a pair of binoculars; he, too, had a pair in his hands, and for several minutes we all stood in silence.

It took me some time to adjust the binoculars and find the object at which I was to peer. I saw in the sky, perhaps five or fifteen miles distant, a bright light cradled in a shallow arc shaped like a cigar end. In the August night thronged with stars the light blazed like a planet; from time to time it whipped downwards a few feet, then soared to its former position. It whipped not only to the right, but sometimes to the left, and this gave me the idea it was some kind of balloon, perhaps a meteorological balloon. I was foolish enough to suggest this, and received for my pains incredulous, starlit looks from both Cummings and his wife, who thereupon returned to their saucer-gazing, diregarding me.

I did not know until the next morning that I had gone to bed disgraced. The subject came up at breakfast, and I stuck to my view: it was a meteorological balloon.

Did I agree it did not look like any balloon I had hitherto seen? Yes—I had to agree to that.

"There you are," Cummings said.

I said: "What do *you* think was in it, if not meteorological instruments?"

Cummings replied: "Little men from another planet."

"What were they doing there?" I asked uneasily.

He looked at me pityingly; she, scornfully.

"They've come to see about all the mischief we're hatching, and to make their own plans."

Over the eggs, over the marmalade, over the coffee, so delicious in the morning air of New Hampshire, the discussion went on, or rather, discourse—I no longer dared to comment, and merely listened. I did not know what to make of it then, and know even less now.

There was another extraordinary event during this visit.

I had recently published a life of Dr. Johnson based on non-Boswellian sources (*Mr. Oddity*). On my last morning there Mrs. Cummings said to me: "We happen to have a complete set of Johnson's *Lives of the Poets,* and Estlin and I have talked it over and decided that you would most appreciate having those books, and so we are going to make you a present of them."

I stood transfixed—the word "set" can hardly convey the magnitude of the gift, for it was a first edition in sixty-eight calf-bound volumes, and included the works of the poets whose lives Johnson had written. The next thing I knew, both Cummings and his wife had begun to wrap the individual volumes in newspaper—it was a present, they said, and I was not to help—and were placing them in two large cardboard boxes. I took those books onto the train with me; I have them still.

5

Cummings was unlike most of the poets I have known—he was interested in people. His poetry reflects that interest, and *The Enormous Room*, of course, is not so much autobiography as a celebration of individuals under that peculiarly twentieth-century kind of duress, the concentration camp. He went where people congregated—to prize fights, burlesque, and wrestling; he even went to an occasional movie, although he despised the medium. To him, "Hollywood distantly resembled a rather undersized hen's-egg into which has been introduced a rather oversized ostrichchick." Once, during a newsreel—it was just after the current Irish Sweepstakes winners had been announced, and some of them were being shown on the screen—I felt a nudge.

"Want to know why you and I can never win one of those things?" he whispered.

"Why?" I asked, startled—somebody was hissing—and he replied: "Because we don't look like that."

Concerning everything under the sun he had, it seems, what Pound considered essential in a writer—an enormous curiosity. Perhaps it will now be said that he was also psychic.

In 1957 I had known Cummings for thirty-two years. In March of that year R. L. De Wilton, my editor at The Macmillan Company, asked me what I planned to do next. Mr. De Wilton was tall and bore an extraordinary resemblance to the portrait of Yeats that hangs in the Macmillan reception room; he was also the best-read man I had met in the publishing industry. I wanted to please him, but I had made up my mind—or so I supposed—to write no more biographies. I told him I felt I had done enough of them, and anyway, there was no one else I cared to write about, with the exception of E. E. Cummings. (This must have been an unconscious thought, for it slipped out without premeditation.) De Wilton instantly asked me whether he could present the idea to the Macmillan book council, and I asked for time to think it over. I also had to know whether Cummings would co-operate.

I called Mrs. Cummings and told her there was something I wanted to ask Estlin, and she invited me to tea. In the course of the next hour or so, after we had talked of everything else, she said: "I thought you had something to ask—now what can it be?" Cummings, looking at her, said very quietly: "Perhaps he wishes to write a book about me." Quite startled, I exclaimed: "That is it—if Your Highness will permit." He replied, with a bow: "My lowness will be honored."

# XVI

## *A Last Look*

**1**

Cummings, May, 1961. The crowded front room in Patchin Place, overflowing with books, is even more crowded with boxes and bags. He and his wife are waiting for the car that will take them to the airport, and they are having a final cup of coffee; he is also eating a hot cereal. "I am trying to fatten him up," she says. He sits in the straight-backed chair, talking as usual like a "cheerfulest Elephantangelchild;" but when she leaves the room to get another cup, he whispers earnestly: "All I ask is one more year."

He is sixty-six. The years that have brought him honors and awards no longer sit lightly on him, for they have also brought illness; I recall glimpses of him in Greenwich Village streets in recent winters that had left me full of foreboding. There had been another trip abroad—to Sicily, and Greece, where he and his wife had visited his daughter and grandchildren. Now he lived only for the farm, finding the city he had loved increasingly harsh and untenable; poems in his posthumous volume reflect his discontent. To me he said: "We were lucky—we both knew New York when it was enchanting." His plan, as I afterwards learned, was of a central-heating system so that he and his wife could leave earlier and stay later.

Thoughts and talk of New Hampshire—of thrushes and hummingbirds—and an eager and overriding anticipation of work to be done, quickly revive his spirits. He had been writing steadily; on the farm he could paint, too, to add to his vast store of lyrical landscapes.

I had observed that latterly, whenever he returned from Europe he was more of a chauvinist, a regionalist even, and it was American virtues he praised. It was only by chance that I learned that part of his feeling of frustration abroad on at least one of his trips was due to the fact that he had missed the blossoming of the crab-apple tree in Washington Square.

It was cut down in 1961.

## 2

In 1962, on the eve of another and—as it turned out—final departure for the farm, he said: "I need at least another hundred years to finish my work." My wife recalls that he said this twice; my own recollection is of a particular dinner with us. He may have said it again when we had him to tea to see the wall of his paintings, a new arrangement that pleased everyone. The tea—May 23 —was the last time I saw him, for he and Mrs. Cummings left for the farm a day or two later.    . .

It was on the occasion of the dinner that he suddenly said he had come around to liking something by Frost. I looked at him in astonishment.

"What?" I asked.

Pause.

" 'Stopping by Woods on a Snowy Evening.' "

Then I saw he had that triggered look on his face—he was biding his time.

"Yes," he declared. "It's this side of platitude."

He was better that year, and in excellent form that night. Even

at his most serious, his mind was never far from humor or burlesque. He had a light voice that seemed to go with the whimsical
side of his nature; it was a very cultivated voice, but though light,
was capable of extraordinary modulations—indeed, as far as from
Harvard to hoodlum—and made an excellent accompaniment to
his habitual mimicry.

It was Cummings who finally prevailed on his wife to publish
a volume of her photographs, and it was he who made the selection from her work. It appeared in 1962 as *Adventures in Value—
Fifty Photographs by Marion Morehouse, Text by E. E. Cummings.* The book reflects their common enchantment with roses,
light, clean line, nature, and certain people, including Marianne
Moore and Harvard's John Finley. He has praise for Patchin
Place, "a certain diminutive deadend lane of hundredyearold
houses," in one of which he lived for almost four decades. And for
a rock like a cloud overhung with birches, photographed on the
farm, he recalled his youth: "beside this mercifully how enormous
friend, a Harvard teacher's small son memorized(after multifarious
strugglings)the alphabet of ancient Greece."

He did not live to see the beautiful book on which he had
worked. But he had seen the proofs at the farm, and made final
corrections; and there he had added to the poems, which he habit-
ually put in a folder for inclusion in a new collection. He also "done
his chores," like his hero in 1 x 1, and in addition had painted
a great deal; his last note to me, which reached me Saturday, September 1, was an urgent request for a dozen canvas boards. He
enclosed twice as much money as was necessary. The following day
he had the cerebral hemorrhage from which he died.

A few minutes after nine on the morning of September 3,
Willard Trask called me on the phone. He had just heard a news
broadcast: Cummings was dead. Other friends phoned. (Silent
crowds had begun to form at the entrance to Patchin Place, and
were there throughout the day.)

I called the farm; Mrs. Cummings answered. She was surprised
that the news had reached the world so quickly. She told me that
on Sunday Cummings had been chopping wood. It was very hot,

and she asked him to stop. He took the ax to the barn, sharpened it, and put it away clean—"like the good woodsman he was." They returned to the house, and he went upstairs to change. Waiting for him, she heard what she thinks may have been a call for help, followed by a fall. Later that day he was taken to Memorial Hospital in North Conway, New Hampshire. He died at 1:15 A.M. Monday without regaining consciousness. He was buried near his father and mother in Forest Hills Cemetery, Boston, after a private service. The central heating system, being installed at last, was half-completed when he died.

In a will filed on September 22 he had written: "I suggest that Marion give my daughter Nancy (Mrs. Willard Roosevelt) and my dearest friends, Mr. and Mrs. J. S. Watson Jr., and my sister Elizabeth (Mrs. Carlton C. Qualey), whatever she, Marion, feels they'd enjoy remembering me by."

## 3

Cummings left a manuscript that now bears the title 73 *Poems*. (Several others, obviously in preliminary stages, were withheld by his wife.) His touch was sure, his range as wide as before. He was still the magic-maker:

> bells cry bells

and

> —open this ghost with millionary knives of wind—

and, once more, there are many nests for birds. Another mouse poem, No. 12 in this collection, may take its place alongside the now well-known "here's a little mouse" whose eyes peer out of a parenthesis.

His place seems secure by this simple criterion: forty years after *Tulips and Chimneys* the mere mention of his name can bring entire poems to mind. To this bright cluster, some of the posthumous poems will be added.

73 *Poems*, published in October, 1963, was followed by two

retrospective shows—at the Downtown Gallery, New York City, and the Rochester Memorial Art Gallery.

So lived and died this "author of pictures" and "draughtsman of words" who, in the pursuit of his twin arts, had cultivated

> scrupulously the Inimitable which
> is loneliness . . .

# Index of Persons and Places

Adams, J. Donald, 33
Aiken, Conrad, 110
Alsberg, Henry G., 161, 168
American British Art Center, 180
American Embassy, Paris, 67, 70, 74, 78, 79, 83, 84, 86
American Red Cross, Section Vingt-et-Un, 63
Anderson, Hon. George W., 74, 78, 79, 81, 83, 85, 88
Anderson, Margaret, 116
Aquarium, 106
Aragon, Louis, 143, 182
Arlington Street Church, 37
Art Students' League, 113
Auden, W. H., 217
Autun, 93

Baldwin, Maria, 30
Baltimore, 181
Barnett, Rev. Samuel A., 13
Barrymore, John, 109
Bartlett, Spaulding, 83
Barton, Anne, 160, 179
Battery, The, 106
Baumgarten, Bernice (Mrs. James Gould Cozzens), 196, 229

Belasco, David, 109
Bennington College, 6
Bianco, Francesco, 106, 125
Bigelow, Mrs. Josephine, 136
Bishop, John Peale, 127
Black Knight, The, 103, 138
Blake, William, 37
Blond, Georges, 216
Bodenheim, Maxwell, 110, 117, 165
Bolton, Lawrence, 164
Boni, Albert and Charles, 103, 127
Boni & Liveright, 92, 95
Bordeaux, 87
Boston, 10, 13, 14, 35, 56, 239
    Arts Festival, 219–24
    Public Gardens, 222, 224
Boulogne, 62
Bourne, Randolph, 115, 117
Breit, Harvey, 211
Brevoort Hotel, 103
Brice, Fanny, 109, 142
Briggs, Dean, 36
"Bringing Up Father," 109
Brinnin, John Malcolm, 216
Bronx Zoo, 106
Brooke, Tucker, 31
Brooks, Van Wyck, 108, 115

Brotherhood Synagogue, 114
Brown, William Slater, 60, 62, 63,
    64, 65, 66, 69, 72, 75, 76,
    78, 79, 81, 83, 85, 86, 87, 92,
    99, 100, 101, 104, 106, 107,
    121, 137, 138, 141, 142
Brown University, 219
Buck, Paul H., 226, 227
Burke, Kenneth, 124

Cabell, James Branch, 109
Café de la Paix, 138
Café Royale, 100
Caldwell, Erskine, 193
Cambridge, Mass., 16, 17, 19, 21,
    23–24, 25, 30, 31, 34, 37, 56,
    74, 75, 83, 88, 92, 219, 227;
    see also Harvard
  Dramatic Club, 34
  High and Latin School, 30
  Public Library, 31
Cantor, Eddie, 142
Carpenter, Estlin, 13
Carroll, John, 152
Carver, Catharine, 229–30
Castle, Irene, 109
Cézanne, Paul, 19, 41, 63
Chaplin, Charles, 100, 109, 142, 177,
    179
Chicago, 181, 218
Christopher Street, 99, 103
Clarke, George, 21
Cleveland, 181
Coblentz, Stanton A., 133–34, 195
Cocteau, Jean, 143, 144
Collier & Son, P. F., 58, 60
Collier's Weekly, 52, 58
Columbia University, 60
  School of Journalism, 64, 104
Columbian saloon, 103
Compiègne, 63
Coney Island, 9
Cooper Union, 101, 113
Copland, Aaron, 108
Cornell, Julien, 203–4
Covici, Friede, 178, 187
Covici, Pascal, 187

Cowley, Malcolm, 35, 45, 60, 61, 62,
    96, 120, 121, 141, 142
Cram, Paul P., 40
Crane, Hart, 108, 138, 208
Crosby, Harry, 136
Crowninshield, Frank, 151
Cummings, Rev. Edward, 8, 12–14,
    25–26, 28, 34, 37, 56, 57, 69,
    70, 71, 72, 73, 74, 78, 79, 80,
    81, 82, 83–85, 88, 91, 92, 93,
    94, 140, 176
Cummings, Elizabeth, 16, 17, 19–20,
    21, 25–26, 68, 106, 239
Cummings, Marion Morehouse (Mrs.
    E. E.), 9–10, 28–29, 198, 204,
    207, 216, 224, 228, 232–33,
    235, 238–39
Cummings, Nancy (Mrs. Willard
    Roosevelt), 239
Cummings, Rebecca Haswell Clarke,
    15–16

Dale, Alan, 170
Damon, S. Foster, 35, 36, 38, 42, 45,
    47, 48, 56, 59, 121, 219
Dana, Henry W. L., 188
Delacroix, Eugène, 174, 177
de Mille, Cecil, 109
Demuth, Charles, 104
Derry, Cecil, 30
Devens, Camp, 99
De Wilton, R. L., 234
Dial, The, 4, 6, 12, 33, 59, 92, 96,
    105, 107, 108, 114–36, 138,
    158, 177
Diamond, David, 171
Dos Passos, John, 33, 34, 36, 45, 48,
    49, 50, 51, 52, 53, 54, 55, 61,
    93, 107, 127, 138, 139, 155,
    206
Dos Passos, John R., 51, 54, 121
Downtown Gallery, 240
Duchamp, Marcel, 41, 104
Dunne, Finley Peter, 109

Eames, Claire, 157
Eastman, Max, 132
El Greco, 9, 37

Eliot, T. S., 34, 36, 110, 119, 120, 121, 213, 216, 217
Emerson, Ralph W., 114, 189
Europe, Jim, 39
Evans, Donald, 37, 43

Farrell, James, 193
Faulkner, William, 60
Felix's, 114
Finley, John H., Jr., 225–26, 238
First Church of Boston, 14
Fitsch, Eugene, 162
Fitzgerald, M. Eleanor, 161
Flowers, Tiger, 157–58
Franck, César, 41
Frazier, Arthur Hugh, 71
Friedman, Norman, 228
Frost, Robert, 217, 219, 237
Fuller, Margaret, 114

Galantière, Lewis, 140, 143, 146, 147, 150
Gay, Miss, 106, 107, 135
Giroux, Robert, 230–31
Golden Swan, 103
Gomme, Laurence J., 49, 50, 51, 52, 54, 55, 56, 57, 58
Gordon, Mrs. J. R., 55
Gould, Joseph Ferdinand, 31, 110-13, 136, 179
Grand Ticino, 103
Graves, Robert, 92, 126
Greb, Harry, 157–58
Greenwich Village, 3, 4, 102, 110, 111, 114, 169
Gregory, Alyse, 124
Gregory, Horace, 47, 126

Hale, Rev. Edward Everett, 13–14
Ham, 63, 65
Hansen, Harry, 124
Harbord, Gen J. G., 74
Harjes, Henry H., 54, 60, 61
Harvard, 13, 17, 19, 22, 30, 31, 32, 33, 34, 35, 36, 37, 38, 40, 59
    Advocate, 31, 32, 33, 35, 40, 45, 96, 97
    Alumni Bulletin, 40

Charles Eliot Norton Professor of Poetry, Cummings as, 225–28
Commencenment, 1915, 40–45
Eliot House, 225
Fund, 219
Graduate School of Arts and Sciences, 45
Monthly, 31, 33-34, 36, 37, 45, 46, 47, 97
Musical Club, 37
Poetry Society, 45–47
Sanders Theatre, 13, 35, 40, 42, 227
Thayer Hall, 34, 35
Union, 33, 45, 52
University Press, 226, 228
Widener Memorial Library, 40
Yard, 40
Hemingway, Ernest, 192, 206
Hergesheimer, Joseph, 109
Herriman, George, 109, 137
Hillyer, Robert S., 33, 34, 36, 45, 48, 49, 52, 55
Holt, Guy, 125
Howard Athenaeum, 35, 105

International Theatre Exposition, 157, 158
Irving Place, 108

Jacobs, S. A., 124, 170, 179, 187, 191, 194
James, William, 13
Jarrell, Randall, 231
Jefferson Market Court, 3
Jerome, Jerome K., 34
Johnson, Martyn, 115
Johnstone, William S., 163–65, 167
Jolson, Al, 109, 142
Josephson, Matthew, 141, 142
Joy, Ephraim, 25
Joy Farm, 25, 211

"Katzenjammer Kids," 109
Kazin, Alfred, 228
Keats, John, 38, 39
Kennerley, Mitchell, 49
Khouri's, 106

Kiesler, Friedrich, 158
Kiev, 190
Kilmer, Joyce, 49
"Krazy Kat," 35, 109, 137
Kreymbourg, Alfred, 108

Lachaise, Gaston, 6, 104, 106, 113, 117
Lafayette Hotel, 103
La Ferté Macé, 76, 78, 83, 86, 87, 91, 92, 97
Lansing, Robert, 85, 88
Lardner, Ring, 109, 142
Larionov, Michael, 127, 144, 179
Levenson, Lewis G., 75
Light, James, 161, 162, 163, 164
Lincoln, Abraham, 14, 101
Lippmann, Walter, 110
Littell, Robert, 170
Little Book Shop Around the Corner, 49
Little Venice, 114
Liveright, Horace, 92, 93, 94, 165
Lodge, Henry Cabot, 87
Loeb, Harold, 141
Lovett, Robert Morss, 115
Lowell, A. Lawrence, 40, 43
Lowell, Amy, 42, 43, 46–47, 59–60, 121
Lower, Dr. Gerhardt, 75
Loyola University, Chicago, 218

McAlmon, Robert, 192
McBride, Henry, 121
McCord, David, 219–20, 222
Macdougal Street, 103
MacIver, Loren, 177
MacLeish, Archibald, 146–47, 205–6, 217, 219, 220, 224
MacNeice, Louis, 217
McSorley's Old Ale House, 101, 102
MacVeagh, Lincoln, 128
Madison Square Garden, 157
Mandarin House, 114
Manet, Edouard, 41
Marin, John, 106
Mario's, 114
Marlowe, Christopher, 31, 119

Marta's, 126
Marvell, Andrew, 130
Masefield, John, 103
Matisse, Henri, 41
Meurice Hotel, 138
Milhaud, Darius, 108
Millay, Edna St. Vincent, 152–53
Miller, Theodore, 38
Milton, John, 39
Mitchell, Stewart, 33, 34, 48, 49, 50, 55, 92, 107, 118, 124, 127, 140, 144
Monet, Claude, 41
Moore, Marianne, 108, 121, 123, 124, 126, 134, 200–1, 217, 238
Morand, Paul, 139, 140
Moscow, 183, 186, 190
   Art Theatre, 157
   Museum of Western Art, 190
Moscowitz's Romanian Restaurant, 100
Mumford, Lewis, 108, 115
Mussolini, Benito, 152, 165

Nagle, Edward Pierce, 104, 106, 107, 160
Nash, Ogden, 217
Nathan, Robert G., 33
National Association of Educational Broadcasters, 218
National Winter Garden Burlesque, 105, 106, 107, 117, 177
Neilson, W. A., 52, 58, 59
New Hampshire, 10, 25, 57, 92, 135, 164, 178, 179, 181, 198, 216, 223, 227, 232, 233, 237, 239
Niagara Falls, 9
Norris, William A., 48, 49, 50, 56
North Conway, N. H., 239
Norton, Charles Eliot, 19, 69
Norton, Richard, 69, 70, 71, 73, 79, 80, 81, 82, 84, 85
"Norton's Woods," 19, 177
Noyon, 63, 65

O'Brien-Moore, Erin, 163–64, 168
O'Connor, Luke, 103
Odessa, 186

O'Neill, Eugene, 103, 161
Ornstein, Leo, 108
Orr, Elaine, 123
Oxford University, 13

Pach, Walter, 41, 117
Paris, 59, 62, 63, 67, 83, 86, 138–40, 143–51, 182, 185
Parker, Col. Frank, 76, 86
Parkman, Henry, 40
Pearce, Charles A., 196–97, 198, 200
Perry, Bliss, 52, 58, 184
Phillips, Charles Francis, 75
Phillips, William, 81, 82, 88
Picasso, Pablo, 109, 213
Place St. Michel, 138, 139
Polly's, 103
Poore, Dudley, 48, 49, 52, 55
Potter, Jack, 57
Pound, Ezra, 38, 97, 108, 113, 119, 121, 148, 182, 191, 202–4, 213
Powys, John Cowper, 140
Précigné, 86, 87
Provincetown Playhouse, 103, 161, 162–70
Psomas, S., 4

Quai de Béthune, 140, 143
Quai d'Orsay, 139, 140
Qualey, Carlton, 16
Qualey, Mrs. Carlton; see Cummings, Elizabeth

Randall, Clarence B., 40
Rapallo, 190
Rascoe, Burton, 142, 146–50, 154
Redman, Ben Ray, 95
Robinson, Edwin Arlington, 116, 117
Rochester, N. Y., 178, 181, 218–19
    Memorial Art Gallery, 176, 181, 240
Rodman, Selden, 199
Rogers, Bruce, 115
Romany Marie's, 102
Rosenfeld, Paul, 12, 30, 108, 117, 182, 216

Rossetti, Dante Gabriel, 32, 36
Roxbury, Mass., 15
Royce, Josiah, 23
Rue Gît-le-Coeur, 138
Rue Notre Dame de Champs, 192
Rue St. André des Arts, 140
Russia, 182–90, 193

Salons of America, 180
Sandburg, Carl, 117, 200, 219
Santayana, George, 23
Savoy, Bert, 167
Schneider, Isidor, 95
Schönberg, Arnold, 42
Schwartz, A., 4, 5
Scollay Square, 35
Scott, Evelyn, 117
Scott, Winfield Townley, 219
Seeger, Alan, 60
Seldes, Gilbert V., 33, 39n., 121, 124, 137, 138, 139, 144, 177, 179
Seltzer, Thomas, 127
Sennett, Mack, 109
Shahn, Ben, 162
Shargel, Jack, 105, 106, 177, 179
Sharp, William G., 78, 79, 87, 88
Sheeler, Charles, 121
Shelley, P. B., 36
Sitwell, Dame Edith, 217
Smith, Philip Hillyer, 91
Society of Independent Artists, 104, 180
Society of Painters, Sculptors and Gravers, 180
South Congregational Church, Unitarian, 13, 14
Spender, Stephen, 217
Stander, Lionel, 164–65
State Department, U. S., 64, 67, 74, 83, 84
Stearns, Harold E., 109, 115
Steichen, Edward, 10
Stein, Gertrude, 37, 43, 44, 47, 109
Stevens, Wallace, 173, 217
Stieglitz, Alfred, 108
Strauss, Richard, 41
Stravinsky, Igor, 42, 63, 106

Sumner, John S., 95, 126, 154
Sweeney, Jack, 219
Swinburne, A. C., 36

Tate, Allen, 216, 218
Temple, Peter, 221, 222
Thayer, Scofield, 33, 108, 115, 123, 138, 179
Theatre Guild, 103
Thomas, Dylan, 216, 217
Thomashefsky, Boris, 105
Thompson Street, 102, 103
Thoreau, Henry D., 5, 7
Tone, Franchot, 163
Toynbee Hall, 13
Trask, Willard, 238
Tumulty, Joseph P., 85

Varèse, Edgar, 108
Veblen, Thorstein, 115
Village Presbyterian Church, 114

Warburg, Felix, 161
Ward, Sam, 211
Washington Irving House, 50
Washington Square, 4, 5, 29, 102, 108
Washington Square Bookshop, 103, 126
Washington Square Players, 103

Watson, Hildegarde (Mrs. James Sibley Watson), 178, 181, 207, 234, 239
Watson, James Sibley, 33, 108, 115, 116, 117, 121, 123, 161, 178, 179, 239
Wendell, Barrett, 36, 52
Werner, M. R., 104, 105, 107, 113, 152, 179, 187, 201
Wheelwright, John Brooks, 46
Whiteman, Paul, 142
Whitney, Mrs. Harry Payne, 161
Williams, Gluyas, 110
Williams, William Carlos, 193, 217
Wilson, Arthur, 59, 60
Wilson, Edmund, 108, 121, 129
Wilson, Woodrow, 69, 81, 82, 83
Winchell, Walter, 169
Wood, Clement, 49
Woollcott, Alexander, 154, 168–69
Wright, Cuthbert, 48, 49, 50, 52, 53
Wynn, Ed, 142

Y. M. H. A. (Young Men's Hebrew Association), 217

Zaturenska, Marya, 124
Ziegfeld, Florenz, 109
Zipser, Stanley, 164